Twelve Years of Correspondence With Paul Meehl

Tough Notes From a Gentle Genius

Twelve Years of Correspondence With Paul Meehl

Tough Notes From a Gentle Genius

Donald R. Peterson

Psychology Press
Taylor & Francis Group

New York London

First published by
Lawrence Erlbaum Associates, Inc., Publishers
10 Industrial Avenue
Mahwah, New Jersey 07430

First issued in paperback 2012

This edition published 2012 by Psychology Press

Psychology Press
Taylor & Francis Group
711 Third Avenue
New York, NY 10017

Psychology Press
Taylor & Francis Group
27 Church Road
Hove, East Sussex BN3 2FA

Psychology Press is an imprint of Taylor & Francis, an informa group company

Cover design by Kathryn Houghtaling Lacey

Library of Congress Cataloging-in-Publication Data

Peterson, Donald R. (Donald Robert) 1923–
[Correspondence. Selections]
Twelve years of correspondence with Paul Meehl : tough notes from a gentle genius / Donald R. Peterson.
p. cm.
Includes bibliographical references and index.
ISBN 0-8058-5489-4 (cloth : alk. Paper)
ISBN 978-0-415-65464-7 (Paperbak)
1. Peterson, Donald R. (Donald Robert), 1923– —Correspondence. 2. Meehl, Paul E. (Paul Everett), 1920– —Correspondence. 3. Psychologists—United States—Correspondence. I. Title.

BF109.P48A4 2005
150'.92'273—dc22

2005040048
CIP

To Paul E. Meehl, who taught thousands of students how to think and blessed the lives of those who knew him well.

The Master in the Art of Living makes little distinction between his work and his play, his labor and his leisure, his mind and his body, his education and his recreation, his love and his intellectual passion. He hardly knows which is which. He simply pursues his vision of excellence in whatever he does, leaving others to decide whether he is working or playing.

Adapted from an ancient Zen Buddhist text

Contents

Introduction

Paul Everett Meehl died on Saint Valentine's day, 2003. Five days later, his obituary appeared in the *New York Times*.

> Dr. Paul Meehl, a University of Minnesota psychologist whose writings on research methodology, mental illness and other topics influenced generations of researchers and psychotherapists, died on Friday at his home in Minneapolis. He was 83.
>
> The cause was chronic myelomonocytic leukemia, his colleagues said.
>
> The names of other American psychologists—B. F. Skinner, for example—might be more familiar to the public. But many experts say Dr. Meehl's influence within his field was equally profound.
>
> His writings are widely cited and prescribed reading for every graduate student. His insistence on precise thinking and scientific tough-mindedness made him a scourge to some and a role model to many others.
>
> In the early 1960's, when a vast majority of psychiatrists and psychologists believed that schizophrenia was caused by bad parenting, Dr. Meehl argued that the illness must have a strong genetic component, and discussed the subject in his 1962 presidential address to the American Psychological Association. Forty years later, the genetic basis of schizophrenia is widely accepted.

In a 1954 book, "Clinical Versus Statistical Prediction: A Theoretical Analysis and Review of the Evidence," Dr. Meehl, who retired in 1990 but continued to teach at the university until last year, enraged many colleagues by pointing out, in meticulous and acerbic detail, why clinicians were not very good at predicting people's behavior.

A far more reliable method, he argued, was to analyze the information gained from personality tests, psychiatric interviews and other sources using mathematical formulas. Dr. Meehl referred to the volume as "my disturbing little book." And many clinical psychologists reacted accordingly.

"Essentially," said Dr. William Grove, director of the clinical science and psychopathology research program at Minnesota, "he was saying that as far as predicting the prognosis of a mental disorder or predicting future recurrences is concerned, clinicians could be replaced by a clerk with a hand-cranked Monroe calculator."

Dr. Daniel Kahnemann, a psychologist at Princeton who last year won the Nobel in economic science, cited Dr. Meehl's work as an influence on his own.

"What he did there was more than show the limitations of clinical judgment," Dr. Kahnemann said. "He also showed that the subjective confidence that people have in their judgment is not necessarily a good indication of their accuracy."

Born in Minneapolis, Paul Everett Meehl received his bachelor's degree from the University of Minnesota in 1941 and his doctorate in 1945. He was trained as a psychoanalyst and kept a couch in his office.

Dr. Meehl's effectiveness as a critic of sloppy thinking in psychology was aided by a conversational writing style and a knack for coining phrases. In a now-classic paper, "Why I Do Not Attend Case Conferences," Dr. Meehl listed the logical sins routinely committed by psychologists when they gathered to discuss patients.

One was the "'Me too' fallacy." In it, psychologists, upon hearing of a patient's odd behavior, insist that it is normal because "anyone would do that." The "Uncle George's pancakes fallacy" is exemplified by the clinician who, told that a patient stored leftover pancakes in the attic, declares, "Why, there is nothing so terrible about that—I remember good old Uncle George from my childhood, *he* used to store pancakes in the attic."

Dr. Meehl was the author of one of the scales of the Minnesota Multiphasic Personality Inventory, one of the most widely used personality tests. In recent years, he played the central role in developing taxometrics, a field concerned with using mathematical formulas to determine the natural groupings of biological or psychological variables.

> He is survived by his wife, Leslie Jane Yonce; his daughter, Karen Enid Hill of Seattle; his son, Erik Rolf, of Hopkins, Minn.; and three grandsons. His first wife, Alyce Roworth Meehl, died in 1972.

Given the limits that newspapers require for the obituaries of all but popularly famous celebrities, the *Times* account of Meehl's career was adequate. But to me, who had begun to study with Paul Meehl 55 years before and had maintained a continuing and often intense personal correspondence with him through the years that followed, the cold print of a newspaper obituary could not begin to suggest the force and quality of the effects Meehl had on those who knew him best.

As soon as I learned of his death, I wrote to his wife Leslie, who often collaborated with her husband in their taxometric studies and had served as an e-mail intermediary between Paul and his correspondents during the final year of his life, when macular degeneration robbed him of his reading vision:

> *As free of sentimentality as Paul was, I don't suppose he'd have sympathized much with my response. I tried to be manly and rational about it at first, but then said, "Aw hell," and wept. I owe everything I have ever done in my career, the good life I live, to Paul Meehl. That sounds hyperbolic but is not. I have some talent and I've received lots of help from other good people, but nobody in my experience—not my parents, none of the other fine teachers I have known—has influenced me as deeply and pervasively as Paul did. Of course he greatly expanded my intellectual horizons, as he did those of everyone who knew his work. And he gave me the critical boosts we all need to enter a profession—brought me into clinical psychology, guided my education, got me my first job, did all the other helpful, encouraging things seniors do for juniors in any academic field. But for me, as no doubt for some others who were closest to him, the effects went far beyond cognitive enlightenment and professional fortune.... He taught me a form of integrity unmatched by anyone else I have ever known. No nonsense. No bullshit. No lying to oneself or others. Be thou true, through and through, but don't get grim or sanctimonious about it.*

Before Meehl died, I had started to write another book, but I could not drive thoughts of the man and his work from my mind. Now and then, I would go back to our correspondence, to the many ideas we had traded over the years, and I would always find something fresh and provocative in his letters, especially the penetrating, eventually illuminating way he opened new windows on old issues by raising questions neither I nor anyone else I knew had ever thought to ask. After some time, I came to believe I had a special opportunity, perhaps an obligation, to let others in on the wit and warmth and wisdom that came through in the handwritten pages he sent to me. Besides, I am grieving and want to write one last long letter to my friend. Thus this book, which consists mainly of letters Paul Meehl and I exchanged during the last 12 years of his life.

I have described elsewhere my experience as a graduate student at the University of Minnesota, conspicuously including my relationship with Paul Meehl, and have no inclination to repeat the story here. The images that flash through my memory now, as I move through my 80th year, are still dominated by Meehl. My first meeting with him—I just back from a grisly war, armed with the GI bill, a sophomore English major bumbling about in my search for some way to make a living in an intellectually challenging, morally satisfying way; he just 2 years beyond his PhD but already nationally recognized as the *Wunderkind* of psychology, taking a full hour to describe clinical psychology to me and leaving me determined to enter a field I had barely heard of before I came through his office door. The delicious mix of excitement, authority, and humor that suffused his lectures. The long sessions in his office after he became my advisor—cheerful conversations about vexing questions, always enriching. My astonishment when he asked me, just short of my own PhD, to take over his graduate class in clinical psychology while he was out of town on a colloquium tour, and offered me money for work I'd have been delighted to do as token return for all the intellectual gifts and personal benevolence Meehl had showered on me. He calculated the fraction of his salary attributable to teaching the course and gave me a check in that precise amount.

In 1952, I completed my own doctoral studies and joined the faculty of the psychology department at the University of Illinois in Urbana–Champaign. For long years afterward, my contacts with Meehl were those of friendly exchange between academic colleagues with some common interests. We sent manuscripts and reprints to one another, more from me to him than the other way around, now and then a congratulatory note, letters when one of us had a question and wanted to talk as we had during my years in Minneapolis. We continued to write to each other whenever our interests and activities coincided, as they often did.

Our correspondence continued after I moved to Rutgers University in 1975 as dean of the newly established Graduate School of Applied and Professional Psychology. I was the first and am still the only psychologist who has directed a research-oriented PhD program in clinical psychology, a practice-oriented Doctor of Psychology (PsyD) program in an academic psychology department, and a school of professional psychology in a major research university. These engagements have required me to pay unusually close and persistent attention to the "Great Struggle of the Psychoclinician," never better described than by Meehl in the preface to his classic book on psychodiagnosis:

> "How do I help my clients or patients, practicing an art that applies a primitive science?" Or, on the other side of the coin, "How do I preserve my scientific mental habits from attrition by the continual necessity, as a helper, to think, act, and decide on the basis of 'scientifically' inadequate evidence—relying willy-nilly on clinical experience, hunches, colleagues' anecdotes, intuition, common sense, far-out extrapolations from the laboratory, folklore, introspection, and sheer 'guesswork'?"

As Meehl's letters show, his preoccupation with that struggle continued into his latest years, as it has in mine. If a single theme can be found to dominate our correspondence, it has its source in our attempts to reconcile the demands of science and profession in the practice of psychology.

In 1989, I "retired." Paul made the same move a year later. After that, our correspondence intensified. During some periods, we wrote to each other every week. Meehl corresponded actively with colleagues in each of his many areas of interest—with his "gene gang" on genetics, with those who shared his interests in research on schizophrenia, intelligence, personality, and learning; with special "pen pals" among his peer philosophers of science; with his collaborators, especially Niels Waller, on taxometrics; with David Faust in developing the "Faust–Meehl hypothesis" in cliometrics. Many a memo was sent to faculty members in the University of

Minnesota psychology department, addressed simply to "Crew." The contents of the messages varied from hastily scribbled, always amusing, often very funny comments on some particularly stupid article he had read in a newspaper, through his handwritten speed notes and letters, to major typewritten essays, many of which he dictated after cogitative composition during the 5-mile walks he continued into the last years of his life. His secretary and/or his wife distributed his correspondence, along with his published articles, among the several mailing lists that he maintained. Meehl not only wrote personally to all these people, he served as a kind of intellectual matchmaker by putting colleagues with common interests in touch with one another. For example, it is unlikely that I would have enjoyed correspondence with David Lubinski concerning his elegant, penetrating research on cognitive abilities, or with the philosopher Susan Haack on the pertinence of her views to applied psychology, had not Meehl written to each of them suggesting that they send some of their writings to me.

His frequent correspondence with me was therefore not unique. However, it differed from much of Meehl's other correspondence in several ways. One was the length of our association—more than a half-century altogether. Another was the unusually broad range of our common interests. A third derived from the accident of our physical separation. Several of Meehl's colleagues probably shared as many interests with Paul as I did, but many of those were fellow inhabitants of Elliott Hall in Minneapolis who could talk to Paul whenever they wanted to; hence, many of their exchanges were not registered on paper as ours were. I kept his letters and copies of my own in an orderly way so I could recover what we had written before whenever we returned to a topic we had discussed at an earlier time. All of this, I think, brought a continuity and coherence to the long series of our letters that would probably be difficult to find in his correspondence with others.

At the time we wrote our letters, neither of us dreamed that they would go on public display. I had no thought of converting them into a book until my wife suggested that I do so. But once I started to read our letters from the earliest to the latest, a previously unnoticed order began to emerge. Consecutively, each topic seemed to flow naturally into the next. A cumulative effect also appeared as we dug deeper and deeper into some of the issues that concerned us most. I no longer consider it accidental that the final chapters in this book epitomize the merits of science by summarizing our thoughts on "the scientific mentality," as well as the limits of science by defining the boundaries of scientistic confidence in our efforts to understand the human condition. For me, writing the book was both a therapeutic experience and an intellectual joy. Each day I could not wait to get back to the office to see what would turn up next. The book wrote itself. Four months after I started putting it together, the first draft was finished.

Of course, some of the content of our letters is personal. Besides our perorations and reflections on the conceptual matters we addressed, Paul and I wrote to one another as person to person. In that regard, the correspondence becomes more than a series of scholarly essays. At another level it is a story of the relationship between Paul and me, at first as mentor to student, but later as colleague to colleague, and at last as aging friend to aging friend—two elders "explaining ourselves to each other."

Inevitably, people who write frequently to one another develop a kind of shorthand that will not always be comprehensible to others, so I have spelled out some of those. I think most of the remaining abbreviations and other idiosyncratic usages that Paul and I employed will be readily understood. Of course, some of the names we mention will be unfamiliar to people who do not share our academic history, but I think most of the ideas we discuss are common fare in the social, biological, and behavioral sciences. At least I hope that a reasonably coherent sense of our concerns and considerations will be apparent to readers whose interests are similar to ours.

It is not easy to guess who those might be. Probably most of them will be other psychologists. I hope that the book will attract some of the most serious scholars in our field—people who know Meehl's work as well as my own and would like to examine what we say to each other in the candor of a private correspondence. The book includes an extensive set of endnotes that identify the many works to which we refer in our letters and often add explanatory comments on remarks that are unclearly or incompletely expressed in the original exchanges. Readers who go beyond the correspondence to the various primary sources that Meehl and I discuss may find their intellectual stores enriched.

I believe the book should eventually make its way to a larger audience. Most of all, it would be useful reading for the armies of psychologists coming along these days who have never read Meehl's work, do not even recognize his name, and need to learn far more than they typically learn about *how to think*. Paul Meehl was the grand master of critical analysis in psychology. In my opinion, all students of psychology need a thorough grounding in his major works, many of which are now conveniently available in the *Meehl Reader*. It seems to me that a book based on his correspondence would be a particularly informative companion volume to the *Reader* in any course designed to help students learn "how to think like a psychologist," the most valuable cognitive commodity anyone in the discipline—teacher, researcher, or practitioner—can offer the public. In Meehl's dialogue with a career-long student and colleague, readers can gain an inside perspective on his remarkable mind at work.

Beyond psychology, Meehl's stature as a philosopher may attract some readers in that discipline. Still further, both Meehl and I read extensively in such fields as history and biography, and in the ease of private correspondence felt free to comment about well-known authors and their works. Whether any of those or their followers would be interested in our comments I cannot guess, but I have a hunch some highly literate readers, whatever academic union cards they happen to carry, might enjoy reading the book simply as an intellectually challenging human story.

I have to say something else before I get to the letters. To me and to many others, Paul Meehl was a genius, but he did not attach the label to himself. Keen as he knew his intelligence was, Paul did not consider himself a genius. He thought this overused term should be reserved for the likes of Einstein and Freud. Probably Darwin too, although, as Meehl's letters show, he was critical of evolutionary theory as commonly received, and annoyed by those, including otherwise respected colleagues, who treated the Darwinian formulation as gospel.

Whatever *he* thought, Paul Meehl—Regents' Professor and honorary Doctor of Science, University of Minnesota, with joint appointments and histories of active teaching in law, medicine, and philosophy; co-founder, with Herbert Feigl and Wilfrid Sellars, of the Minnesota Center for Philosophy of Science; author of ground-breaking work in such broadly diverse fields as learning theory, psychopathology, psychometrics, forensics, political theory, behavior genetics, and philosophy of science; recipient of every major award organized psychology has to offer; member of the National Academy of Sciences; chosen by the Society of Clinical Psychology of the American Psychological Association (APA) as one of two Clinical Psychologists of the 20th Century and in my opinion the only one who fully deserved the accolade—comes as close to genius as anyone I ever expect to know. For me, correspondence with Paul Meehl was a priceless privilege. It is a further privilege to let others in on it, to give them a chance to see the intellectual sparkle, erudition, human kindness, and moral passion that Paul Meehl brought to his everyday exchanges with one of the fortunate few who knew him well.

I am grateful to my wife Jane, who sensed my gloom after Paul died, encouraged me to compose this book, and offered helpful editorial suggestions from start to finish of the manuscript. I am also grateful to Paul Meehl's wife, Leslie Jane Yonce, for permission to publish her husband's personal correspondence, further encouragement as I prepared the manuscript, and essential help in editing and enriching the text. Without Leslie's collaboration, the book would contain some unacceptable errors and lack some of the nuanced knowledge of Paul's ways that only his wife could provide. I thank Scott Lilienfeld and Niels Waller, who read the manuscript and urged its publication. Without their enthusiastic approval, it is not clear that the book would have appeared in print. Finally, I thank Debra Riegert, senior editor in the house of Lawrence Erlbaum Associates, who insisted wisely on a change in the title I had initially proposed, but unlike other editors I have known did not insist rigidly on squeezing the unique creature that is this volume into a standard "scholarly" format that would have destroyed the spontaneity and spirit of the work.

CHAPTER

1

Meekl

When I retired from my decanal duties in 1989, the editors of the student newsletter asked me to identify the experience outside the classroom that had most influenced my career. I dashed off the following handwritten note:

> *My personal relationship with Paul Meehl. Meehl not only led me into clinical psychology, but was mentor and model to me throughout my graduate study. He was my advisor, so naturally he helped me plan my coursework, complete my dissertation, and meet all the other demands of the rigorous Minnesota PhD program, but he did far more than that. He always greeted me warmly. When I came in the door of his office, he would say "Donald Robert Peterson!" and I would say "Paul Everett Meehl!" and then our conversation would begin, a respectful discussion, often punctuated by laughter, between two people interested in the same topic. We were never close, equal friends. To this day, I feel that he is the professor and I am the student. But by prizing me, he helped me value myself. I have never written an article, chapter, or book without thinking, at some point, "What would Paul Meehl say about that?"*

Some months later, I learned that Paul had retired, so I dug out the copy of the newsletter that contained my statement and sent it to him, along with a letter that said, in part:

> *I don't think I have ever told you directly what a powerful influence you have had on my life. I enclose a couple pages of a newsletter managed by the students in our school. Last fall, they asked me to comment on the experience outside the classroom that had mattered most in my career. My response appears on the second of the two pages I have enclosed.*
>
> *I also enclose my latest try at the science* x *practice issue. I do not expect written comment from you (too late for that—the article is scheduled for the April American Psychologist) but I think you will be interested in the argument.*

Then, the following summer, I performed my annual duty of sorting through accumulated correspondence to see if anything in the pile still needed attention. For the first time, I read the newsletter statement closely, gasped when I saw that Meehl's name had been misprinted as "Meekl," and wrote another letter to my one-time advisor:

> *August 8, 1991*
>
> *Dear Paul,*
>
> *Jesus Christ. I just finished my annual clean-up of outdated correspondence, and noticed for the first time the way our newsletter editor spelled your name. I am embarrassed less by the typographical laxity of the newsletter staff (and my own) than by the harsh realization that at least one of our students failed to know your name well enough to spell it correctly. My handwritten h's are easily mistaken for k's, but I still would expect any of our students to respond with "Meehl" to "Paul . . ." as a free-association stimulus.*
>
> *I have also had some afterthoughts about my comment. You are one of several smart but kindly critics who inhabit my brain and read over the stuff I write—D. G. Paterson and Herbert Feigl from Minnesota, Hobart Mowrer and Lloyd Humphreys from Illinois, among others. You, however, have been the most persistently helpful. (I'm sure you understand that I don't always agree with my mental commentators.)*
>
> *With best regards,*
>
> *Don Peterson*

This helped, but my shame did not subside immediately. Three days later, I mailed another letter:

August 11, 1991

Dear Paul,

Last night I was in the kitchen, wife Jane was in the living room, and she came in and said, "What are you groaning about?" And I said, "I was thinking about that Paul Meekl thing, but I didn't know I was doing it out loud." In a laughing way she said, "Oh hell, he's big enough to get a kick out of it. Why don't you tell him about some of the really stupid things you've done."

Not a bad idea, I thought. It takes me awhile to process mistakes like this, and it usually works best when I do it directly. So here's another story.

When I resigned as editor of the Journal of Abnormal Psychology, I was asked to nominate some successors, with special interest in women as candidates. So I dashed off a note to Al Hastorf [Stanford psychologist], who was chairman of the APA publications board at the time, suggesting consideration of Mavis Hetherington, Lucy Rau Ferguson, and Ann Magaret Garner. I wrote the note in my usual script, handed it to a new secretary to be typed, signed it hurriedly the next day, along with a pile of other stuff, and left it all to be mailed.

A week or so later, I received a letter from Hastorf that said, "Thank you for your recommendations. Blah blah. I am not sure we are prepared to place Morris Hetherington or Lucy Rare Ferguson on our short list, but Ann Margaret appears to be an eminently interesting candidate."

I thought I learned at that time to proofread everything I ever mailed to anybody, but I seem to require repeated trials to learn all the important lessons of life.

With best regards,

Don Peterson

P.S. That takes care of me. I will chew out our students in (carefully proofread) print next fall.

While my letter of August 11 was on its way to Meehl, a letter from him, in response to mine of August 8, was in the mail to me:

8/12/91

Dear Don:

I think I've seen the "Paul Meekl" item before. Amused rather than irked. Re student not recognizing my name, we had an APA site visitor on our clinical program who clearly didn't recognize it. Such is fame!

I'm used to name corruptions—a rare name like Meehl is subject to them. Commonest, of course, is "Meal," and if orally on phone, "Neal" or "Neely." Locally the old Meehl–Dahlstrom rules [for configural scoring of the MMPI] were called the "Neely–Dahlstrom rules."

I love retirement. Should have done it at age 63 when first $$ feasible. Gross irrationality not to.

Paul

Still later, I received another letter from Meehl, this one following his receipt of my letter of August 11:

8/16/91

Dear Don:

I'm high on Minn. Clerical [Minnesota Test of Clerical Aptitude], so is Leslie, we proof things carefully, but see the attached blooper! [page from a chapter by Meehl and Golden on taxometric methods in which the running head "The Maxcov-Hitmax Model" appears as "The Maxcov-Hitman Model," with the error circled and a note written in: "So I'm Mafia-connected?"]

Remember poor old Ned Springer at VA [Veterans Administration]? Before arriving, I reckon buttering me up in advance, he sent request for 2 reprints, got titles as "Private [for Profile] analysis of the MMPI (etc.)" and "The K Factor as a Suppository [for Suppressor] variable (etc.)" I sent them, mentioned the parapraxes, and jokingly added, "Perhaps you are thinking, 'These results won't replicate, and you can stick them up your ass.'" If I'd known him I'd never have done that. He was one of the half-dozen most anxious people I've ever known outside a mental hospital. Died very young of Ca, I'll bet stress played a part.

Do not fret over "Meekl." Gave us excuse for a little exchange, hah?

I'm still puzzled by your interest in hermeneutics in psy. How is it different from interpretation? Or mebbe that's too long for letters, requires talk?

Paul

Shortly after the university opened the next fall, I placed an item in the student newsletter. It began with a report of the "Meekl" mistake and continued as follows:

ATTENTION ALL STUDENTS

Perhaps it is not quite as important for you in your time to know as much about profile analyses and suppressor variables as it was for me in my time, but I hereby declare any student in our school who does not recognize the name of Paul Meehl, and who cannot write a thoroughly informed statement about clinical versus actuarial prediction, construct validity, and the other issues in clinical psychology that Meehl has so brilliantly elucidated, to be psychologically illiterate and undeserving of the Doctor of Psychology degree.

Donald R. Peterson, Ph.D., D. Sci.

Professor Emeritus

CHAPTER

2

Hermeneutics

When the newsletter appeared the following autumn, I sent a copy to Meehl. In the meantime, I had requested, received, and read a particularly powerful article he had published in *Psychological Inquiry*, a journal in which outstanding contributions to the philosophical and methodological foundations of psychology are distributed to several recognized experts for comment, and the author of the "target article" then replies to the critics.

Meehl's article extended some of his previous arguments. In a widely cited essay published in 1978, he had claimed that most research in the "soft" areas of psychology had failed miserably to advance the discipline as a science: "I consider it unnecessary to persuade you," he wrote, "that most so-called 'theories' in the soft areas of psychology (clinical, counseling, social, personality, community, and school psychology) are scientifically unimpressive and technologically worthless." This was so for two reasons. One was the inherent difficulty of psychology's subject matter. Early in his statement, Meehl listed 20 serious impediments to scientizing the human mind, ranging from problems in defining response classes (how do we slice up the raw behavioral flux into meaningful intervals identified by causally relevant attributes on the response side?) to ethical constraints on research (crucial experiments to determine, say, whether a particular pattern of family dynamics would produce clinical depression are easy to design, but obviously immoral to conduct). Meehl saw nothing for investigators to do about psychology's subject matter except to keep examining it in ever more sophisticated studies, but he thought the second condition that determined failure to develop a science of personality, social behavior, and other soft material could be corrected by a basic change in methodology. He believed that the vast majority of researchers in psychology had adopted the wrong approach. Seduced by the renowned mathematical statistician, Ronald Fisher, and bedazzled by the appearance of scientific rigor cast by elaborate statistical analyses, psychologists were pumping an endless flow of statistically "significant" findings into their journals, but getting nowhere in developing the self-correcting theories that form the core of authentic scientific knowledge.

In psychology, everything is more or less correlated with everything else. Meehl called this phenomenon the "crud factor." To get publishable results in a study, therefore, all investigators have to do is contrive *some* kind of theoretical rationale (whatever topic is currently "hot" will do), see that their study is "properly" designed, and examine enough subjects to push any difference between the groups they are examining beyond the level attributable to chance. The study might or might not show something that supported or refuted sound theoretical principles. Most, in Meehl's easily documented opinion, did not. "It is simply a sad fact," he wrote in his essay on "theoretical risks," "that in soft psychology theories rise and decline, come and go, more as a function of baffled boredom than anything else; and the enterprise shows a disturbing absence of that *cumulative* character that is so impressive in disciplines like astronomy, molecular biology, and genetics."

Instead of relying on significance testing, researchers might profitably test their theories by generating the most precise predictions the theories would allow—numerical point estimates, if possible—do so in multiple ways, and then examine consistency among the various estimates. The article in *Psychological Inquiry* at once criticized Meehl's own previous formulation and advanced a more refined development. Failure to confirm point estimates, he noted, could lead to premature abandonment of a salvageable theory, there being many plausible alternatives to theoretical failure as explanations for discorroborating evidence. Ad hoc tampering with the theory to make it fit new data, although often done, was no way to go about the theory-building endeavor. With scrupulous care, Meehl showed that defense and amendment of an apparently falsified theory was justified only when the theory displayed a substantial history of prior success (a good track record) in predicting improbable outcomes, and then defined two rough indexes for numerifying the track record.

I considered his article another typically Meehlian, beautifully elegant contribution to the social and behavioral sciences. In the letter that accompanied my "Attention All Students" notice in our school newsletter, I described the piece he had written as "the best statement on research strategy I have seen in years," and added that I had even found it useful in thinking about a current preoccupation of mine: a large-scale institutional effort to reduce racial tensions, sexism, homophobia, and other forms of social prejudice at Rutgers University. Meehl thought I had misunderstood his article:

To: Donald R. Peterson — *SPEED MESSAGE*

From: Paul E. Meehl — *Nov. 19, 1991*

Subject: Your letter 11/15/91

Don't spend too much time analyzing which parts of my Lakatosian article [he had borrowed some concepts from the philosopher Imre Lakatos] bear on your current "social engineering" concerns. Even my anti-null hypothesis-testing line may not apply to technological issues, as I believe my paper says somewhere. Only the cognitive goals of the "pure scientist" (in psy, sociol, poli sci, etc.) are directly impacted. Another issue: I fear one cause for (always latent, ready-to-grow) racism is reverse discrimination. I strongly oppose it. In our department, reverse discrimination has had a really malignant effect on excellence and amity.

11/27/91

Dear Paul,

Do not fear that I will over-generalize your 1990 Psych. Inquiry argument to my technological analyses. You set the limits clearly in your article, and my concerns are more closely akin to those of Don Campbell (making maps that fit) & Lloyd Humphreys (getting good empirical data) among your commentators than to those of pure scientists. Still, the questions you raise, if not your answers, must also be addressed by would-be social engineers. (Do I seek to falsify or merely amend the "theory" that direct education for practice in psychology produces more effective practitioners than other educational alternatives? How could I design useful evaluative research and detect a degenerating research program in appraising the conception?) The literature on program evaluation is of course directly pertinent, though the political nature of the social enterprise is discouraging. The last I read Lee Cronbach's good works on the topic, he seemed to have been driven into cynical withdrawal by seeing his efforts, to bring more rather than less fact and rationality into the social process, frustrated by the political interests of those in power.

I agree with you about the adverse effects of reverse discrimination but cannot publicly oppose "affirmative action" in most of the circles in which I am involved without being disqualified as a racist. One of the clearest findings from our local studies is the fury of many White males, especially working-class, at the unearned advantages they see being offered to women and people of color. The backlash is building, and all will suffer. Best hope I see is coming from Black intellectuals (e.g., Shelby Steele, Thomas Sowell) who argue that affirmative action, as currently practiced, has not only failed to help minorities but has hurt them by demeaning basic assumption and diversion of energy from development to entitlement.

Happy holidays,

Don

12/2/91

Dear Paul,

Semi-perseverative p.s. to my note of 11/27:

My enthusiasm for your Psy. Inquiry piece on appraising and amending theories was not confined to questionable extensions into my technological/political campaign against prejudice (all forms) and discrimination (all directions). I have maintained an interest in philos. of science ever since you got me to reading P. W. Bridgman & Carroll Pratt and suggested several courses with Feigl as a "collateral field" alternative to German and French. My scholarship is scant and spotty and my contributions nil, except indirectly. I sponsored a conference on hermeneutics as general editor of a series of symposia on applied psychology that produced in its course conferences and books on assessment, cognitive development, self-injurious behavior, and corporate competitiveness. In all fields, we assembled the best scholars we could find on a topic previously defined by one of our faculty teams, got them together for a conference (after preparing and exchanging draft statements), got the conferees to comment critically on work of others, and developed the most coherent statements possible out of the exchanges. I helped assemble the cast for the hermeneutics symposium & helped edit the book, but the main job was done by Stan Messer, Rob Woolfolk, and Louis Sass of our crew. I remember asking Stan to ask you if you would take part. (I was worried about the Positivist-bashing I saw among card-carrying Hermeneuts and wanted some post-Popperian to speak up.) You declined, we got one of my Illinois students, Don Meichenbaum, to come in as a voice of empiricism, and he did OK but didn't quite treat the topic with the depth and force you might have given it.

My interest in your Lakatosian argument is also tied to my continuing involvement in conceptualization, methodology, & research in one of the softest of all the soft areas of psychology: close relationships. I have worked with Hal Kelley, Ellen Berscheid, & others in this field, and find conceptual analyses (we never reached a theory), methodological guidelines, & even some of the instrumentation we developed useful in examining interaction process just about anywhere people influence one another, but I wish we had had advantage of your recent thinking when we were putting our ideas together. I think everybody involved (9 authors) had read your 1978 "Theoretical Risks …" article, but the people who wrote the research methodology chapter in our book (H. Kelley et al., 1983, Close Relationships) wound up defending most conventional null hypothesis-refuting research, and by then I was either too tired or negligent to argue with them.

Meanwhile, all anybody asks me to talk about is the education of professional psychologists. I'll be giving a talk at CUNY this Thursday titled "A PsyD Program Is Not a Clinical PhD Program Without Research," but I don't expect it to do much good. Development of practitioner programs has not occurred in strong universities, as I once hoped and predicted, but in little departments where people seem to think they can add a couple faculty lines & a half-time secretary to a Master's program in counseling and do a decent job of educating doctoral-level psychologists for practice. I feel like the Sorcerer's Apprentice.

Well anyway, Merry Christmas

Don

12/8/91

DRP: I didn't know whether you had maintained an interest in metatheory [I don't say "philosophy of science" unless I forget—propaganda reasons, plus shorter + adjectival form exists] or I wd not have felt it necessary to "warn" about my paper's intended relevance. As to positivist-bashers, can you mention a few points they make that (a) you didn't know already and (b) helped you think abt psy? I can think of almost none. By 1950, Feigl was an "empirical realist," as his "Existential Hypothesis" paper (1950) shows. Influence of Popper and Sellars, mostly. I can show, in my work, where I was helped by Feigl, Carnap, Reichenbach, Salmon, Popper, Hempel, up to 2 dozen I recently listed (when wife challenged my "2 dozen"). Lakatos helps re diachronic emphasis, but not much otherwise. Feyerabend is a brilliant nut. Kuhn never helped me one bit in thinking about psy matters, and his current effect in "soft" areas is positively cancerous. People now defend their theories by invoking his name (in ways I'm pretty sure he would dislike—he says early in his book that he doubts social science even has a paradigm yet!)

The important revisions of logical empiricist line came mostly from themselves, such examples as Carnap, Feigl, Hempel. I'm curious what you think the "new crew" really contributes.

PEM

From the Desk of P. E. Meehl

12/8/91

APPENDIX

Even my post-Lakatos theory testing formula is due to Feigl (center period 1950+) as much as Lakatos. And Lakatos doesn't stress a big Feigl (anti-Kuhn, anti-Quine, anti-Duhem) point, stressed recently by physicist Franklin, that we can usually test the auxiliaries separately, i.e., without regard to theory T.

On reverse discrimination, I strongly oppose it on several grounds, to wit:

1. *Violates the statute*
2. *Violates XIV amendment*
3. *Reduces excellence of organization (e.g., our dept. here)*
4. *Bad social engineering*
    a. *For group itself*
    b. *Backlash, reinforces latent prejudice*
5. *Unethical to punish Smith at x, t_1, for harm done Jones at y, t_2.*

#5 is the Biggie, with me. Suffices absent the others.

PM

12/19/91

Dear Paul,

OK, metatheory, as long as we understand that we're considering not only T [the substantive theory] but the auxiliaries, for me especially A_i [auxiliary theory of instruments]. The term is better than "philosophy of science" not only for the secondary reasons you mention (brevity, adjectival form) but primarily for its semantic accuracy—theory of theories.

Your challenge, to mention a few points that the postmodern, contextualist, hermeneutical, constructivist gang have offered that I didn't know already and that helped me think about psychology, yielded a pretty skimpy list.

Kuhn may not have helped you, probably because your grasp of history of science was at least as broad and deep as his, so you knew it all before, but he helped me, and I'll bet lots of other amateurs like me, gain a broader perspective on the process of scientific advance than I had before, tho I learned more from the questions he raised than from his answers, and agree that misinterpretations and over-extensions of his argument have probably done more harm than good in the social sciences.

I have learned from Ken Gergen to look more closely at social process as history (tho I already did in a limited way before reading him) and to consider the generativity of theory, along with verisimilitude, in appraising its value. Again, however, I fear his well-written, persuasive, but substantively questionable arguments re constructivism as an <u>alternative</u> to positivism will have evil effects on the field.

What else? Not much, now that I think of it. Don Spence on narrative vs. historical truth; the whole idea of the hermeneutic circle. Even these ideas, to me, are more confirmatory than revealing. The central demand of the Hermeneuts, "Thou shalt contextualize," I had already written about as the leading premise of my 1968 book, <u>The Clinical Study of Social Behavior</u>, and I came to that idea, as did Walter Mischel, by examining data rather than responding to rhetoric.

I think, as you do, that the most powerful advances in metatheory have come from the empirical realists themselves. Feigl always, Pap on open concepts, for me—you, more than anybody else. As soon as you and MacCorquodale & then you and Cronbach unlocked the operationist trap by way of constructs, construct validity, nomological nets, etc., the early confinements of primitive positivism were gone, as far as I was concerned. To me, the biggest mistake psychology made in its first 100 years (more serious even than the Fisherian misdirection you exposed so beautifully) lay not in its statistics but in its premature rush to assume the form of an advanced science (elegant theory, precise experiment) without first developing a broad, firm base of descriptive fact. We yearned for a Newton, when we had not yet seen a Kepler, and could not possibly have done so because there were no Tycho Brahes around willing to take the time and devote the care required to find out what was what in the natural world. I'm no Tycho, but I decided early that any contribution I might make to the field would come by way of description and the methods required to refine description.

In all of this, nothing has provided a more sturdy guide for inquiry than the criteria I learned mainly from Feigl so long ago: intersubjective testability, sufficiency of confirmation, precision (so far as subject matter allows) and comprehensiveness.

With best regards,

Don

CHAPTER

3

Kudos and Confusions

Throughout the time Meehl and I were corresponding about hermeneutics and related matters, two of his colleagues, C. Anthony Anderson and Keith Gunderson, were assembling a collection of Meehl's philosophical and methodological papers for possible publication by the University of Minnesota Press. The editors of the Press asked the philosopher Wesley Salmon to referee the submission, and Salmon's remarks appeared later in a foreword to the book:

> This collection of essays is a veritable goldmine. I had previously read a number of them—though by no means all—but rereading them brought back vividly the range and profundity of Meehl's work as well as the sheer delight of his writing style. This collection should be published, and it should be required reading for anyone seriously interested in such areas as philosophy of mind, philosophy of psychology, artificial intelligence, methodology of the social sciences, as well as such specific topics as the foundations of statistics, psychoanalysis, free will, moral responsibility, determinism, punishment, rehabilitation, and ESP.

> The world is full of scientists—especially senior scientists—in the physical, biological, and behavioral sciences who are eager to talk and write about the philosophy of their particular branch of science. The vast majority of them do it very badly. Paul Meehl is an outstanding—perhaps *the* outstanding—exception to that general rule. There are two main reasons. First, he is extraordinarily learned in philosophy, having mastered the thought of a wide variety of important thinkers. Second, he has a superb gift for philosophy, especially philosophy of science. He has benefited from and contributed to the Minnesota Center for Philosophy of Science in important ways over a period of several decades. When he philosophizes, philosophers and psychologists should listen. For example, in essays 2–7, he makes profound contributions to the age-old discussions of freedom of will and its relationship (or lack thereof) to determinism, and the mind–body problem. The great strength of these discussions arises in large part from his philosophically knowledgeable application of scientific details from psychology and neurophysiology to these problems.... I cannot praise this collection of essays too highly. They are clearly the product of a superb intellect ranging over a broad sweep of areas and issues. And, they are fun to read.
>
> From: Anderson, C. A., & Gunderson, K. (Eds.). (1991). *Paul E. Meehl: Selected philosophical and methodological papers* (pp. vii–viii, xiv). Minneapolis, MN: University of Minnesota Press. Reprinted by permission.

Shortly after the book appeared, Meehl sent me a copy, inscribed "To Donald R. Peterson, with esteem and affection." During the same period, I had been working with a team of editors and authors to produce a book on the history of psychotherapy. In 1992, the American Psychological Association (APA) celebrated the centennial anniversary of its establishment. Every one of the divisions of the APA, by then nearly 50 in number, organized some effort to examine the history of its own specialty, and I was asked by Donald Freedheim, then president of Division 29, Psychotherapy, to work with several others in exploring and describing the history of that field. Stanley Messer and Paul Wachtel agreed to edit a section on theory, Hans Strupp a section on research, Herbert Freudenberger and Donald Freedheim a section on practice, and I a section on education and training, with Freedheim as editor-in-chief.

We all knew each other, and all except Freedheim lived within easy reach of New York City, so we met for a series of organizational discussions in Herb Freudenberger's Manhattan office, decided on the authors we would invite to write the several chapters that would make up each section, and set to work writing overviews, prodding authors, and shaping what became a voluminous manuscript into publishable form. With helpful boosts from Jane Kessler, who wrote an introductory chapter to the entire volume, and Gary VandenBos, Editor of APA Books, we managed to get the book into print in time for the copyright date of the centennial anniversary, 1992. By APA standards, the book became a best seller, and all the editors were given extra copies in reward. I sent a copy to Meehl. In my inscription, I wrote, "to Paul E. Meehl, in gratitude for a lifelong education." In a cover letter, I said, "I haven't written any books lately with which I might repay you [for the book you sent me], but enclose one in which I was involved. It's so expensive I figured even a rich regents' professor emeritus would be unlikely to buy it."

5/18/92

Dear Don: I much appreciate the book gift, and the so-kind inscription. I find that when my research and writing don't go well (they almost always do, *but . . .) reflecting on the contributions of PhD's I either "advised" or influenced a lot, is therapeutic. Via persons like you, and Gough, and Dahlstrom, Buchwald, Seeman, Rorer, Lykken, Marks, Sundberg & Co., a "causal fan" spreads out thru still others I don't know, to yield knowledge contributions and literally 1000s of patients who were somewhat better diagnosed and treated than they would have been otherwise. I'm sure you feel the same way.*

The book gives me ammo for my 1990 (Boston) ABPP Prize lecture, which I'm revising for Amer. Psy'ist. Probably stupid referees will reject it. I'm urging tenured people, who needn't impress the Dean, to submit stuff to Carol Ammons [Editor of Psychological Reports]. She's great.

The book's photos are fun. Leslie says [about a photo of psychologists who attended the 1949 Boulder conference on training in clinical psychology], "Why, Jack Darley was a mere child!"

Regards,

Paul

Once the psychotherapy book was out, I started working on another. I had been invited by some of my colleagues in the National Council of Schools and Programs of Professional Psychology (NCSPP) to publish a collection of my papers on the education of professional psychologists. I agreed to try, but realized that the book would be incomplete without a thorough statement on the epistemological foundations of psychology as a profession and of the education required to prepare psychologists for professional careers. I felt adequately familiar with the work of analytic philosophers—critical realists like Meehl, Feigl, Carnap, Popper, et al.—but had not read the works of the postmodern, constructionist philosophers—the "new crew" that Meehl and I had discussed—either as diligently or as sympathetically as had some of my friends in the council. Fortunately, Roger Peterson, chair of the clinical psychology department in the Antioch New England Graduate School and more knowing about the fictionists than I was, agreed to collaborate in writing a chapter that would embrace both the analytic and constructionist perspectives. Roger and I, who had had many a long conversation about these matters before we began working together, talked some more, prepared drafts, and discussed them as collaborating authors do, and within a year or so had prepared a manuscript that we entitled "Ways of Knowing in a Profession." I sent a copy to Meehl, mainly to draw on his wisdom in correcting any mistakes I had made in interpreting the masters. Early in 1994, I received a puzzling letter from him:

1/17/94

DRP: I must say I admire your charitable tolerance of the dogmatic "positivist-bashers" in your surround, but I couldn't do it. The repeated allegations that the logical empiricists excluded theoretical concepts, or said they all must be "operationally defined," reduced explicitly to indubitable observation statements, that merely probable inferences were disallowed, etc., etc., are intellectually slovenly and—what deeply offends me—historically unjust, to some great minds I learned from, with brains considerably better than the current bunch of detractors. I recently came across the enclosed (I'm doing a bit of emeritus free lecturing for Will Grove, who took over my methodology class) which refutes the bashers. This paper was read in 1954, I believe, two generations ago!! And Feigl's amendments go back to 1950, the "Existential Hypotheses" article.

I really think the twisted history and false attributions are scandalous, and find it hard to respect such persons. I also disrespect their motives, which are obscurantist.

Regards,

PEM

P.S. Did I tell you that Bergmann, Carnap, [and] Feigl were all psychoanalyzed? Dumb to do, if one held probabilistic concepts to be inadmissible!

2/2/94

Dear Paul,

Thank you for your note re my "Ways of Knowing ..." paper & the page from Carnap's 1954/56 piece on theoretical concepts. I was puzzled, however, by your description of my attitude toward dogmatic positivist-bashers as one of "charitable tolerance." My composite crystallization of the postmodern attack on positivism (p. 3), which is made up entirely of literal or near-literal quotations from Gergen, Polkinghorne, et al., seemed to me so obviously dogmatic (& mistaken, to anyone who has actually read Carnap, Feigl, Meehl, et al.) that I assumed it would be immediately recognized as a caricature. The rest of my statement on the analytic philosophers was intended as a refutation of the "postmodern," positivist-bashing position, showing what the logical empiricists/critical rationalists actually said (rather than what their critics claim they said) by quoting Carnap (p. 6, his 1936 paper on "Testability and Meaning" written 3!! generations ago), and others, including Bridgman's (1959) relaxed operationism. Above all, I quoted Sir Karl [Popper] (pp. 9–10 and elsewhere) so extensively that I figured even those who lump Popper in with the positivists could not help but recognize the distortions in their views, and might be encouraged to desist from their misinterpretations.

I share completely your contempt for the shoddy scholarship, obscurantism, & moral injustice that many of the postmodern crowd display in their false attributions, and try to show, in my section "On Constraint and Inspiration in Disciplined Inquiry" (pp. 13–14), what study of the analytic philosophers has meant to me.

With best regards, Don

To: Donald R. Peterson *SPEED MESSAGE*

From: Paul E. Meehl *2/7/94*

Subject: Yr letter 2/2/94 re my note and yr "Ways of Knowing"

I hadn't read yr paper when I wrote that note, and I think I hadn't received it, although having no copy of my note, I can't check dates. You surely must have been puzzled by my note, if read as a response!! I think the only stimulus for my note was my Xeroxing pages of Carnap for Will Grove's Philos of Psy class, where I did 4 sessions at his request. No "external" event from DRP was involved. Sheer coincidence→mal-communication. Will respond when I finish your article. Meeting a deadline. Have to set aside for now.

Paul

2/16/94

Dear Paul,

Thanks for your note of 2/7. Sorry about misunderstanding. I'll appreciate any comments you care to make on my "Ways of Knowing" paper. No hurry. I'm on another deadline too.

Don

To: Donald R. Peterson *SPEED MESSAGE*

From: Paul E. Meehl *3/9/94*

Subject: Yr "Ways of Knowing"

Terrific, superb, brilliant!! I think of myself as one of the best interpreters of philos of sci to psychologists, but I could not do it that well. When I feel depressed about the field, it helps to think of my PhD's like you—Seeman, Welch, Golden, Grove, Rosen, Korman—smart guys whose minds were stimulated by me. I have only one small complaint, your use of Popper's word mistake. Aren't there 2 kinds? One (his usage) inevitable, as we can only guess. The other avoidable, epistemic error. I can err by betting on a poor horse. But betting on best horse, I can err, and no one cd do better, given my data. Agree?

Paul

Annoyed by the hypocrisy of practitioners who rejected the "medical model" of psychopathology but lobbied to include *all* mental health services in governmentally supported healthcare plans, I had written, "We cannot expect Manhattan cab drivers to help pay psychoanalysts large sums of money for strengthening the ego boundaries of the Woody Allens of the world." Just 2 days after I received his latest speed note, I learned that Paul had had the same idea:

From the Desk of P. E. Meehl

3/11/94

DRP: I've been saying (for 3–4 years now) that "not clear why the widow charwoman's taxes—when she doesn't seek psy help—should pay for Prof. Glotz's 100 couch hours, complaining that he dislikes his boss, with official Dx of reactive depression." So I enjoyed your remark about taxi-driver paying for Woody Allen! We think alike about many things. That was surely not a topic discussed here when you were my student. It's a type of mind!

PEM

3/22/94

Dear Paul,

Thanks for your very kind comments on the "Ways of Knowing" paper. Pellets like those, from you, should be enough to keep me going the rest of my life.

Re your "small complaint" on my use of Popper's word mistake. Indeed there are 2 kinds: the inevitable errors of bold conjecture, and avoidable epistemic errors where data point one way and the erring one goes another. Any clinician who cannot read the signs of clinical depression and does not know the statistical risk of suicide, for example, is not to be forgiven for human fallibility, but should be ousted from the profession on grounds of incompetence. I'll take another look at my paper to see if I can make the distinction clear.

Yes, we do think alike on lots of issues. I know reliability does not guarantee validity, but the thought of our concordance comforts me all the same, especially since I seem to be disagreeing with so many others.

Thank you again for your comments.

Don

CHAPTER

4

Prizewinners, Perils, and Parapraxes

In 1995, officers of the APA Division of Clinical Psychology (Division 12, now called the "Society" of Clinical Psychology) decided to identify the person they considered the "Clinical Psychologist of the Century." At the end of their surveys and deliberations, they chose two luminaries: Paul Meehl and Hans Eysenck. Meehl's contributions were uniformly recognized. I doubt that anyone questioned his selection. Eysenck was equally well known. He had first come to international notice among psychologists during World War II as head of the only notable clinical psychology program in Great Britain. His was a sternly "scientific" operation at the Maudsley psychiatric institute, devoted exclusively to the functions Eysenck considered useful and appropriate for clinical psychologists: research and assessment, valued in that order. Psychotherapy, popular among clinicians in America, was specifically excluded from clinical psychology as Eysenck defined it. To him, psychotherapy was a nondescript "healing art" of dubious value.

In 1954, Eysenck published an article purporting to show that psychotherapy, as then practiced, was no more effective than were the psychological self-corrections that occur naturally with the passage of time. To clinical psychologists who were devoting their careers to the various kinds of "talking cures" that Freud, along with Freud's followers and dissenting creators of alternative approaches, had invented, Eysenck's article was a bombshell. Nobody in the field could ignore his argument. Studies and articles questioning his interpretations soon flooded the journals.

All along, Eysenck had been producing his own flood of research on the description of psychological disorders. Instead of diagnosing people with "mental illnesses" by naming the "disease" they had—schizophrenia, manic-depressive psychosis, obsessive-compulsive neurosis, or whatever—Eysenck urged psychologists to develop an alternative descriptive system based on research, rather than the opinions of committees of psychiatrists who formulated successive editions of the *Diagnostic and Statistical Manual of Psychiatric Disorders* (DSM) that was, and still is, the standard schema that all mental health professionals are required to use in diagnosing patients for purposes of legal protection and insurance-based financial reimbursement. Eysenck proposed that psychologists begin by describing the actual symptom patterns that people with psychological problems displayed, and then develop, through factor analytic research, a diagnostic system composed of continuous dimensions along which all people, normal and abnormal, could be located. The main factors that emerged in many of his early studies were neuroticism, psychoticism, and introversion-extraversion, although many more specifically refined variations were presented in the 80 books and some 1,600 articles he published in his long career.

In midlife, Eysenck changed his mind about the therapeutic capabilities of psychologists and psychiatrists. He remained as contemptuous as ever of psychoanalysis and other forms of conversational psychotherapy, but he saw promise, and then began to accumulate data, on the efficacy of treatment procedures that were rooted in established principles of learning and shown to be effective by rigorous experimental research. Along with Joseph Wolpe, who had invented a learning-based procedure that he called "systematic desensitization" for the treatment of phobias, and B. F. Skinner, whose principles of operant behavior control formed the basis for a range of "behavior modification" procedures, Eysenck was widely recognized as one of the founders of behavior therapy. Nobody who read the research literature in clinical psychology could dispute the impact that Eysenck's research and writing had had on the field.

Nevertheless, I had reasons of my own to question Eysenck's elevation alongside Meehl as "Clinical Psychologist of the Century":

4/24/95

Dear Paul,

I just heard that you had been selected "Clinical Psychologist of the Century" by Division 12. Congratulations! I cannot imagine a more fitting tribute.

I am less pleased by the Division's other choice, Hans Eysenck, partly because he is not & never was a clinical psychologist (per my definition), but even more because I have long questioned his integrity. When I was working with Ray Cattell on personality structure in children, & had already come around to an Eysenckian position on number of dependably replicable factors (a few rather than many), I tried to replicate a study Hilde Himmelweit had done in Eysenck's lab, using the "objective tests" E had developed. Eysenck was very helpful in giving me detailed info about the tests & I ran my own study in the U.S. employing the tests, but my results were garbage. No structure. Unreliability throughout. I didn't publish the study. Presumably couldn't have if I had tried. I came to suspect that Himmelweit had either concocted or cooked the data. Maybe she was the prime culprit, but Hans cited the study without qualification, didn't offer a word of caution in his correspondence with me, & I never quite trusted his work after that.

Again, please accept my congratulations on this, your latest well-deserved honor.

Don

5/3/95

Dear Don: Thanks for the "pellet" letter. I really can't feel I deserve it, but who does. Our field is a funny one, that way. Think of paradox that the co-winners Eysenck & Meehl disagree strongly about some very big, basic issues (e.g., he denies schizophrenia even exists, he has faith that factor analysis can test taxonicity, he spits on Freud, he believes factor-based questionnaires more valid than MMPI). I've never made up my mind about his lasting contributions, and, like you, I'm suspicious of him. He says dogmatic things about nosology, ignores a half-dozen different evidence domains on existence of Sc (e.g., pharmacologic specificity, psychosomatic patterns, family genetic studies, soft neurology, recent psychophysiology). He's really unscholarly in this respect. It shocks me.

And he persists in the (undergraduate) error that unless a factor emerges, there can't be a latent taxon. Awful....

Regards.

Paul

P.S. I've been gravely ill, subacute bacterial endocarditis, but now 95% recovered. Before penicillin, it was 100% fatal—still some 15% die.

5/8/95

Dear Paul,

I was very sorry, & greatly concerned, to learn about your illness. Pray God the antibiotics work. I shall hold a special set of good thoughts for you.

I found your comments on Eysenck not only interesting, but especially disturbing. Wouldn't be so bad if the two of you merely disagreed re etiology of Sc, relevance of factor analysis to taxonicity, etc. The trouble is he is wrong, dead wrong, on those issues, but is either too little of a scholar or too much of a big-head to acknowledge it. Re your honor, as clinical psychologist of the century, of course you deserve it. Who else, among the living?

I don't know whether you feel up to reading much these days, but I enclose some stuff I hope you will enjoy. My colleagues in the Council of Professional Schools have asked me to put together some of my papers on the education of professional psychologists for publication as a book, & suggested I write an autobiographical piece for the beginning and some afterthoughts for the end. I did that, and you figure large in both statements. If you're not up to reading what I wrote, I'll have to take a chance I got most of it right, but if you can read it, I hope you will let me know about any inaccuracies you spot, or anything you find in questionable taste. I have included some of our personal correspondence (e.g., the "Meekl" exchange), edited to exclude anything you or others might find offensive or that ought to remain private. If I missed, I hope you will tell me.

Please get well.

With best regards,

Don

5/18/95

Dear Don: I am 95% recovered, out of danger, only residual is a bit of fatiguability, a common result. Echocardiogram shows no further mitral valve damage. Antibiotics are great. Do the social constructionists call in a witch doctor if they fall ill with s.b.e., I wonder?

I find no historical errors (relying on my memory as "criterion") in your account. Some stuff I had forgotten, or mebbe never knew. A fun read! I'm curious to know who was the psychoanalyst from Chicago that couldn't tolerate your searching questions. Could it be C. Knight Aldrich, who was here for awhile and disliked psychologists, barely concealed it?*

Too bad you can't print my paraphrase of ole Ned Springer's slips, I suppose too crude. But if you wanted to, I'd not mind.

Yes, there really is something haywire with Hans Eysenck, worse with age + prestige. Despite his "productivity," I never did see him as all that super. And I agree with you, he isn't really a clinician. No seasoned clinician could believe that simplistic theory.

Regards,

Paul

P.S.: Leslie & I were warmed by your expressions of concern.

6/13/95

Dear Paul,

I just returned from a 3-week stay in Vermont to find your letter of 5/18, with its good news about your near-complete recovery. Thank God—or rather Waksman et al. & modern antibiotics.

The psychoanalyst I tangled with in Illinois was Howard Weatherly, who never wrote anything, as far as I know, & died some years ago in California.

Thanks for checking my autobiographical stuff. I left out your paraphrase of Ned Springer's parapraxis mainly because I thought you might find print-

*In my chapter, I had written the following statement about my early work at the University of Illinois psychological clinic:

In those days the concept of the psychiatric team was very much in force. Intake was handled by our social worker. Psychologists gave tests and did psychotherapy. Because the University of Illinois medical school was in Chicago, we had to import medical coverage and psychiatric supervision by way of a psychoanalyst who commuted to Urbana by train once a week. Our father figure was a dapper man, handsome and expensively dressed. Intelligent and compassionate too. His interviews showed a penetrating skill, and the effects were sometimes dramatically revealing. I learned a great deal from the demonstrations he offered from time to time. However, he was given to interpretations that I sometimes considered far-fetched, and whenever I challenged one of those in a case conference he grew visibly irritated. On two or three occasions he raised questions before the group about the dynamic origins of my hostility. I didn't think I was hostile. I thought I was seeking clarity and truth. But he may have read me better than I knew. I began to get headaches during the conferences and avoided them as often as I could.

ing it in poor taste, but if you wouldn't mind I'll reconsider. I can't see where it will hurt readers to know we're human.

With best regards,

Don

6/17/95

DRP: My paraphrase of Ned S's 2 parapraxes is too funny to erase, but I do understand your worry.... I have no objection to quoting it. As you say, shows we're human.

PEM

About a week later, I sent Meehl a revised draft of my chapter, with his statement to Springer restored to its original form. I added a note to say, "If some prissy editor objects, I'll argue":

6/30/95

Dear Don: The quote reads fine, but I'll bet they won't allow it. One way psychologists try to feel "scientific" is stuffy prose (e.g., indirect discourse, passive voice, never use pronoun "I"). Let me know how it goes.

Paul

3/27/96

Dear Paul,

I had some trouble finding a publisher for my book ["too personal" plus low sales potential were the common objections] but APA Books recently agreed to take on the project & I am hard at work on a final revision.... By now, the ms. has been repeatedly reviewed, and no one so far has said a word about the Springer-Meehl exchange. I have kept quiet about it and will continue to do so. We'll see what the copy editor has to say.

Don

The copy editor had nothing to say. The book was published in 1997.

CHAPTER

5

Morality

In 1996, the APA held its annual convention in Toronto. Both Meehl and Eysenck gave invited addresses in response to their selection as Clinical Psychologists of the Century. By this time, I had stopped attending APA meetings regularly, but I didn't want to miss this one, so I had a chance to hear both talks and congratulate both recipients—Eysenck sincerely, for his genuine contributions to the field, and Meehl personally, rather than by letter. I also had a chance to talk with Paul face to face, a pleasure I had not had for several years. In the course of one of our conversations, I mentioned that I had just written an autobiographical narrative entitled, "The Professional Psychologist as a Moral Agent." Meehl asked me to send him a copy. I did so, along with a note saying how good it had been to see him in Toronto:

8/27/96

Dear Don: We found your chapter MS on moral agent fascinating. Perhaps you had told me of your childhood but I have forgotten it. <u>Most</u> interesting. The shaping of values (the goddam politicos have made me antsy about the world, more than Feigl did!) is, I think, a DEEP sociopsy business that we don't un-

derstand well, agreed? I'm sure it's an interactive mix of modelling, reward/punishment, and precept-teaching. (Our colleagues tend to dismiss #3, but I believe that's mistaken.) I am still surprisable by the shabby ethics one finds in academia. Persons with security, prestige, autonomy, interesting work, who are spiteful, petty, who lie, who keep enemies' lists, etc. Recently I was on a PhD oral (philosophy) where a full prof, whose intellect and work I admire, tried to flunk an A+ candidate because he hates the major advisor. Disgusting—and hard to understand.

I've fussed about ethics as a "cognitive" domain since high school. Wrote a small book on it (memo to Feigl) and dismissed it.

Yes, Toronto was nice, but I got a BAD tooth the next day, aaagh ... and we are mourning our cat Otto Rank, who died shortly after our return.

Paul

Addendum

I knew Mowrer [a section headed "Psychology and Morality" in my chapter had begun with the sentence, "The first severe jolt to my simplistic identification of truth and virtue came through my relationship with O. Hobart Mowrer"] was subject to severe D spells (unipolar or bipolar? ever strongly "up"?) but somehow I got idea his suicide was a rational one, given Dx of disease of some sort. Was it the obit [in the American Psychologist] that said, or implied, that? Can unipolars be that productive and creative? They're usually "down" a bit between episodes, I find.

I thought he was muddled about religion, so it intrigues me that you began to react positively—especially as most psychologists did not, for various reasons, some good, some bad. My view is deviant, differs from the "sympathetic non-believers." The best scholarship (Roman, Lutheran, Anglican, agnostic, Jewish) has converged pretty much to non-Christian conclusions as to Jesus of Nazareth. So one can examine his alleged moral teachings "on the merits," as one would Aristotle, Confucius, Buddha, Bertrand Russell, Albert Ellis, or Ayn Rand (HAH!) By that inspection, Jesus fares very poorly. Rehash of contemporary rabbinical dicta, repeats of the earlier prophets, and a main stress on the immanent arrival of The Kingdom, which didn't happen. Bluntly, why should I care what this confused, fanatical itinerant thaumaturge/exorcist said? (Hardnosed response of an ex-Lutheran skeptic. Residue of my "Lutheran Phase," sound but unpopular in these days of subjectivism. Thesis: If Jesus was not what Paul et al claimed, or even what he himself claimed, tho that's doubtful, with what authority does he speak?)

RD 1, Box 975
Windsor, VT 05089
September 13, 1996

Dear Paul,

Thank you for your letter re my "moral agent" piece.

I agree passionately that the shaping of social values is a DEEP sociopsychological morass that (a) is very poorly understood, (b) is vitally important not only to our whole society but to me personally, as a therapist, as an educator, as a citizen, as a person, as a parent—every which way, (c) lots of people in positions of influence (Bill Bennett, Ralph Reed, et al.) are appallingly sanctimonious about, and (d) is beyond my personal ken at this stage of my life.

About 10 years into my time at Illinois, I considered devoting much or most of the rest of my career to the topic. I'd been studying juvenile delinquency with Herb Quay and parent–child relationships with Wes Becker and others, & thought to focus on moral development for the rest of my time, but on closer inspection decided not to try any further research in the area for the same reason you said you didn't do any research on psychotherapy. I didn't know how. I think Piaget, Kohlberg, Gilligan, & others have brought us along a little way in our understanding, but credentialed knowledge, as against fervent opinion and rigidly determined insistence on moving the opinions into public policy through political action, is in very short supply. I am more than "antsy" about what the politicos are doing to the world. As Daniel Patrick Moynihan said about the Gingrich-type Republicans in Congress, "They are so sure of themselves, and they know so little. They chill my butt."

My qualified acceptance of Hobart Mowrer's views brought these issues to a head for me forcefully. Mowrer's meta-ethical position was about as close to hard-core ethical realism as I ever found in a psychologist I admired, though he usually spoke of ethical rules as products of "the hard-won wisdom of society," and never, within my hearing, as God-given mandates. Some interesting discussions with Missouri Synod Lutherans & Jesuits revolved about this point in the Lilly Foundation seminars [initiated and run by Mowrer to encourage dialogue among theologians and psychologists on questions of value in human affairs]. His mood swings were bipolar. Most of the time he was in a mild to moderate hypomanic state—cheerful, very energetic. We could all see the D coming on. He'd slow down, wouldn't show up at the office, etc. As you probably know, he tried everything to deal with it—2 psychoanalyses, at least 1 non-psychoanalytic psychotherapist, every kind of anti-depressant drug, ECT (he accepted evidence on biogenic origins) plus the integrity groups that he and Mollie ran weekly in their home, as much, he acknowledged, for his own benefit as for benefit of others. His suicide was "rational" in the sense that it did not occur when he was in the throes of a deep depression, tho I have a hunch he felt one coming on. His dear (but also vexing) Mollie had died, his children were grown & gone, he felt that his work was done, & saw little but pain and trouble to others in the future. So he went around to say private good-byes to his children and after that one night swallowed a large number of sleeping pills. I was very fond of Hobart and wrote a personal obituary for a minor journal after he died. I'll send you a copy when I get back to New Jersey. Right now we're watching the slow advance of autumn in Vermont, and I'm mixing golf & social pleasures with equally pleasant reading of history & biographies of some admirable but ethically troubled, and often muddled forebears. As you said once about your own life, I love retirement.

I found your comments on Jesus of Nazareth fascinating, but this letter is already too long for counter-comment, which, if I tried one, would be less well informed but largely in agreement with yours. I'll send you a copy of a sermon I gave at Rutgers' Kirkpatrick Chapel while I was involved in my work on social prejudice. I describe my own religious leanings as those of a "fallen-away Unitarian." No, I don't think you & I ever talked about my childhood. Like the Army, all behind me & too many more interesting subjects to discuss.

Don

10/4/96

Dear Don: That's a fine obit you wrote. A very interesting and admirable man, he was. I only met him once, he talked on religion, not a very persuasive talk, people were disappointed. I was urged to give a post-visit lecture in reply, which I did. People didn't much like mine either, but for different reasons.

Perhaps you can help me in tracking a cite. In a fat book of his "integrative" kind, he had said (in MS?) that Stephenson first used inverse factor analysis in the 1950s (or late 40s, I don't recall exactly). I told him Ed Bordin did it in 1939 or 1940, his Ohio State PhD thesis. Mowrer made the correction in a 2nd book, or mebbe in a footnote to original text? But would I have seen MS or galley? We were not on such terms that he would have sent me an MS or whatever. I've tried to track this but failed. I thought it was a book on psychotherapy and learning theory (in title, that is). I do recall the big box showing P, Q, and R type correlations was in it, same locus as the Bordin footnote. DON'T toil on this—I thought it might be easy for you being more familiar. I may be conflating two totally unrelated loci.

I gather you tend to agree with Mowrer on ethics & behavioral "dis-ease." [Mowrer claimed that neurotic distress, i.e., dis-ease, was generally a conse-

quence of undersocialization and too little conscience, rather than oversocialization and a harshly punitive superego, as Freud had said.] I don't, much, but am open to it. For the major disorders (schizophrenia, bipolar, unipolar depression) I don't think it's a helpful conceptualization. I doubt it for panic disorder and for "classic" obsessive- compulsive disorder. But that leaves a wide field of other neurotic & psychopathic stuff where he has a point.

Paul

10/5/96

Dear Don: Bang-up sermon you gave! We differ on egoism/altruism thing, too "deep" for letters to work. And probably reflect very deep personality differences. I am a non-groupy fellow, first noted at age 7 or 8 when the teacher's Big Pitch was for our room (grade 2 or 3) to have best showing in supporting this cause or that. It had no effect on me—I always brought a little token batch—and I was puzzled that almost everyone responded. This defect in Trotter's "Herd Instinct" is probably a moral defect, as you (and Mowrer, and Don Campbell) view things. If so, I plead guilty. It's how I am, and I feel no impulse to change. Partly because I'm sure others perceive me as a reliably moral agent, in fact I suspect am above (academics') average in fulfilling my obligations and avoiding wrong-doing. But your sermon asks for more than that.

I wrote a critical reply to Campbell's APA prexy address, but never published it, or sent it to him. I am unconvinced that Herd Instinct does more good than harm. You expound the biological basis for the harm at the sermon's beginning, very nicely. I think war, racism, class-ism, ideological conflict, etc., derive largely from the Herd Instinct. Only a few persons (e.g., Hitler) are extremely evil, but most people are gregarious + stupid, so they fall for the Hitlers. Altruism impels a few people to send money or clothes or food to Greece after an earthquake; OK, that's peanuts. But it impels many people to swallow the goddam rulers' Vietnam lies, and for years.

Paul

Addendum

Bertrand Russell said (in autobiog? I d.k. where), "In my youth I was troubled because most people selfishly pursue their own happiness; I now realize that the main problem is their not doing that because they're trying to generate unhappiness in others. If we could get people to pursue their own happiness rationally and stop trying to make others unhappy, we would usher in the millennium." Altho of course exaggerated—as Russell often was on moral and political questions—his statement has a lot of merit, I think. But one must add, to "rationally," the term ethically. That opens up the can of worms. I am an "ethical minimalist-rigorist," which sounds an oxymoron but is not. It says, "Only a few moral rules, but try hard to obey them." I have a colleague who worries (or claims to?) about the peons in Peru, but he once left PhD prelims unread for 5 weeks while students sweated. There's a lot of that in academia, and I strongly disapprove of it. "Charity begins at home" is a good motto.

October 29, 1996

Dear Paul,

Your letters of 10/4 (re Mowrer obit) & 10/5 (re sermon) were in the mail headed for VT while I was in my car coming back to NJ. My fault—I'd failed to notify secretary of sudden change in travel plans. Please forgive delay.

I'm pretty sure the citation re Stephenson, Bordin, and inverse factor analysis that you were seeking per your letter of 10/4 is Mowrer's chapter on Q technique in Psychotherapy: Theory and Research (1953). I didn't "toil" to find this, but I did penetrate the local stacks to look it up & find that Hobart credits W. Stephenson & Godfrey Thompson for first use of Q-technique in 1935, & Ed Bordin for first use of Q-tech. in his OSU dissertation (1942). My guess is Hobart hadn't known about Bordin's work until you told him about it. He thanks you, Starke Hathaway, & others for "particular info." in a chapter footnote in the 1953 edition of the book.

My agreement with Mowrer on ethics and behavioral "dis-ease" is heavily qualified. I agree with you that for the major disorders (Sc, bipolar, unipolar D) the conception is not only "not helpful" but is seriously misleading. Mowrer came to this same view in his later years, but by then was off on his "new group therapy" kick & did not, to my knowledge, publish a retraction/correction. I share your doubts about pertinence of the idea for panic and obsessive-compulsive disorders, but know no research on the topic, and the research I do know (I did some of it) on garden-variety low-level anxiety and depression of the kind most of us see in outpatient Rx support Mowrer's hypothesis.

I think we differ less on our views of egoism/altruism than your letter of 10/5 (& my sermon) suggest. I agree that many of our species-endangering evils (war, mass murder based on racial/religious hatred, etc.) derive largely from some kind of Herd Instinct, & try to say so in my sermon. I also agree emphatically that "Charity begins at home" and am as disgusted as you are by the hypocrisy of colleagues who are big on altruistic generalities at cocktail parties and sometimes in lectures and writings, & then do the kinds of outrageous things you mention in your letters (leaving exams unread while students sweat, going after political enemies in their dept. by punishing adversaries' students—I've seen that one a lot) in their personal lives. One of my colleagues at Illinois (no longer there) wrote high-sounding prose about social justice in the early days of the community psychology craze, but, while married, screwed every pretty female grad. student he could seduce & skipped town leaving a pi-

ano dealer holding the bag for the price of a grand piano, less the down payment that brought the piano into his possession.

Without ever talking about it, you influenced my attitudes & behavior in these matters. I wouldn't expect you to remember it, but you asked me to take over your lectures in Intro. to Clin. Psy. on a couple of occasions when you had to leave town for colloquia elsewhere. I was honored by the request & would cheerfully have done my best for nothing, but you actually paid me for my work. On reflection, I thought that was fair. I was especially impressed with your practice of seeing that the students in the course got all the content they were paying for (or at least the best a sub. like me could offer) instead of just canceling the classes. When I went to Illinois, I followed the pattern you had set, except a few times when my lecture notes were too sketchy to inflict on anyone else.

Anyway, I certainly agree that the first obligation for all of us is personal integrity. That was Hobart's main point. He and I would also agree with you in your mimimalist-rigorist position (few rules, but stick to them) in a general sense, but may differ in emphases on "involvement" & "responsibility," the 2 moral imperatives that Mowrer added to "integrity" in his definition of core values. I don't know how wide the differences between you and me are, but suspect they are smaller than your comments appear to presume. I'm non-groupy too, in my way. Never went for the "go-team" stuff in school, never joined a study group, enlisted in the Army, but not because I felt a passion to save our society (tho I was plenty worried about prospects of Nazi/Jap victory). I enlisted partly to get into a program that sent me to college to study engineering for awhile & promised a shot at a commission (which I never received), and partly for the adventure that war service provided. In psychology, the only organizations I've ever joined are APA and Div. 12 (none of the sections), & the National Council of Professional Schools, which I helped found as a leaky organizational bulwark against lousy professional training & for which I felt responsible. There was talk about "doing your part" in my growing-up years, and I'm sure I absorbed some of it, but the main reasons I've done things that have an altruistic look to them are (a) that somebody asked me to and the challenge looked interesting, & (b) because I feel best when I'm doing something that seems to have a chance of helping somebody else. I'll bet we're fairly even on need: Nurturance, which has to be involved somehow in motivation of altruistic behavior. In one of our conversations a few years back—I think to discuss failure of PsyD plan at U of M—you casually mentioned that you were thinking of increasing your practice, & said something like, "I don't feel quite right unless I'm helping somebody."

But as you say in your letter of 10/5 all this is too deep for letters to work. As you presume, I went along with Don Campbell's APA pres. arguments without questioning them cognitively, and with heartfelt sympathy for the spirit of the piece. I'd be interested in your objections, if you still have a copy of your critical reply to D.C. & are willing to send it to me.

Don

11/9/96

Dear Don: Thanks for Mowrer reference. There was no urgency—I tend to be a "quick responder," as you are, but that doesn't imply urgency.

I seem to have given the impression that I consider you a "groupy" type, which is not the case. I suspect you are below the mean, as some of your self-reports would suggest. I even think you may be a trifle introverted, like me. Persons with high g, fluency, ambition, n[eed]: Achievement, energy, social potency, get rated "extrovert" by less perceptive judges, I think. There are several paths to an altruistic group-oriented ethic, and temperamental n: Affiliation (= "groupiness") is only one of them, I believe. I can't find my draft of anti-Campbell—pencil only, I think—but it is somewhere. I can't believe I just trashed it. The 2 main complaints were (a) Herd Instinct often harmful, mebbe more often than helpful, and (b) accepting religion in a "symbolic" (= not true) sense is a cop-out and muddle-headed.

Hendrickson book on McNamara is powerful, as strong as Mc's was feeble. He never once admits "We were evil-doers," only "We made mistakes." That disgusts me. Those crumbs lied and lied and lied, killed 58,000 young men for nothing except their own libido dominandi. Yech!

Paul

P.S.: Leslie points out the goddam politicians don't even say, "I made mistakes," they say, "Mistakes were made," as if the cosmos did it.

11/18/96

Dear Paul,

Report of solitary ways during my childhood & beyond was intended not so much to correct possible misperception on your part as to note remarkable resemblance between the dispositions you felt and showed as a kid & those I felt and saw in myself. There may be, as you said in your prior letter, "deep" personality differences between us, but I have seen no sign of them yet, and whatever diffs. there may be, standing on n: Affiliation does not appear to be one of them. Sure enough, I've come in on the introversive side on every I/E test I've ever taken.

If your anti-Campbell comments ever turn up, I'd appreciate your sending me a copy, but I'm sure I'd agree with one of your complaints and suspect I'd agree with the other. In my view, the Herd Instinct not only may be but is more often harmful than helpful in society today—atavistic remnant of disposition that brought the species thru the first few million years but must be transcended now. I would need to reread Campbell's paper & see yr comment (to see what you mean by "true" religion) to decide about your second complaint.

I haven't read McNamara's book, & from reviews & knowledge of his history don't think I want to. He and his ilk not only killed 58,000 black and white American men but at least hundreds of thousands of brown & yellow Asian men, women, & children. And then he wants to come clean by saying, "Some mistakes were made." Jesus. I haven't seen Hendrickson's book but will keep my eyes open for it.

I'll be out of commission for awhile. I'm scheduled for surgery Monday to ream out a carotid artery & once recovered from that [will have] another operation to repair an abdominal aortal aneurysm. I hate to see this once perfectly dependable body show some cracks, but the odds are on my side (risk of "complication" during the carotid job = .01; risk, absent operation, for one of my history and numbers, of major stroke within a year (=) .25–.30). I expect to come through fine.

Don

P.S. Modern imagery technology is <u>*fabulous*</u>*. Ulceration in my carotid and bubble in aorta clearer than any 1940s x-ray of bones. Praise God for modern science.*

Around this time, Meehl resumed his practice of rubber-stamping the envelopes in which he mailed his letters with a political slogan:

Caligula

For

Proconsul

Later I learned that Paul had the stamp made in 1968, following Lyndon Johnson's decision not to run for president and the bloody Democratic convention that nominated Hubert Humphrey, and during Humphrey's campaign against Nixon. It was meant to reflect his opinion of politics and politicians in general. He brought out the stamp again and again in subsequent elections, along with a t-shirt he wore at the office and campaign buttons bearing the same slogan. When anyone showed amusement or curiosity about the button he pinned on his jacket, Paul would take it off and cheerily hand it to the other. When he got home, he would take another from a box in the basement and wear it the following day. Johnson and McNamara, Nixon and Kissinger, Humphrey, McGovern, Reagan, Bush—it didn't matter. Meehl never voted in a presidential election after Vietnam.

CHAPTER

6

Peterson's Sermon

During the final 2 years in my job as dean of our school of applied psychology at Rutgers, I had spent at least one third of my time as chair of a group called "The Committee to Advance Our Common Purposes," which was charged with the formidable task of "strengthening the social fabric of the university" by combating intergroup animosities—racial tensions, homophobic attacks, and the like—that were flaring on campus in those times. I was not responsible for the name of the committee; that was the work of the late Edward J. Bloustein, then president of Rutgers, who had asked me to organize the activities of the group. Bloustein himself was very active in the effort. He set aside funds to support our activities and appointed an executive committee that included the vice president for student affairs and the vice president for personnel. We met briefly as a steering committee every week, and went on about our business in between.

To bring the work of the committee to the attention of the Rutgers community, Bloustein and I gave many talks to constituent groups. He called our number "The Don and Ed Show." Early in the second year of our operation, John Cooney, an ordained minister in the Dutch Reformed Church and university chaplain, asked me to talk about prejudice and bigotry as the sermon for a Sunday service in Kirkpatrick Chapel, historic site of the worship services that all Rutgers students had once been required to attend. I gave my talk on October 2, 1988. As is my usual custom for brief presentations, I spoke without notes. As I left the chapel, Cooney asked me to prepare a written version, so I did. This is the sermon I sent to Meehl:

The Phylogeny of Prejudice

Or Why We Love Our Own and Hate Those Others

Donald R. Peterson

Rutgers University

Over the past two years, several ugly expressions of racial, sexual, and religious bigotry have appeared on the campus of Rutgers University. Last year a swastika was spray-painted on a wall at the B'nai B'rith Hillel Foundation. "Kill Jews." "Boot Power." Posters advertising Black and Hispanic events have been defaced. "Deport Puerto Ricans." "Kill Niggers." "Spics and Niggers go home." Several incidents of date rape were reported, and women organized a march to protest. Our own fraternity boys sat on the porches and shouted obscenities at them. Someone painted the word "FAG" on the car of a homosexual man, who wasn't quite sure then whether or not to report the incident to the police. He was very uneasy about the way he might be treated.

The outrages we have seen at Rutgers are no worse than those that have appeared on many campuses across the country, public and private, large and small. The Universities of Colorado, Michigan, and Wisconsin, the Citadel, Smith College, Purdue, and Pennsylvania State University are among those that have felt the "rising tide of racism," as some have called it. In some cases, the tensions have erupted in physical violence. White and black students got into a head-bashing fight at the University of Massachusetts a couple of years ago.

Except for the perpetrators, we are all appalled by these events. In a university, of all places, the fount of knowledge and free inquiry, the hideous corruptions of bigotry seem especially out of place. But we should not be surprised. The roots of prejudice run deep in the human spirit, and the potential for violence is latent in us all.

The capacity to love and the capacity to hate are fundamentally connected in human beings. The urge to protect and the urge to destroy are connected in the same way. We attack other people in the belief that we are protecting ourselves, our loved ones, and the group with whom we feel the closest bonds. Altruism—but only toward our own—and aggression—but only toward the other—are tied together in the fiber of our beings.

This link, between love of our own and hatred based on fear of others, has a long evolutionary history. Except for the human brain, and now I add, except for our organization into intimate groups, the human species could never have survived on this planet. The little naked hominid running through the bushes 4 million years ago didn't seem to have much of a chance. He had no natural protective armor. He wasn't as strong as the big cats, nor nearly as fast. He had no fangs or claws of any consequence. He couldn't fly like a bird or swim like a fish. Life was precarious, and not many of those early creatures made it to maturity. When agriculture was invented, around 10,000 years ago, there were probably more baboons on earth than people. To survive as a species, human beings had to band together. Nobody wanted to take on a mastodon alone, but if the group hunted together as a pack they could chase a mastodon over a cliff and eat it. As near as we can tell, human beings have lived together in small groups—extended families that became tribes—from the very beginning. Not only their wits and their tools, but above all their solidarity, mutual support within the small, intimate group, has kept the human species from extinction these millions of years.

Besides the advantage in getting food and fending off the perils of nature that social organization provided, close membership in a strong group allowed one tribe to fight off the invasions of other tribes, who were perfectly willing to kill them for access to a scarce water supply or the rights to a productive hunting ground. To survive as an individual, every person had to be a loyal member of his or her immediate group. Acceptance was life; exclusion was death. To survive as a group, cohesion had to be strong, and solidarity complete. Fighting for their lives against another tribe, everybody had to stick together and win—or all would die. As short a time as 2,000 years ago, it was commonly assumed that protection of one's own always required destruction of the enemy. It was simply understood that military conquerors would put their captives to the sword or enslave them.

As societies organized in larger groups, and as the tool-making capabilities of human beings developed, warfare became more efficient and technical means of murder more effective. At the same time, however, the idea of civilization began to take root. With growing economic interdependence, people came to realize that it often paid off to work with other people instead of against them. With trade and travel, people learned that others who often looked much different from themselves had loved ones too. The others had needs and feelings, felt joy and gladness, grief and sorrow, just as they did. Not only the economic sense of cooperation but the emotional spirit of "civilization" began to grow. Civilization literally means the expression and development of civility: respect for others, the best possible encouragement of every person's cultural and spiritual resources, the proper weaving of each individual into the fabric of society. The voices of religious leaders were very important in this revolution. In the message of Jesus Christ, for example, the revolution that was needed had to be rooted in a spiritual love of others. Civilization advanced in its emotional as well as its technical aspect. By the end of the 19th century, it was widely believed that we had put the horrors of primitive barbarism behind us.

But of course we have not. Within [the 20th] century, 1½ million Christian Armenians were massacred by Muslim Turks. The German people, a Christian nation thought by many to be one of the most "civilized" in history, led by a demagogue and gripped in a racist doctrine, tortured and killed 6 million Jews. We ourselves have nearly exterminated the North American Indian, and little more than a century ago held Black Africans in slavery. Only a quarter century past, in the belief that we were fighting a Communist enemy, we killed hundreds of thousands of Vietnamese and Cambodian people, mainly women, children, and helpless old people in the villages that we bombed. At this very time [1988], Protestants and Catholics are killing one another in Northern Ireland. Muslims and Jews are killing each other in the Near East. Competing Muslim sects are killing each other in Iran and Iraq. Hindus and Muslims are killing each other in Sri Lanka. The old instincts still lie within us, far closer to the surface than most of us would like to believe.

The underlying attitude that drives all this horror is the universal human tendency toward egocentrism and ethnocentrism, and the related tendency, also universal, toward prejudice against others. We can only look from the inside out, and the first inclination of the human creature is to see himself or herself, and then the others of our own close and beloved group, as the center of the universe. The first inclination toward another who is different is all too likely to be one of distance and distrust. We have to categorize others. No person can ever know another completely. We all have to make some inferences and assumptions about everyone we deal with to get on with the business of living. Prejudice, in the literal sense of prejudging others, is an inevitable part of the social process. We are all subject to it. Any man who thinks others are prejudiced but he is not is simply displaying his own egocentricity. Any group with the shared idea that "they" are prejudiced but "we" are not has fallen prey to its own ethnocentrism.

Prejudice only becomes dangerous, however, when it extends to an over-generalized attitude, based on irrelevant appearances, with fear and hatred at the core of the feeling. Without correction, human beings are prone to dichotomous thinking. We not only see ourselves as the same and others as different, we think that we are right and they are wrong. And then, all too readily, we convince ourselves that we are superior and they are inferior, that we are good and they are evil. The lie we tell ourselves is easier if the others are visibly different from us in some way: if they are black and we are white; if they are short and we are tall; if their hair is kinky or coarse while ours is straight and fine. If there are no obvious signs to go by, but we have an emotional need to debase others, we can always find a way to set them apart from us. We can make them wear yellow stars or pink triangles. And we can always find a way to humiliate others, by calling them "gooks," or "niggers," or "spics," or "wops," or "kikes," or "honkies," if we need to dehumanize them in order to justify ourselves in attacking them.

These are some of the nasty facts about the prejudicial process. These attitudes—love and loyalty toward one's own and their emotional shadows, fear and hatred of others—kept human beings alive for the first few million years on this planet. But we cannot get by with those same expressions any longer. Our planet is getting more crowded all the time. The technical advances that began with the industrial revolution, above all the recent scientific advances of medicine and public health, set the human population on a course of exponential growth little more than a hundred years ago. Some populations are growing more rapidly than others. White European Americans, who often seem to act as if they were the hereditary rulers of the universe, have become a small minority, set against the 1 billion Chinese, the 800 million people in India, at least 300 million Black Africans, 400 million Latin Americans, and all the other non-White, non-European people packed together on this tiny globe. Somewhere around the middle of the 21st century, White people will cease to be a numerical majority in the United States, outnumbered by Black, Hispanic, and Asian people growing within and flowing into the land. The speed of modern transportation, and the speed and vividness of modern communication, bring us all in constant touch with one another. Isolation is no longer possible. Our economic and political interdependence no longer allow exploitation. And of course the new tools of destruction that we have so cleverly devised, always defined ethnocentrically as instruments of defense rather than as weapons of attack, can now destroy us all.

If we are to survive now as a human species, we have to learn to live with our diversity. The balance we need is difficult to reach. We have to maintain the unity that comes from loyalty to our own. Love of country, pride in our people, close cooperation among ourselves is required if we are to maintain our own integrity, if we are to compete successfully with economic rivals, and even, God forbid, if we have to defend ourselves against warring attack. But we must at the same time be sure we know who our enemies are. We must avoid exaggerating the dangers of others who seem to threaten us. We must resist the temptation to buttress our own pride by debasing others. Everywhere we can, we must seek out the common values we all share, and work together to attain them.

I am not sure what I can do personally about Russian–American relationships or an Israeli–Palestinian settlement, but I have always believed that we all need to do what we can where we are, and there is plenty to do right here at Rutgers University. When Queens College was founded in 1766, it was made up entirely of White, male, Dutch Reformed Protestants. The problem of diversity was solved by exclusion. Until 20 years ago, Rutgers was still mainly a White, male school. All that has changed. Now we have 47,000 students, men and women about equally represented, of every race and creed, nearly every national origin, and every major culture on earth. We should not be surprised to see some prejudicial antilocution in a community so diverse and so closely crowded. The excrements of bigotry are flowing all around us. We must do what we can to stem the flow, to wash away the corruption in a tide of decency and respect.

The first thing we have to do is acknowledge our problem, and pledge an unyielding resolve to do something about it. Yes, there is prejudice everywhere. Yes, we shall confront it. No, we will not let the right to free expression allow anyone to diminish in any way the right of every person to safe and respectful treatment. Leadership from the top is essential to the force of the movement. It is not enough for the president of a university to be "behind the project." The president has to be out in front, leading the campaign. At Rutgers, President Bloustein's courage and determination in facing these issues is vital to the success of our efforts.

Then we must organize to advance our common purposes, by systematically strengthening our university community. That is what the Committee to Advance Our Common Purposes is designed to do. This is not the place to discuss our activities in detail. I have written some reports that describe our work this past year and propose plans for action in the year ahead. In this brief time, I can only outline our major goals and suggest the kinds of things we need to do to reach our goals.

As we move in our efforts to improve cohesion, we need to be sure we know what is going on. Poorly planned social programs, usually begun with the best of intentions, make matters worse. We need to assess patterns of prejudice subtly but accurately, design corrective and preventive programs with cautious vigor, evaluate the effects of our programs in a realistic way, and change the programs as the facts of experience suggest. Although careful assessment is needed, it is important not to study the problem to death, as academics are often prone to do. Action and assessment go hand in hand.

Some of our needs are obvious. We need to replace ignorance with understanding. Many students come to this school knowing next to nothing about the civil rights movement. They barely know about the Civil War. Students, as well as faculty and staff, need to learn more about the cultures of others. We can accomplish this by changes in curricula, special educational programs, and other means.

We need to find ways to break down the segregation that isolates one group from another. Nearly all the students in our Africana studies programs are Black. Women enroll in women's studies. Informal segregation can be seen in housing, in classroom seating, in dining halls, and on the mall. This discourages the contact that can lead to understanding and respect. We need to find ways of bringing people together without forcing them into unnatural or debasing contacts that only encourage animosity.

We need to provide incentives for working together rather than in isolation or in opposition. Last year, President Bloustein initiated, and our committee managed, a grant program to reduce prejudice and encourage cohesive student activities. Proposals came in from Asian groups, gay groups, women's groups, Jewish groups, Black groups, White groups, large groups, small groups, Hispanic groups, Black/Hispanic coalitions—43 organizations in all. Many of the students who wrote the proposals had terrific ideas about better ways of working together. All they needed was encouragement and a little money. A related call for works of art—essays, stories, poems, paintings—that showed the ugliness of bigotry and the promise of understanding produced some moving entries.

We need to teach people how to resolve conflicts. Some conflicts are bound to arise in any diverse society, because the interests of one group are sometimes incompatible with those of another. But people can learn to be resolute in holding on to their basic goals, yet more flexible than they ever imagined they could be in finding ways to attain those goals. They can learn to avoid the coercive and abusive tactics that escalate conflicts and harden antagonisms beyond recovery. Above all, they can seek out superordinate goals, the common purposes we all share, and find ways to help one another work toward those aims.

In a conglomerate culture like ours, finding common purpose is not always easy. When Clark Kerr was president of the University of California, he said that every university was composed of three main constituencies: students, who are interested in sex; alumni, who are interested in football; and faculty, who are interested in parking. Maybe so. But beyond that, we are all interested in good education and thoughtful inquiry. We all want to see that every student has the best possible chance to learn what he or she needs to learn in a safe and respectful environment. We need to see that every faculty member has the emotional support, as well as the financial and administrative support required for good research and teaching. We need to take advantage of our diversity. We need to find ways to work together to serve the communities of which we are all a part.

At the core, each of us needs to acknowledge his or her own human loyalties as well as the aversions that often arise in the first response to others who are different from us. We need to turn our loyalties toward the larger human group. You might wonder what a White, male, Protestant, heterosexual Aryan is doing talking about racism, sexism, and homophobia. I stand before you as a living endorsement of Gunnar Myrdal's idea that the "race problem" in America is a White problem. So also is the Jewish problem a problem for Christians and Muslims to resolve. No less is the Muslim problem a problem for the Jews. Sexism is primarily a male problem. Homophobia is an issue that heterosexuals need to confront.

You may also wonder what a secular psychologist is doing behind a pulpit in a church, but maybe you know the answer. The issues we are facing are moral issues, and the work we are doing is shot through with value. To be sure, we need to study behavior, but we also need to make life better.

I'm going to close with an exercise and a prayer. The prayer may seem odd coming from a person regarded by some of his sectarian friends as a fallen-away Unitarian. Whatever your own beliefs may be, I hope you will look beyond labels and join me in these thoughts.

Just sit back. Relax. Close your eyes. Now imagine that you are with your loved ones. You hear their voices. You see their smiles. Someone especially dear to you comes to join you, and you embrace.

Now imagine that you see another group of people, talking together some distance away. They are different from you in some way. Maybe they are of a different color. Maybe they are different in some other way. You're not too comfortable with them. Maybe you fear them.

Now imagine that a mother and child come away from that group and walk toward you. They come closer and closer, and you see their faces. There is sadness in the face of the child. They are right before you, and you take the child in your arms. And silently you say, "Little one, I want you to be safe and healthy. I want you to know the joy that life can bring. I want you to have a good and decent life. I will comfort and protect you all your days."

Let me find the light to see the world, in all its sorrow and all its beauty, through the eyes of my brothers and sisters.

Let me gain the sense to know the difference between outer appearance and inner reality, and reach the common good in all people.

Let me have the heart to care for the loved ones of others as I care for my own.

Amen.

CHAPTER

7

Meehl's Response to Campbell

Donald T. Campbell, longtime member of the psychology faculty at Northwestern University, noted primarily as a hard-headed methodologist who had contributed mightily to the social sciences by bringing all attainable rigor to social field research, was elected president of the APA in 1975. He had some trouble deciding on a topic for his presidential address. He didn't think he had anything new to say about the work for which he was best known, and he was far too intelligent and responsible to lapse into the vague generalities and exhortations so commonly seen in the addresses of APA presidents who followed him in later years. Fortunately for all of us who had elected him, Campbell had a strong avocational interest in biological evolution. He wrote a long, abundantly documented essay entitled "On the Conflicts Between Biological and Social Evolution and Between Psychology and Moral Tradition." I thought he did a fine job, daring to address such matters as the genetics of altruism and the psychology of religion in ways that I considered both learned and wise. As usual, Meehl was more incisively critical than I was, and saw cause to question some of Campbell's arguments. Thorough understanding of Meehl's critique obviously requires prior study of Campbell's paper, but a reasonably accurate sense of the dialogue can be gained by reading Meehl's remarks on their own:

12/5/96

Dear Don: We found it, an old pencil draft, here typed, you may retain. Still seems sound, basically. I'm unsure why I didn't publish it, perhaps seemed a bit harsh, on someone I liked & admired? Don't know. I also think I intended to write some more but broke off. The "end" is abrupt, non-closured.

Only major alteration I would now make is split the altruistic component of "Herd Instinct" from other (bad) components (e.g., gullibility, hatred for out-group, adulation of leader, coercive conventionality). But I d.k. the most recent ethology about that cluster, how separable it is.

Paul

P. E. Meehl, Response to Campbell's 1975 Presidential Address Draft II 1/20/76

As always, Professor Campbell's conjectures are perceptive, stimulating, and reflect that combination of erudition, methodological sophistication, and human concern that makes us proud to have selected him APA president. In this necessarily brief response, it would be pointless to waste words on echoing him. For example, I think we social scientists should cultivate a bit of humility toward the wisdom of our grandparents (cf. my "Law and the Fireside Inductions," 1971, etc.). Again, like Campbell, I have a strong interest in religion and find irritating the combination of arrogance and ignorance with which some of our brethren approach (or avoid) the "great questions." In this communication I aim to advance the dialogue by (a) qualifying what he says about psychotherapists, (b) offering a counter-conjecture to his approval of altruism, and (c) strongly dissenting from his "liberal Protestant" defense of religion. Since we are both (at least semi-) Popperians, I make no apology for not here "proving empirically" my conjectures—offering them on the same conjectural basis he gave as his.

As to the permissive, counter ethical, "accept your impulses" attitude of psychotherapists, probably no one will dispute this as a vague cultural consequence of Freud, Rogers, Ellis, and Co.'s teachings and tactics. But as a sometimes psychoanalytic, sometimes RET [Ellis's Rational-Emotive Therapy] practitioner, I am impelled to emphasize the crucial difference between "Do not deceive yourself by defensive unknowing" (Freud) and "It is okay for anyone to do as he pleases" (Who?). The author of *Civilization and Its Discontents* was surely not saying, or implying, anything like the latter. Somewhere Freud says explicitly that mere non-gratification of instincts as such never made anyone ill, and he says the same thing about hard work. The "do as your momentary impulses seem to suggest" view of mental health is a corruption of our dominant Western psychotherapy tradition.

As to altruism [which Campbell advocated without qualification], perhaps I can further Campbell's good cause by offering a provocative, far-out conjecture (which I myself only half-, and sometimes, believe) and urging reflection upon it to sharpen the empirical differences for long-run tests, which will mostly be "reforms as experiments" [one of Campbell's most widely cited, practically valuable conceptions]. Meehl's counter-conjecture: A socially optimal ethic *within the achievable range* would be a minimal ethic, not a strongly altruistic one. Sentiments of altruism, group identification, loyalty, and the like may do as much harm as good, maybe more. By a "minimal ethic" I mean, roughly, one that says: "(1) *Primum non nocere;* (2) fulfill your contractual obligations; and then (3) do as you please."

The vaguenesses in this language are well known and, of course, largely incurable on present knowledge even if I had the space. The "contractual obligations" phrase is particularly messy, as I intend by it to include not only explicit agreements (business contracts, personal promises) but those so-called "implicit agreements" that are relied on in much of political theory to explain why we are obliged to pay taxes, obey the law, vote in elections, etc. One may think of these as being analogues to the lawyers' notions of quasi-contract, unjust enrichment, etc., writ large. Probably Professor Campbell will ask me, "Well, Meehl, but would you really want to live in a world with people who practiced such a minimal ethic? Don't you want to love and be loved? Don't you care whether your friends and colleagues and family are there to give (and receive) help, affection, sympathy, etc.?" Sure I do. But I am conjecturing that unless a person is genetically aberrated or dreadfully twisted by a loveless childhood, my third non-altruistic precept "then do as you please" will be sufficient to cover most of that. Putting it crudely, "I want my wife to darn my socks because she *agreed* to (maybe in what my daughter and her husband call a 'mini-contract') and is, therefore, *obligated* to; but I would prefer that she be fond of me for non-ethical reasons, spontaneously, arising out of the pleasant coincidence that I meet some of her deepest needs. I do not much like the idea that I am being loved "altruistically," and I'm not at all sure that I can love a spouse (or student, or colleague, or patient) that way. I can, however, strive to keep my promises.

Other than because of deep temperamental factors, why does this minimal ethic have plausibility for me? Herewith a brief summary of two sorts of considerations. Take war, which Professor Campbell (like me) is deeply concerned about. I shall assert without proof that war is mankind's greatest scourge, whether assessed by physical and psychological suffering, deaths, or economic waste. An "achievable" ethic that would reduce appreciably the amount of war would have a strong case despite its other defects, even if major. Now I gather that Professor Campbell conjectures more altruism would be desirable on this score. I do not believe it. Bodaciously I urge the exact opposite: War is not mainly due to mass aggressiveness or territoriality but is due to dominance, aggressiveness, and territoriality in the leaders combined with stupid, gullible altruism and group-feeling by the mass of followers. The alpha baboon is mean (that's partly why he gets there!), the beta baboons are hangers-on, and the gammas are dumb suckers. I suggest that if we could eradicate the sentiments of group identification, loyalty, patriotism, and altruism *in the large* from the human animal, wars would cease. If each gamma baboon were (rationally!) brain-washed by Albert Ellis to ask, "What's in it for *me*?" the alphas and betas would have one hell of a time getting a good war started (or, at least, keeping it going). This idea is not confined to political warfare between states, but applies to the history of religious, racial, and other kinds of group conflict. There are, to be sure, some circumstances in which it is to *my* (individual, selfish, rationally calculable) advantage to risk injury, death, or major inconvenience in a group struggle, but very rarely. A rational egocentric calculus would, I suggest, almost never lead one to risk his life killing capitalists, communists, Catholics, Calvinists, Whites, Blacks, greens, or whatever. I will buy in on a world of minimal ethics rationalists any time.

It may well be objected that we don't know how to achieve such an ideal. I think we do, at least as well as we know how to achieve Campbell's super-altruistic one. Some Christian apologists like to say, "Christianity works fine, it's just that it's never been tried." That, of course, is a preacher's easy cop-out. A doctrine and institution that possessed a total educational monopoly (not to mention great political power) for over a millennium and a half has, I submit, been "tried" about as well as a social scientist expects anything to be tried. It made a few saints—very few—and it didn't prevent war, poverty, social exploitation, race hatred, subjection of women, judicial torture, or slavery. On the other hand, I am not aware of any time or country in which a comparable large-scale, long-term near-monopoly of education aimed at shaping a rationally egocentric minimal ethic has been tried. I would be curious to learn whether Professor Campbell can provide me with an example of such. As I read the record, even today, in the shadows of our Spenglerian decline (where megalopolitan man is, according to ole Oswald, supposedly unfeeling, rootless, and hyper rational), the child is brainwashed by parents, sibs, peer group, teachers, scoutmasters, clergy, and so on to believe rigidly in all sorts of "musts," "cannots," "shoulds," about life and self which he is not encouraged to examine (and, in fact, is usually punished for so doing).

Which brings me to my second example. I believe I have learned a little something about mind and society in the course of logging over 10,000 hours as a psychotherapist, although the riskiness of relying on such clinical impressions is well known. I am not persuaded by my clinical experience that an ethic located well toward the altruistic end of Campbell's scale is better for people's mental health than one closer to my minimal ethic. Of course, one does not see very many saintly people in psychotherapy—no doubt partly because true sanctity is conducive to contentment, but also because the base rate for saints is pretty low, as it always has been. What we see in psychotherapy is, rather often, persons who are pseudo-saints, or who are married to pseudo-saints, or who think, "Shame on me for *not* being a saint," whether they use that term or not, usually not. Suburbia and academia teem with people whose lives are 95% controlled by a cluster of shoulds, oughts, and quasi-moral group identifications that tend to make them unhappy, as well as other people. One need not be a hippie, a hedonist, a crook, or even a disciple of Albert Ellis to notice the ubiquity, severity, and recalcitrance of life-postulates that patients simply never question. That one must live for others, conform to the group's expectancies, define one's identity via the group's list of roles—in short, "be a good baboon" in the baboon troop's sense—these are near universals for business executives, faculty (and faculty wives), lawyers, doctors, and the rest. I think a "mental hygiene" case can be made against these manifestations of group feeling that is as strong as any case Professor Campbell could make in their favor. I repeat, I don't claim to be able to "prove it scientifically," but I know he doesn't expect that of me, any more than he demanded it of himself in the address.

Finally, I cannot resist the impulse to chastise my friend Campbell gently for the one short (but important in his eyes, I infer from our conversations and correspondence) passage that, I think, is tendentious and below the usual Campbell standard of intellectual craftsmanship. Discussing the "need for epistemic humility" he faults behavioral scientists for holding religious discourse to a direct realism, a literal veridicality that they recognize is impossible for science itself. Now, brethren, I submit that this is really a bit thick—more what we would expect from a bankrupt Methodist sky-pilot than a philosophically sophisticated psychologist of Professor Campbell's brains. Three brief comments, of necessity somewhat dogmatic due to my space limitations.

First, his text seems to conflate the probable (uncertain, corrigible, fallible) character of human knowledge, scientific or otherwise, with sentences not meaning what they seem to say. If an astronomer tells me, "The sun is, very probably, a sphere of hot gas 93 million miles away," he means what he says. The assertion is admittedly approximate (e.g., the sun is an oblate spheroid) and only probable (being inductive); but it is informative, makes a truth claim, and is (despite its imprecision in some respects) not compatible with "The sun is Apollo's chariot" or "The sun is a glowing lump of lead." It is misleading to suggest that because theoretical science involves (a) idealizations in the embedding text, (b) approximations in the formalism, (c) error in the empirical measurements, and (d) probability rather than certainty, *therefore* scientific statements are pretty much like religious statements which our ancestors believed but we do not. Professor Campbell states explicitly that he disbelieves in teleological or supernatural explanations. I take it this disclaimer entitles me to assume that he does not hold, for instance, that one Jesus of Nazareth was sent by God (let alone was Nicaea—identical with God), performed miracles, rose from the dead, and so forth. For some 19 centuries the Church believed these things, and today some people still do. I am at a loss to understand why Professor Campbell thinks it is unfair or inconsistent for the unbelieving psychologist to set aside the teachings of Jesus, and his followers, and the social institution they built. What competence, expertise, qualifications, or authority do these possess, on his naturalistic premises? I cannot think of any. It sounds somewhat as if he were telling me that I should have a proper epistemic humility toward a medieval housewife's views on the economics of the modern dairy industry, even though *she* believed that brownies curdle the milk whereas I know that it is due to enzymes secreted by *Lactobacillus bulgaricus*. Does it help my reflections on buttermilk production to say, "Oh well, after all, let's not be snooty about the Middle Ages. Remember, our knowledge of bacteria is incomplete, approximate, oversimplified, and only probable. It's really kind of a metaphor, properly understood. I mean, brownies are little animated beings invisible to the naked eye, and so are bacteria." To which I say, bluntly, "Baloney." Parts of science are understandable quite literally, and even in using "models" (loose term here) the scientist can normally, on request, distinguish what Mary Hesse calls the negative analogy from the positive analogy. A chemist does not literally believe that his tinker-toy model, which colors sulfur atoms yellow and carbon atoms black, "corresponds" to the external world. But nothing he tells us qua chemist, or does in his laboratory, depends on any such misattribution of the negative analogy to the alleged reality. On the other hand, when the chemist asserts that the angle Cl B Cl in a boron chloride molecule is 120° and the nuclei are approximately 1.76Å apart, he means what he says, and his calculations and experiments are based upon that literally intended feature of his positive analogy.

Nor is this true only of the exact sciences. If I conjecture that schizophrenics have a different parameter of synaptic function because at a certain locus of their DNA one of the four organic bases adenine, cytosine, guanine, thymine is different from the normal, I *mean* that, literally as it reads. If Skinner tells me that you get much higher rates on FR than on crf, he *means* that, literally as he says. The trouble with Professor Campbell's brand of liberal Protestantism is that when the negative analogy in the received corpus of Christian theology is shaved off, Occam's razor leaves nothing of substance. We have some deluded fanatics following a somewhat aberrated (grandiose, judgmental, riot-fomenting) prophet, and a resulting social institution that taught a bunch of stuff that isn't so. The "non-supernaturally-linked" components—if there are any such, which I doubt—are ethical (= moral and life-style) exhortations which are politically unworkable, philosophically indefensible, and sincerely practiced by almost nobody. I do not understand why Professor Campbell advises us to regard them with such respect, or why he thinks that the approximate and probable character of scientific knowledge has much of anything to do with that question.

Of course, one may say that wise and "epistemically humble" thinkers will be open to instruction from any source. To this, as a very general remark, I cheerfully agree. If it appears that I can learn something interesting, valid, or useful from a Hogo-Bogo witch doctor, I should do it. But I quickly add two caveats: First, you really can't hear everybody or devote serious study to all claims, even if you

> officially subscribe to open-mindedness and epistemological humility as a policy. Secondly, Professor Campbell asks us to do more than this. If I read him rightly, he urges us to cultivate a positive, actively receptive attitude toward the religious tradition. Our Bayesian priors on its moral deliverances should, one gathers, be sizable. I cannot see that he has told us why. On the Campbell non-supernatural ontology (and, I take it, epistemology), John the Baptist and my sainted namesake were pretty thoroughly muddled about practically everything that is testable, and for the rest they held a world picture that Campbell thinks he (and we) cannot. Why, if I do not buy St. Paul's theories of the cosmos, the creation, the origin and destiny of man, the creation of the world, the source of sin, the future life, the verbal accuracy of the Scripture, the resurrection of the dead, or the authority of Jesus as a prophet and teacher, should I think his views about human society, moral conduct, or the "good life" deserving of respectful attention?

Along with the reply to Campbell that Paul sent me, Leslie enclosed a line graph that had appeared in a Christian fundamentalist newspaper. It showed the precipitous, decade-long decline in national average SAT scores that began around 1960, bottomed out around 1980, and then began to climb again. The most commonly accepted interpretation in the educational community was that the accelerated democratization of higher education through the 1960s had changed the composition of the college population by including many students who would not have been considered for admission in previous times and hence lowered the average score. But the Christian fundamentalists offered a different explanation—they showed that the decline began shortly after the U.S. Supreme Court removed prayer from the schools and that the recovery after the low of 1980 began soon after Elvis Presley died. The journal *Chance*, which had reprinted the figure and the Christian interpretation, added a legend: "We need a whole lot more of Jesus and a lot less rock 'n roll." Leslie had added a note: "Do not feel obliged to respond to any of this. We understand 100% about life post-surgery."

12/23/96

Dear Paul and Leslie:

Thanks for mailing of 12/5. I'm glad you found comment on Campbell, but I'm not up to any heavy lifting these days, physical or intellectual, so will defer any studied thoughts I may have until I can reread DC's article & ponder PM's objections.

Leslie, I got a chuckle out of the SAT function with inflections marked by school prayer and Elvis events. I'll pass it on to our main research methods teacher, who spends considerable time in her classes on quasi-experimental design & related topics.

With best wishes for the new year,

Don

My AAA repair turned out to be more precarious and my recovery more prolonged than I had expected. I didn't feel much like writing letters or doing anything else "extra" for several months. Then, in late March, I received another note from Paul. Leslie had run across a book review in the *Wall Street Journal* that she thought might interest me:

From the Desk of Paul E. Meehl

3/26/97

DRP: I dk whether u read the WSJ (Leslie, who does the stock market, scans news & reviews for me). I thk I recall u ment'd the Times once? Let me know.

I served on a crime deterrence panel with J Q Wilson (before he became famous). He is one very smart, clear-headed man with a sensitive shit-detector. But I suspect I like him more than u do (my "state-phobia" touches everything, perhaps too much).

How are you? I've been reprieved for now from open heart surgery, although cardiologist says cheerily, "If you were age 38 we'd have replaced that valve 2 years ago." Hmm …

PEM

4/8/97

Dear Paul,

Thanks for J. Q. Wilson's review of "The Origins of Virtue." I don't read the Wall Street Journal with any regularity (Jane scans news & reviews for me, as Leslie does for you, but mainly in the Times) and had not known about the book. I will add it to the list I want to read when & if I go deeper into the moral/ethical questions you and I have corresponded about. Wilson's Moral Sense (1993 or thereabouts) is already on the list + some other work of his. I agree JQW is very smart and clear-headed, but I don't know his work in any depth. Origins of Virtue should be interesting. I thank you and Leslie for the lead.

I wish you well with your heart valve problems. Arnie Lazarus [Rutgers colleague known primarily as founder of multimodal therapy], at age 65± had one replaced about the time of my AAA repair. Came through OK, but the surgery was tough. He & Daphne, Jane & I are planning a celebratory get-together. I'm doing fine now. No heavy lifting yet, but office work is all right (nearly done correcting proofs of Educating Professional Psychologists) & doc told me two days ago I could start swinging golf clubs any time.

Don

I still have not read *Origins of Virtue* or *Moral Sense*, although I did read Wilson's fine collection of essays, *On Character*, later on. After I got the proofs of *Educating Professional Psychologists* back to the publisher, however, I reread Donald Campbell's APA presidential address with greater care than I had given it before, and lined it up against my sermon, as a comparable approbation of altruism, and Meehl's response to Campbell, as a critique of altruism. The difference between Meehl's "responsible minimalist" ethic and the "cautious activism" that Campbell and I advocated was clear to see, but I saw no point in attempting to reconcile the views. It seemed to me they both encouraged behavior that was at least prosocial and at best genuinely virtuous. I was content, as I knew Paul was, to attribute the variation between us to deep temperamental differences that were neither changeworthy nor changeable by any known means.

CHAPTER

8

Selling an Unpopular Book

I had some trouble finding a publisher for my book on the education of professional psychologists. To begin with, the thrust of my argument went upcurrent against mainstream opinion. The prevailing view was that all psychologists, practitioners and researchers alike, were and ought to be scientists at the core of their being, and were best prepared for their careers in academic departments of psychology. The problem with this view was that practice and research in psychology, like practice and research in medicine and engineering, are not identical enterprises. That is why we have different curricula and educational settings for physicians and biochemists, different curricula and educational settings for engineers and physicists, and needed, I claimed, different curricula and educational settings for practitioners and researchers in psychology.

In academia, of course, the controversialism of an argument is never in itself an impediment to book sales, with which publishers are never unconcerned. Unless an author is hugely famous, collections of previously published papers are usually rejected on grounds that the contents are easily available elsewhere. My book had a considerable amount of new material in it but was still about two thirds reprinted matter. Above all, the market for books on graduate-level education in any specialized field is tiny. Fewer than 300 accredited doctoral programs in professional psychology were in operation in the United States and Canada at the time I finished my manuscript. The international market was minuscule because nearly all "applied psychology" programs outside the United States and Canada were at the master's level (although that is changing now). Besides research libraries, the only buyers who might feel obliged to purchase my book were the people responsible for the design and administration of doctoral programs in professional psychology, scarcely a population that might promise a best seller. So I was not surprised when two publishing firms that trade in the kinds of subjects to which my book was devoted declined to review the manuscript at all, and another rejected it on advice of marketing staff.

Despite these disadvantages, however, many of the papers included in the book had long been required readings for graduate students in professional psychology and were seen by some as the defining conceptual statements for the education of practitioners in the field. Gary VandenBos, editor-in-chief of APA Books, agreed to send the manuscript to an anonymous referee, whose review not only recommended publication but offered some valuable suggestions for reorganization that enhanced perception of the volume as a basic ideological and conceptual template for the profession itself. I welcomed the suggestions, made the required changes, and worked closely with the in-house editor on further minor revisions. Roger Peterson, respected president of the National Council of Professional Schools, wrote a laudatory foreword to the book, past presidents of the council endorsed the sense of Roger's statement, and the book was ready for such promotion as the publisher might decide to give it.

In fact, APA gave the book about the amount of exposure I had expected: full-page ads in several successive catalogs, a broadly circulated brochure, and review copies to relevant journals. My single disappointment was that the back cover was used to advertise some other books on education in psychology that were "also of interest" rather than containing the "blurbs" that I thought might have been obtained from the list of distinguished colleagues I had provided the marketing staff. Still, the book had an attractive, "scholarly" look, opened easily, was priced appropriately, and seemed otherwise suitable for distribution. I sent copies to friends, several of whom wrote thank-you notes that included the kinds of statements I had hoped to see on the back of my book. From Arnold Lazarus, "Extraordinarily insightful and informative ... the definitive tome on professional psychology." From Milton Schwebel, "In years ahead, long after we are gone, a work that will be identified as a landmark in psychology ... shows clearly the inextricable bond between the theoretical and the applied, the researcher and the practitioner, psychology-in-general and professional psychology." Of course I sent Paul Meehl a copy. This time his response was typed:

July 19, 1997

Dear Don,

Herewith belated thanks for the gift copy of your professional education book. I started to read it immediately, but set it aside when we ran into some grave programming problems in connection with a paper that has a quasi-deadline, plus the fact that, due to concern about my cardiac condition, I have been focused intensely upon completing a couple of long-delayed, high-priority tasks—the concrete impact of the concept of mortality! My recent echocardiogram has given me another reprieve from valve-replacement open-heart surgery, which I was, of course, not anticipating with glee. I am asymptomatic, except for a bit of breathlessness on going up stairs or lifting storm windows, plus I sometimes have to stop and rest in the course of my daily five-mile walk, and around half of the time I end up calling Leslie to come rescue me. "Dissolution is inherent in all component things," as the Blessed One said. I trust that your recovery from aneurysm surgery has proceeded satisfactorily. It is not easy to parse the indirect influence via the psyche and the direct influence of organic disease on how much energy and zeal one has, is it? I observed this many years ago in working with patients who had organic diseases, and decided that, while it wasn't easy to tease them apart, neither was it necessary, so the heck with it. I recall one of the earliest findings on the MMPI, even before the manual was published, was the elevation of the depression score during physical illness, including illnesses that are not life-threatening or particularly painful, and also the interesting finding that women, when sick, become less depressed than men.

On reading the first chapter in the section on quality control, I was struck with the fact that within my otherwise excellent contribution to Holt's book [a chapter entitled "A Scholarly, Scientific, Nonresearch Doctorate for Clinical Practitioners"], I seem not to have discussed that highly important issue. I did discuss *quality*, both as to the selection of students and the scientific character of the pre-clinical curriculum, and the intensity and diversification of clinical exposure, but discussing quality is, of course, not the same as discussing quality *control*, and I find it strange that this objection to the PsyD idea was avoided. I can think of two psychological explanations. The first is a funny one, and doesn't perhaps make much "logical" sense, but I believe it operated, and that is that I believe I had a very low opinion of the quality control of the traditional PhD program in clinical, so in a way it seemed odd to say, "How will we have quality control of the PsyD?" implying that there was some special different problem here that didn't already exist.

I had this negative impression on the basis of examining perhaps 200 candidates for the clinical diploma when I served on ABPP [American Board of Professional Psychology] for six years. It was shocking to find how just plain ignorant many of these PhDs from accredited institutions were. I am not talking about ignorance of some high-level Meehl-type philosophy of science, or some advanced mathematical business. I am talking about ignorance of elementary psychometrics, statistics, probability, and quantitative reasoning, which any decent Minnesota BA would normally possess. This kind of ignorance of undergraduate measurement matter is widespread, as I know from many examples David Faust and Will Grove have told me about from their forensic experience. For instance, you have a clinician who is writing a report and testifying under oath in a lawsuit or criminal case, and has done the usual over-interpretation of subtest patterns on the WAIS [Wechsler Adult Intelligence Scale], who does not know what the standard deviation of the subtest scores is, does not know approximately how much various subtests are correlated with total score, or how much they are correlated with one another, when asked to define the term "standard deviation" cannot even do that, and then, when asked roughly what percent of cases lie above plus one standard deviation on a normal curve, confesses he hasn't any idea. There are all sorts of people out there practicing clinical psychology whose knowledge of the tools that they are using would be like a physician who has no idea about the range of systolic and diastolic blood pressures, and can't tell you even qualitatively the difference between them. I do not exaggerate. I think you would be astounded and horrified at how ignorant some of these people are. David Faust assisted a lawyer in cross-examining a psychologist who had charged $300 to interpret an MMPI, and whose interpretation included the statement that since the patient had a very low K score, we can assume he was highly defensive in taking the test. I am inclined to think that this ignorance is even worse than it was forty years ago, when I was an ABPP examiner, and it certainly isn't confined to people from PsyD programs, since most of the experts that Faust and Grove deal with are PhDs.

It has occurred to me to wonder whether there is any other legally recognized profession that involves degrees from institutions of higher learning with such a low level of ordinary competence as clinical psychology. Perhaps there are. How could we tell? An architect friend of mine, who was a professor at Clemson, and then went into private practice to make more money, told me that in his opinion if you picked a random architect out of the yellow pages to build your house you'd get a crappy house. I know that during the Great Depression there was a study made of the mechanical competence of personnel working in service stations, and it was extremely low. And then there was the MD who ran around the country pretending to be a sick patient and reported about how many times an examiner listened to his chest through his shirt and undershirt, or never looked in his eyegrounds, or never elicited kneejerks, and so forth. So I am not prepared to say that clinical psychologists are worse at their job than physicians, architects, and automobile mechanics, but I certainly hope that the average lawyer or physician is not as ignorant as the average clinical psychologist of things that he really needs to know in order to make rational decisions.

I have been trying to arrange that a few diagnostic items about basic ideas of statistics, measurement, and probability, and the meaning of diagnostic signs can be inserted in some of the examinations that one of the APA committees is preparing. I make a confident prediction that people with PhDs will display a horrifying ignorance of these basic matters. And it's not just the Minnesota emphasis on statistics and measurement that I'm complaining of. I got into the habit on ABPP of asking a few questions about descriptive psychopathology, focusing during the last two or three years on the board, on candidates' ability to decide whether the patient was suffering from a major depressive disorder, in which he had a

15%–20% lifetime suicide risk, or was mildly or moderately depressed in one of the other varieties (reactive, neurotic, schizoid, anhedonic, organic illness). I asked the candidate to imagine that a student comes up to him after class, where he has been teaching a general psych or abnormal psych class, and expresses worry about the uncle who is living at their home. They know he is depressed (he admits that he's feeling sad), and the student wonders if he is a major suicide risk, that they should see to it that he gets psychiatric attention whether he wants it or not. Then I would say to the candidate, "Look, you don't have any test data on this man, and apparently you will not have the opportunity to examine him yourself, but this student is asking you for clinical advice, and the advice involves what might in effect amount to a psychiatric emergency. What questions would you ask about the uncle's behavior? Believe it or not, over half of them did not know enough to inquire into the cognitive or vegetative signs of a major depression, but instead started to talk about psychodynamics, or whether he identified with the family members, or all sorts of other stuff that had no prognostic significance. Many of them did not even mention weight loss or insomnia, or the like. I thought this was pretty scary.

Of course, this is sort of a tu quoque, but I am not offering it as a justification for omitting my discussion of quality control, but rather as a psychological explanation. It just apparently didn't strike me that there was anything new or special about controlling educational quality of science or practice, when we were already in a mess in that regard. The other reason, which I find hard to explain, is that the objections I answered in my Holt chapter were the objections that I met in discussions of the Stillwater conference, and many hours of subsequent discussions, informally over the lunch table, and so on, with objectors—which included practically everybody except Hathaway and Wirt, as I recall. People did ask about quality—that is, what preclinical sciences would you require, how would you keep the second rate misfits from filling up the program, and the like. But quality control, for some strange reason, they did not ask about. And if one says, "Well, what are the incentives available to insist upon high quality control in a free-standing institution" it's kind of hard to say what they would be, is it not? That is, if the quality control in the PhD program is as bad as it is, where at least you have some statisticians down the hall, and some professors of experimental psychology in the department, and a graduate dean who checks the makeup of the PhD oral examining committee for academic diversity, and such things as this don't come close to guaranteeing high quality control in departments located in universities—if you take off even those inadequate constraints, it would be plausible to expect things to become even worse, would it not? Of course, the short answer might be in your statement of how proud you feel entitled to be with the Rutgers products, but the obvious rejoinder is, "How do you know that other such places will have somebody like Donald R. Peterson running things?" If Garmezy or Tellegen or Schofield (he later came around) had asked me at Stillwater or later, "Well, all right, you describe a respectable curriculum and selection process, but what makes you think people will do what Meehl says? They haven't much done what you said about anything else have they?" (Hah!!) And to that query, I would have had no answer.

I find this topic somewhat discouraging to think about, and I admire you for your zeal and optimism without being muddle-headed. But it is psychologically interesting that, since I have now myself ceased working with patients and have no supervisory or teaching functions in the clinical area, I discern a marked withdrawal of cathexis from this topic. In fact, my wife says I should accept the fact that I have changed professions, that I should think of myself as (a) a philosopher of science, (b) a statistician, and (c) a retired clinical psychologist. She has a strong point there.

Best,

Paul

Windsor, VT
Sep. 2, 1997

Dear Paul,

At last I can answer your letter of 7/19 re quality in prof. psy & related matters. Your letter reached me here in VT just as we were packing to go to NJ on way to Chicago for APA, then on to Champaign to visit family, back to Jersey to attend to some office & household matters, & finally back up here, where goldenrod & autumn wildflowers are appearing in profusion, & flaming colors are starting to come into some of the maples.

I understand completely your need to set aside my book to focus on long-delayed, high-priority projects, given your heart condition & the nature of human mortality. Since my surgeries last winter, I've had to face the realization that I shall not finish all five of the books I have been collecting materials for over the past 10–15 years, and have focused on one, a huge project on the course of American bigotry from Thomas Jefferson to Ronald Reagan, with no feeling of assurance that I'll even finish that. In one sense I don't care. I've always enjoyed the search more than the finished product. In another way I care a lot. Here I am, 74 years old next week, finally reaching the point where I think I'll have something to say about something that matters and a good chance to say it well, & it's not at all clear I'll live long enough to do it. I'm relieved to hear you are not facing valve replacement surgery right now. It's a mean operation & you know the risks. Please continue to take care of yourself and do the work that you are uniquely, now and forevermore, equipped to do.

On quality control, I have felt from the beginning, as you did when you wrote that fine chapter for Holt's book, that the issue is not specific to the PsyD programs and that, in general, our PhD programs are doing a lousy job of teaching practitioners the essentials required for competent, responsible professional work. That's why I went to all that trouble. I'm not happy with the way the movement turned out. I'm especially concerned about the free-standing schools, as I have said from the beginning, repeated in keynote addresses to NCSPP groups, & say again in my book. But there they are. Neither you nor I nor anybody else had any control over Cummings, Kovacs, & the rest. Once it was clear to me that the free-standing schools were here to stay (very early) I decided the best thing I could do was join them and lead a force for quality. This has been at least a partial success. I also was the prime mover in a nationwide self-study of professional schools which has just been completed & will be available soon. We tried to get the PhD clinical programs to join NCSPP in this, thru CUDCP [Council of University Directors of Clinical Psychology] but they ignored us, in the view, I guess, that what they were doing couldn't possibly be anything other than first class. Jesus. So, I gave it my best shot. What I had to say is in my book. I hope you can get to it some time. It wouldn't take you long. Except for the section on quality control & a couple of other chapters, you've already seen draft or final copies of everything there, tho you've never seen it all in a single statement.

Paul, I hope we can both stay around quite awhile longer. There are things I can talk about with you that I can't discuss in quite the same way with anybody else.

With best wishes, Don

My book sold 401 copies the first year, about what I expected. But I thought it might do better with a little extra promotion, so I talked to Gary VandenBos at the APA convention about running at least one more ad that included some "praise for ..." statements. In a letter after the meeting, he told me to chop the long list of prospective blurb writers I had included in my marketing questionnaire to a much smaller number, so I did that. I listed five, including Paul Meehl, but commented as follows in the letter that named them:

> *I'm not worried about 4 of the 5. They're all grown men and they will or they won't. I am concerned about Paul Meehl. Paul is a very busy man, on in years, feeling his mortality, and properly stingy with his recommendations. I wouldn't be surprised, and would not be offended or hurt if he refused on grounds of incest or some other form of conflict of interest. But Paul too is a grown man, and I don't think it would hurt to ask.*

Then I let a few weeks go by and wrote to Meehl.

3/10/98

Dear Paul,

By now, I suppose Julia Frank-McNeill (or someone from APA Books) has called to find out if you would write something favorable about my book Educating Professional Psychologists. I'm slightly embarrassed by that, don't want to pretend I had nothing to do with the request, want to assure you that I won't be hurt or offended if you decide not to do it, & enclose copy of letter that shows what I said to publisher in response to their request for names of possible promoters. Whatever you say or don't say will be OK with me.

Don

3/19/98

Dear Don: No, McNeill has not called me, nor anyone else from APA Books, which is well because I have just (yesterday) been "officially" diagnosed as having congestive heart failure ("but mild," heh ...). So I'm rather disinclined to take on even a small task, with a speech to write for APS [American Psychological Society] Prize talk and 3 fat MSS in process. I know you will accept this. It's not just time expended, it's partly the psychology of "too many things to be done," which in youth I tolerated well (better than most) but no longer do.

Best

Paul

I have either misplaced or never made a copy of my reply, but of course I understood Paul's situation and was entirely ready to let my book float or sink as the vagaries of academic publishing would determine. In fact, none of the people I had named as boosters for my masterpiece were contacted by APA Books. Further "advertising" was limited to listing in subsequent catalogs. As Gary VandenBos had said in setting my royalty rate at 10%, sales of books on professional education in psychology are not "robust." If sales continue as they have in the past, *Educating Professional Psychologists* will finally top the 1,000-copy mark during the current year and raise my royalty multiplier to 12.5%. Jane and I will probably buy lunch in Manhattan with the proceeds.

CHAPTER

9

Discovery and Justification

One of the contributors to my bounty from the professional psychology book was Peter Dybwad, president of the Wright Institute in Berkeley, California.

Among all the freestanding schools, the Wright Institute had long impressed me as one of the best, burdened as they all were by fiscal dependence on student tuition, but advantaged by proximity and appropriate administrative relationships with the University of California at Berkeley, with a decently talented, hard-working faculty, closer selectivity in admitting students than is usual for freestanding schools, and intelligent administration by Peter Dybwad and his staff. Dybwad was a lawyer by training, in the public defender/consumer advocate tradition, and, as I found during a site visit for accreditation by the Western Association of Schools and Colleges, more learned about the philosophy and practice of higher education than all but a few academics I knew in universities. Peter had given a copy of my book to each of his full-time faculty members. Some time during the summer of 1998, he invited me to join the Wright faculty as a visiting scholar, and in September of that year Jane and I packed for a 4-month stay and headed for Berkeley. A letter I wrote to Meehl later in the term related what I did there:

10/28/98

Dear Paul,

I need some help & hope you can provide it without too much distraction from your other obligations & interests. I'm here at the Wright Institute (this is Nevitt Sanford's creature, grand(iose?)ly designed to educate "clinicians-to-society") on a visiting scholar appt., running a seminar for faculty and key administrators & giving talks around the Bay area on practice of psy as disciplined inquiry (plus living in a million-dollar house in the Berkeley hills). I'm working up a talk that I'll probably call "The Two Disciplines of Professional Psychology" (with apologies to Lee Cronbach) [author of a classic article entitled "The Two Disciplines of Scientific Psychology"], centered around the idiography-nomothesis distinction, which in turn lines up (roughly) in my thinking with several other distinctions, including Reichenbach's differentiation of context of discovery from context of justification. I find R's distinction useful, but I've also seen it described as "much criticized." I'm away from my books & unfamiliar with UCB library across the street. Can you, off the top of your head or with ease, give me references for: (a) Reichenbach's original distinction, & (b) major critique(s) of the distinction? I can't see anything wrong with it, unless R claimed discovery proceeds absent prior conjecture—which I can't imagine he did.

How are you? I wonder often about your health. Please let me know. And please send me anything you've written lately. I can't conceive of anything you would write that I wouldn't want to read.

I enclose a piece [a conversation with Thomas Reid, the first graduate of the first PsyD program at the University of Illinois, and George Allen, one of Reid's classmates in the Illinois clinical PhD program] that I found fun to do, & that might interest you as a report on what some of your intellectual grandchildren are doing. Allen, as director of clinical training at U. Conn. for 15+ years, has affected many students. For better or for worse, our influences do exponentiate.

With best regards, Don

11/2/98

Dear Don: Enclosed is the famous passage. The distinction is about the epistemologist's task in examining the scientist's work product. It is NOT about the scientist's "discovery stage." The study of that is the philosopher's "context of discovery." Almost everyone has this wrong (Golden and I even got it wrong in an article, aaarrgh!! He wrote it but I didn't catch it), as if the scientist were saying "Now, in the (my) discovery process, I am (doing, thinking, noticing) so-and-so." The philosopher of science (or historian of science—HR doesn't mention him but should have, & would if asked) when examining science may be interested in the rationale (evidence, argument, derivation) supporting or refuting a theory. In that (philosophical) "context" he is asking normative-justificational questions, e.g., "What's the evidence that benzene molecule is a ring?" But a historian of science, or psychologist, or sociologist, may ask, "How did Kekulé come to think of it?" That's a question in the context of discovery. To mix them is fallacious. No chemist would reject the theory because Kekulé dreamed of a hoop snake. This incident in the "discovery process" is totally irrelevant to the theory's correctness. So people who wish to eliminate Reichenbach's distinction are inviting us to commit fallacies found in freshman logic texts. I ignore them. Do so.

Note: R did not say, or imply, that the same sentence could never properly appear in both contexts. (He was not silly, unlike some of his critics, a bunch of 2nd raters). The fact that the stoichiometric formula is C_6H_6 is a fact known to Kekulé (it produced the structural puzzle!) and this fact-sentence therefore occurs both in the context of discovery and context of justification. Similarly, the sentence "Freud had 19th century male bourgeois Jewish prejudices" occurs in the context of discovery (history of psychoanalysis) but also in the context of justification, because his interpretations of penis-envy in women have to be critically appraised by us (context of justification). Or that Spence was not very "clinical" about rats, and didn't like them much—helps explain Iowa negative latent learning experiments.

Best wishes, Paul

P.S.: I have "walking pneumonia" but recovering.

To all but historians of science, philosophers of science, and psychologists interested in these matters, Meehl's reply to my question will be difficult to interpret. Those puzzled by the allusion to Kekulé and the hoopsnake need to know that the 19th-century German chemist Friedrich Kekulé, after struggling unsuccessfully for many months to define the molecular structure of benzene, woke up one morning knowing with perfect clarity that it took the form of a *ring*. The night before, he had dreamed of a hoop snake, a mythical creature said to move about by taking its tail in its mouth and rolling like a hoop. Psychologists teaching students about cognition are fond of the anecdote as a way of illustrating differences between rational problem solving and creativity. It will also help to read Reichenbach's typically concise distinction between the contexts of discovery and justification:

> If a more convenient determination of this concept of rational reconstruction is wanted, we might say that it corresponds to the form in which thinking processes are communicated to other persons instead of the form in which they are subjectively performed. The way, for instance, in which a mathematician publishes a new demonstration, or a physicist his logical reasoning in the foundation of a new theory, would almost correspond to our concept of rational reconstruction; and the well-known difference between the thinker's way of finding this theorem and his way of presenting it before a public may illustrate the difference in question. I shall introduce the terms context of discovery and context of justification to mark this distinction. Then we have to say that epistemology is only occupied in constructing the context of justification. Even in the written form scientific expositions do not always correspond to the exigencies of logic or suppress the traces of subjective motivation from which they started. If the presentation of the theory is subjected to an exact epistemological scrutiny, the verdict becomes still more unfavorable. For scientific language, being destined like the language of daily life for practical purposes, contains so many abbreviations and silently tolerated inexactitudes that a logician will never be fully content with the form of scientific publications. Our comparison, however, may at least indicate the way in which we want to have thinking replaced by justifiable operations; and it may also show that the rational reconstruction of knowledge belongs to the descriptive task of epistemology. It is bound to factual knowledge in the same way that the exposition of a theory is bound to the actual thoughts of its author.

11/17/98

Dear Paul:

I'm hesitant to pester you further about Reichenbach's discovery/justification distinction, but your comment that nearly everyone gets it wrong, & report that you and Golden, of all people, did so in one of your articles, leads me to fear that I've been screwing it up too. I read HR's original statement long ago, in the Feegle-Meegle days [seminars in the philosophy of psychology, jointly taught by Herbert Feigl and Paul Meehl, were fondly known as the "Feegle-Meegle seminars" by those of us who had the good fortune to take them], and I think I have consistently understood that R restricted his epistemological considerations to the task of justification. I think I have also avoided the obvious but common error of using constructions of the "discovery" process in examining the work-products of investigators, i.e., appraising theories & testing truth-value of factual conclusions.

As a psychologist, however, & especially as an educator of psychologists, I am interested in putting as much order & rigor as possible into the process of inquiry, including the inquiries of practitioners. I started writing about this in my 1968 Clinical Study book & have continued ever since, all the way through my 1997 book & into the workshop in practice of psy as disciplined inquiry I'll give to Bay Area practitioners on Dec. 4. Along with the brochure inviting people to come to the meeting that I stuck in my last letter to you, the practitioners/clinical supervisors who come to the meeting will have received a copy of my 1991 paper on connection/disconnection of research and practice [in the education of professional psychologists]. The notion of disciplined inquiry has taken over big time in the community of educators of practitioners (NCSPP especially). For me, the analogues of scientific discovery & justification are professional assessment & evaluation, respectively. I separate the 2 conceptually (tho in practice the 2 processes may go on simultaneously), & I do not use Reichenbach's holy name to justify my approach (context of discovery vs. context of justification is only mentioned in passing on p. 428 of enclosed article), but I am uneasy about the possibility of fundamental logical error in my conception. Like the good quasi-Popperian that I am (Popper's caricature of induction is almost the only argument he presented that I find much fault with) I would welcome your help in correcting any mistakes you see in my article.

Don

11/20/98

Dear Don: I don't see anything on your p. 428 that mistakes Reichenbach's distinction or implies its non-existence. Someone might think that the idea of disciplined inquiry collides, or at least is slightly frictional? I think not. But suppose it were, that it conflicts with your push for guidelines in the strategy of discovery, which implies there is such a strategy; so then one can be "normatively evaluated"—a "justificatory" kind of judgment—as a discoverer, by "how you go about it." Well, if Reichenbach's dichotomy requires him to deny that, then Peterson is right and Reichenbach is wrong, that's all.

I don't think he would say that. Perhaps his "thinker's way of finding the theorem" may be taken that way. But it need not, and since he was a bright man, I don't so take it. I avoid attributing dumb errors to smart people.

Popper is worse here, because (for some reason, what?) he harps on there being no rational prescription for discovery. Makes it seem all spooky, all "non-rational" psychological processes, like Kekulé's hoopsnake. But that's plainly incorrect. Kekulé asked, "How hook the 6 Hs and 6 Cs together? Can't be a string, like methane, ethane, etc." Such constraints on the possibilities were rational constraints. So if history of science and metatheoretical analysis of why "good theories" are good (my new book lists 10 properties) give us guidelines, we have a logic of discovery, and you are elaborating it in the context of the scientific practitioner. Seems a clear, clean case.*

Paul

**Funny, KRP's book title conflicts with his view!*

11/30/98

Dear Paul,

Thanks for your comment on Reichenbach's distinction re my disciplined inquiry argument. You captured my concern exactly in remark that someone (Reichenbach? Meehl?) might perceive at least friction, and maybe collision, between my push for logically defensible strategies of inquiry & R's clear restriction of (his) epistemic considerations to context of justification. Your further comments eased my qualms, tho I think we would both agree that definition of a "logic of discovery" is a tough & treacherous task. Not impossible, though. I have never understood Popper's contemptuous "bucket theory of mind" dismissal of the entire inductive process (see enclosed page of my foreword to Dan Fishman's forthcoming book), tho of course he (KRP) is right in saying we can* *never prove synthetic statements by accumulating supportive facts. Until I saw the footnote in your last letter, I had not noticed the inconsistency between Popper's argument & the title of his classic book* [*The Logic of Scientific Inquiry*].

Thanks again,

Don

**I think my fears of misstatement on my part and misunderstanding on the part of my audiences are exacerbated in this California culture, which in psychology seems to be made up 90% of psychoanalytic/existential types who have no interest in data of the kind I encourage, and 10% of people who agree with everything I say, despite my own uncertainties.*

CHAPTER

10

Constructionism, Realism, and Intellectual Honesty

The foreword to Dan Fishman's book that I mentioned in my letter of 11/30/98 began with the following paragraphs:

> Daniel B. Fishman's book, *The Case for Pragmatic Psychology,* is revolutionary, both in substance and in portent. I mean that literally. Instead of assuming, as prevailing ideology would have us do, that practically useful, socially beneficial psychology must begin with a science that is passed on through a closely sifted technology to more or less routine application by practitioners, Fishman proposes that we turn psychology upside down. As practitioners, we begin with our clients, be they people in distress, dysfunctional families, failing corporations, or violent, culturally deteriorating communities. We take them as they come, in all their natural complexity, bring our best knowledge, experience, skill, and creative ingenuity to bear in understanding and improving the condition of each client, and in organized cooperation with other practitioners accumulate a database of successful and unsuccessful cases. On this base, we inform future generations of

professionals and progressively extend the mass of useful knowledge that any true profession must embody and that the people who purchase our services deserve and demand.

If faithfully enacted, the program Fishman proposes will revolutionize the psychological professions. The intuitions and lore on which many professional actions are currently based will gradually be replaced by systematic records of comparable cases, though there will always be room for creative innovation in the ever-expanding range and ever-changing flow of problems that professional psychologists encounter. Results of pertinent research can be readily incorporated in the knowledge base that practitioners bring to each new case. Useful theoretical developments, whenever they appear, can be integrated with prior conceptions in guiding each inquiry. The emerging result will be, of all things, a science-based profession, in the pragmatic sense intended by William James, John Dewey, and contemporary pragmatists like Richard Rorty, Richard Bernstein, and Stephen Toulmin, whose thinking Fishman skillfully integrates in forming the epistemological foundations of his argument.

About a week later, I received an envelope from Meehl dated 12/5/98 that contained this portion of the foreword. The name "Richard Rorty" was circled in red ink, a red arrow pointed to the margin, and the following message was written, in red, on the back of the page:

DRP: I'm surprised you give a plug for Rorty. Just because Fishman relies on his crappola doesn't force Peterson to allude to him. You must read my pen pal Susan Haack's critique. Rorty is intellectually irresponsible, obscurantist. My local philosophers spit on him.

PEM

A rational high-IQ pragmatist like C. S. Peirce would simply laugh at him. As Haack says, Rorty has no right at all to class himself with Peirce, an alpha.

No one who knew Meehl would have been surprised by the force of his statement. The common idea that scientists are cold-blooded, passionless people is of course a myth. I have never known an effective scientist who was anything other than passionate about the scientific mission. The preceding spring, Meehl had circulated broadly among his several circles of correspondents a two-page outline of the essentials of scientific method, with a cover note that read, "Outline of lecture in philosophical psychology seminar, aimed to counteract the obscurantist muddle-heads who deny there is any such thing as 'scientific method.' A rational mind knows something rather special developed in the time of Galileo, Newton, Boyle, & Co. that was different from any previous way of investigating the world, even the genius of the ancient Greeks." I was familiar with Rorty's fictionist arguments and considered them silly, but found acceptable sense in some of his writing, and had never experienced the visceral response to Rorty's work that inspired Meehl's contemptuous denunciation.

12/9/98

Dear Paul,

*Thanks (OUCH!) for your comments on Rorty & my tacit endorsement of his views in foreword to Fishman's book. I'll look up Susan Haack's critique, but I don't need anyone else's opinion to persuade me that Rorty's radical, "postmodern," constructionist argument that there is no such thing as privileged information, that "science talk" is just another vocabulary for dealing with human nature & natural phenomena generally, is irrational, fallacious, misleading, and obscurantist. I've told Fishman how I think & feel about that, in person & in print, & if he had asked me to review his ms. before it went to press, I might have gotten him either to omit Rorty's argument or at least present part of it more critically. But that's not how it went. Dan gave me the finished manuscript (previous drafts of which had been reviewed by Brewster Smith, Donald Polkinghorne, & Yvonne Lincoln) close to the publisher's deadline for production & asked if I would write a foreword. I read the ms., approved his general argument (a pragmatic alternative to postpositivist exclusions a là Robyn Dawes, on the one side, and loose hermeneutics, on the other) and agreed to write the piece.**

Anyway, I don't agree that Rorty is completely wrong-headed. His arguments on the inextricability of human behavior from social context & moral value are valid, in my opinion, and especially important in vindicating a profession of psychology. His emphasis on pragmatic dialogue—willingness to listen to others, to weigh consequences of our actions on other people—is obvious, I suppose, but we don't hear much about that from strict followers of post-Galilean scientific method. That's why I think "disciplined inquiry" is a better term than "applied science" for the work professional psychologists do, & that's why I'm willing to encourage Dan

Fishman's advance of the idea, even if he does include some of the arguments of an arrogant 2nd-rater like Rorty in his statement.

Don

*P.S. *This statement makes Fishman look like a gullible mush-head (as contrasted with clear-eyed, straight-thinking Peterson), which is unfair to Dan. We have argued at length about the merits of hermeneutics & "postmodern" views (words I never use except in identifying people who state the views), and I have published a critique of one of Dan's essays that I thought went too far in disparaging the early analytic philosophies, but I have never confronted him directly about our differing appraisals of Rorty's work. I think Fishman has done a masterful job of integrating analytic & constructionist views in his pragmatic paradigm, & I was glad to write an enthusiastic foreword to his book.*

12/10/98

P.P.S. to letter I mailed yesterday—

Given space Fishman allotted to Rorty, I could not have excluded his name from list of those noted in my foreword without long, inappropriate comment, but I could have found a way to praise the book in a more discerning way, and wish I had.

Don

12/15/98

DRP: Troubles me that my tough-but-correct Rorty remark pressed you to "explain" at length, as I am not a divinely appointed censor of you (or anyone else). I mistakenly thought you must not be familiar with what Rorty actually preaches. It's hard to handle problems of review, preface, comment on colleagues' writing. I sympathize.

I suspect you and I do differ in attitude. Your history (e.g., as a dean in an "applied" school) has not muddled your thinking, but it must surely have enabled you to tolerate others' muddled thinking. We are social animals, have to live peaceably or kill one another. In politics, I much prefer those clowns in Congress to what I am currently reading about the growth of terror & suppression in USSR from 1917 on.

My intense dislike of muddle in psy is partly esthetic, partly narcissistic ("they should listen to me"), but the BIG one is ethical. There are 100s of people serving long prison terms for alleged child sexual abuse of which they are innocent. How can this occur? It's wholly due to muddle-headed psychologists & social workers. That is a major social evil, and I feel justified in my contempt for those who do it, or defend it.

PEM

December 18, 1998

Dear Paul,

Don't trouble yourself, or feel yourself in any way responsible for, the lengthy "explanation" your Rorty remark excited in me. I've never taken your comments as censorious. You have sometimes been a more kindly critic than my works deserve. I suspect some Oedipal n: approval underlies the length of my response, but I am more keenly aware of my discomfort over the realization that my tacit acceptance of Rorty's views in the Fishman foreword, while I privately reject Rorty's most fundamental epistemological arguments, is intellectually dishonest. Too late to correct now.

I've eased up some on myself in matters of this kind through the perverse realization that an attitude I've preferred to think of as "diplomatic evasion" (just keeping my mouth shut when others express views with which I disagree, & thereby letting them suppose I agree with them) has characterized my treatment of many people, in many situations, for many years. I think you are right in thinking that my history as a dean in an "applied" school has a lot to do with that. At Rutgers, I saw my main job as getting a faculty with widely differing, often contradictory views to work together toward common aims, & didn't figure I'd get far along those lines by harping on the "truth" as I saw it. To this day there are people who think I sympathize with their views when, to be honest, I don't. Nationally, working with others in such organizations as NCSPP, I have let many a dean think I approve of his or her professional school when, in truth, I don't. Pragmatically, I have chosen instead to press for higher standards both inside the organization & outside, e.g. in APA accreditation. I hate the deceptions involved, but keep them going as a necessary price of useful dialectic.*

I couldn't agree more with your ethical objection to muddle-headedness that damages others, & whenever I'm sharp enough to see that, I call it what it is.

With best regards,

Don

**When Lloyd Humphreys retired as head of the psy. dept. at U of I, he asked Morton Weir, who had a strong career going as a developmental psychologist, to consider succeeding him. Mort went around talking to old-hand adminis-*

trators about the choice he was facing, & in a conversation with Harry Hake, who had done time as a v.p. for academic affairs, said, "One thing I'll never do is lie to people," to which Harry replied, "You won't last long then." Weir went on to become a fine department head, LAS dean, & later chancellor of the UIUC campus, noted, among other qualities, for his integrity.

December 22 (Christmas cards intervened)

P.S. What really eats at me, & is probably at the heart of my over-reaction to your slashing comment on Rorty, is this: Whatever my intentions [in organizing the first PsyD program] & however rational my actions seemed to me at the time, have I contributed more to the muddle than I have done to reduce it? Dawes, McFall, Hayes, & others clearly think so, and, alas, they have a case. By now evidence (not just anecdote) shows decisively that opening up the PsyD path has dumbed down the profession. It is 4 times easier to get into a PsyD program than to enter a PhD scientist-practitioner program in a research university. Performance on the written part of the national licensing exam (tho not on the oral "show me how you've handled a case" part) clearly favors the PhD programs. I have done my best to bring these disturbing facts to the attention of my colleagues, in print & in my talks, but cannot duck the harsh possibility that all my efforts may have hurt the profession, & our society, more than they have helped it. I am biologically incapable of profound, prolonged depression, but I have spent many a restless hour in the middle of the night in throes of the "My God! What have I done?" syndrome. It won't help now to say, "Sorry, folks, it was all a big mistake." I don't honestly believe that the PsyD/professional school development was entirely mistaken, & will continue to emphasize that side of the argument in public pronouncements & the other work I do.

I apologize for laying my troubles on you, but you are one of the very few people with whom I can be deeply and thoroughly honest about these matters. Please don't feel I need a response from you. It's helpful to me just to unload. If you feel a comment coming on, though, send it to my Rutgers address. We're leaving here Jan. 5.

Merry Christmas, Don

12/26/98

Dear Don: I don't fault any administrator from holding back criticism under some conditions. I haven't been a dean, but chaired psy dept for 6 years, and was on Psychiatry Exec Committee for several. As chair, I never lied "affirmatively," no, not once—to a student, colleague, dean, or another chair. But I sure as hell kept my mouth shut at times; e.g., some of our world-famous social psychologists did studies I considered trivial and of no practical or *theoretical value. But I never let on. I fear the gray-region of "silence = negative lie" is impossible for any ethicist to demarcate sharply, or even roughly. It's a tough moral judgment call. So I am NOT disappointed in you as regards integrity. We're in the same boat.*

*As to substance, I incline to think we do disagree. So what? Gottesman disagrees with me on Sc-genetics. Heston disagrees about Freud. All my super-bright colleagues disagree with me on Darwin. My student Golden disagrees about pseudo-taxa. My pal Faust disagrees about reverse discrimination. Etc., etc. Everyone I know disagrees with me about ESP, except Sherm Nelson.**

Westen's "Freud legacy" paper (November Bulletin) is excellent. But how does he separate the gold from the fool's gold? Quantitative studies, either experimental or correlational. So when Rorty, or Fishman, or you reject mathematics as an essential feature of scientific method, I have to disagree. The reason we've had disagreement about Freud for 4 generations, thousands of articles & books, smart, honest truth-seekers with MDs & PhDs unable to decide (or persuade one another), is precisely the lack of mathematization. I challenge you to show that it's something else.

Cheers, Paul

**Rattle yr cage with Radin, Dean, The Conscious Universe (Harper Collins, 1997). Evidence for ESP > prophylactic aspirin!*

P.S.: I feel bad that you get non-clinical reactive Ds from your heroic PsyD efforts. Be grateful you lack my cyclothymic genes, you might have a rip-snorter. But look, a bit of RET (no white lie!). Your PsyD programs didn't turn out incompetents. Others did. And consider this: I've kept track of my opinions since grad school, on controversial topics. On every major issue but one, I was right. It took 25–45 years for the majority to catch up with me—a variety of topics. The one I missed? The PsyD. At Stillwater, people (all but Wirt and Hathaway) said it wd be a 2nd-rate diploma mill thing. I said no, not the way my selection + curriculum was set up. And it wouldn't have. My error: to assume "they" wd do what Meehl said. No critic asked me why I believed that. Reason: We all just assumed no Flexner Report would be needed. We assumed all PsyD programs wd be in accredited universities. No one even mentioned free-standing PsyD schools. So I can say, "I goofed, I failed to think of that." But I didn't flagellate myself because some 2 dozen smart critics failed to think of it either!! So console yourself. Humans, as Ellis says, are all fallible. I'm partly to "blame," but I lose no sleep over it.

P.P.S.: Xmas Eve, 4 hrs Emergency Room, Dx "paroxysmal atrial tachycardia." Now on K+ and higher Digoxin meds. Scary but rarely dangerous. I never rely on self-Dx in cases like this.

1/4/99

Dear Paul,

Your kind letter of 12/26 arrived as I was packing to leave. Many thanks for it, tho by now self-administered RET, plus talks with Jane, have pretty well dissipated the depression I was feeling when I wrote my previous letter. By now, I've come back pretty close to the mood that shows in my conversation with Tom Reid [the first PsyD] and George Allen [clinical PhD classmate of Reid]. That statement is as honest and open as I dare to be without risking libel suit, and is phrased in a form that offers hope of constructive effect. When I wrote to you in my down-state, I hadn't intended to call you out of your retirement as a practicing clinical psychologist, but I'm glad I did, & I thank you again for all you've done to help me.

If there are substantive differences between us, I don't know what they are. I do not dispute, indeed I agree emphatically with your argument that mathematization of theoretical entities is required for strong science. I claim only that we can improve enormously on current levels of rigor in the disciplined inquiries of our profession without theoretical mathematization (even a little numerification & summary arithmetic would help) & I personally doubt that math'ization is possible in most of the areas of soft psy that underlie practice. I don't know how many times I've reread your "Theoretical Risks ..." article & pondered the final sentences ["I think we ought to acknowledge the possibility that there is never going to be a really impressive theory in personality or social psychology. I dislike to think that, but it might just be true"]. My own forecast is gloomier than yours. I think it is true.

I also agree with you & Sherman Nelson [one of my Minnesota classmates and another of Meehl's students] about ESP. I once ran a demonstration of the Rhine procedure in my intro. psy. class. 280+ students. I asked if anybody in the room considered him/herself ESP "sensitive." Many hands up. I picked a steady-looking older woman in the back of the room. I "sent" the images on the cards. She "received" and hit 13 of the 25. I calculated a Chi-square ($p < .001$) and the students left the room shaking their heads. Not me. Like you, I find the data persuasive.

I'm sorry to hear about your Christmas Eve cardiac episode. I've been in ER for exactly the same condition, & am probably on same meds you are. Bless us both. And many others, including the crew here at Wright. Before my depression sank in, I was exhilarated by the experience of working with the earnest, industrious, in some cases highly talented people who devote their lives to an operation of this kind. Unlike most of their snooty brethren next door (at UCB), these folks are in the trenches, working with the families of men & women in prison (who otherwise are forgotten by the self-righteous, lock-em-up, law & order types, & are 4–5 times more likely than others of comparable ethnicity and SE level to move into lives of crime), running drug pre-

vention programs in Oakland, etc. I have learned from them, as I think they have from me, & in many ways I feel privileged to work with them & others in the NCSPP family toward building a sound, useful profession. I'd like to work also with the CUDCP [Council of University Directors of Clinical Psychology] people, but they, by & large, have disowned me. I tried to get CUDCP to join NCSPP in self-studies, but was coldly ignored. Now, my genial, very intelligent friend, Roger Peterson, has finally arranged a joint meeting of NCSPP and CUDCP. Maybe there is hope.

While still in Berkeley, I received reprints of two articles by Susan Haack, including her *tour de force* "conversation" between Richard Rorty and Charles Sanders Peirce. Haack had composed this by selecting quotes from the writings of Rorty and Peirce, juxtaposing them in the form of a dialogue, and in a playfully devastating way exposing not only the incompatibility of their views but also Rorty's impudence in squeezing himself between Peirce and Dewey in his writing about "we pragmatists." I wrote a note to Professor Haack, thanking her for the articles, enthusiastically commending their quality, and noting how sorely needed in my world, applied psychology, were sound philosophies of the kind she and Meehl expounded. When I returned to my office at Rutgers, I found there a complimentary copy of her splendid book, *Manifesto of a Passionate Moderate*.

CHAPTER

11

Reconciling Differences

In my office, I also found an audiotape that Paul had recorded along with a paper entitled "The Power of Quantitative Thinking" and headed "P. E. Meehl, APS [American Psychological Society] Cattell Award, 5/23/98, Draft X."

1/25/99

Dear Paul,

I haven't read your APS award paper yet, but I have listened to your tape with great interest, plenty pleasure (felt like we were in your office), & occasional apprehensive concern that I will have nothing useful to say about some of the questions you raise (in which case, I'll do my best not to say anything). I look forward to trying, though. Can't do it right away. We're still unpacking from Cal. trip & I have agreed to review an article for AP, on my desk, under deadline. When I've done my duty, expect a long letter.

Don

Paul's audio message ran a full 60 minutes. His paper was 13 pages long. The letter I finally wrote in reply filled 32 handwritten pages. Both of us rambled even more than we usually did in our correspondence. Between us, we registered enough verbiage in this exchange alone to fill a small monograph, so considerable abbreviation is needed. Worst of all, I cannot find the tape. I have looked high and low, over and over in the same likely places, and at least once in all the other crannies I can think of, but my search has failed. I must have put the tape in a special place so I would be sure to find it later on, and then forgot where the place was. This is regrettable, because Paul Meehl's talk is even richer than his letters in anecdotes and unexpected sidelights. Let me try an example from the opening of the tape. I remember this part well enough to feel confident that I can recount the sense of Paul's message as well as the spirit of his language:

Paul E. Meehl to Donald R. Peterson, January seven, 1999, side one.

Don, I've chosen this way to communicate with you because I have some arthritis that makes writing difficult, and what I want to say and ask is too big for a letter. I hope you won't mind.

First is this goddam problem—the most irksome intellectual problem in our field as far as I am concerned—that is, how can we give the proper weight to clinical experience in diagnosis and intervention? Experience is untrustworthy, but we can't just dismiss it. I started to fret about this when I went to work for Starke Hathaway. Starke had a pathological bias against Freud. Partly Minnesota empiricism, which I share, as you do, but there was more to it than that. Hathaway had a dose of sexual Puritanism in him. He had a big collection of pornographic books [Hathaway was one of the first psychologists to bring human sexuality into the medical curriculum and regularly taught the subject to medical students and clinical psychologists of my generation as part of a required course in clinical psychiatry], but he was sort of Puritanical. I have a streak of that in me. For example, I don't enjoy it when a group of men stand around telling dirty jokes. I never have one of my own to add. I predict you feel the same way. [Correct.]

But I digress. Starke was so biased against Freud he would dismiss or dispute almost anything Freud claimed. If I said something like, "Have you ever noticed how some people tell you the exact date of everything that happened in their lives? You know, 'When I got out of the Navy on the 12th of February, 1946....' I believe that's a mild indicator of paranoia. Not pathognomic, not psychosis, but indicative. Have you ever had an experience like that?"—if I said it, Starke would listen, and more often than not he would come back with an anecdote of his own. But if I ran across something like that in Freud and asked Starke what he thought about it, he'd reject the idea. I was tempted to do a little study. Collect 20 observations from my experience and 20 that Freud reported. Try them out on Starke, identifying the source, and put his responses in a 4-fold table. I'd bet everything I own that he'd have gone along with Meehl but not Freud. So there was Hathaway, whom I admired as a diagnostician and therapist, excluding observations I was ready to consider and disagreeing with me fundamentally on the value of a major theory. Who's right? What shall we credit and what shall we reject? I'm seventy-nine years old. I've been fussing with this question since I was in graduate school and expect I'll go to my grave without reaching a fully satisfactory solution. But let's see what we can do with it.

Alas, I can't remember the rest of his talk as clearly as I recall the opening. But I took detailed notes as I replayed the tape later on. I have repeated the substance of Meehl's queries in my written reply, so my letter incorporates most of his challenges along with my responses:

2/10/ (interruptions) 16/17/18/1999

Dear Paul,

At last I've had the pleasure of replaying the tape you recorded 1/7 & some time to ponder the questions you raised. Let me get right to the main one, on which you bet we'll disagree. You phrased the general question in several forms:

What weight should we give to clinical experience in diagnosis and intervention?

Which paragraphs in "The Power of Quantitative Thinking" (Meehl, 1998) would I challenge?

And (here I'll have to combine several statements & rephrase a bit) given a large population of reasonably intelligent, well-meaning practitioners working with individual cases, "noticing things," and reaching some conclusions that generalize beyond the individual, and given further that a considerable group of practitioners say "x is true" while another group say "not x is true" is there any other way to decide the question than to quantify robustly observed "hard" data and examine the data through the procedures known collectively as "the scientific method"?

In approaching the question, you suggested that I read Drew Westen's article on the scientific legacy of Sigmund Freud, an excellent example, I think. Sure enough, here we are, 4 generations after the original Freudian statements, still disagreeing, and still working to separate the gold from the pyrites.

Let me start by sharing your enthusiasm for Westen's paper, as strong a work of integrative scholarship as I've seen in many a year. It is one of those rare statements that changed my mind about something important. Before Westen, I was impatient with psychoanalytic theory, which in my limited reading of it seemed to be growing more & more divergent & obscure. Following Westen, I see his five core propositions as a reasonably sturdy foundation for further research and cumulative knowledge about human mentation. Why do I think so? Because these are the ideas that have survived 4 generations of scientific scrutiny and collective clinical experience. Could any kind of "unforced consensus on what is good for us to believe" (Rorty, et al.) have led me to the same conclusion? No. Why not? The history of human thought shows the ubiquity of error, & often correlated injustice & evil, when widely shared beliefs are justified in that way. Examples: The sun revolves around the earth; the bubonic plague is caused by Satan's legions of witches (Meehl's examples and mine too); no Negro is capable of high-level intellectual activity, and most Negroes in slavery are happy with their lot (Fitzhugh, Calhoun, et al. & the collective American Confederate culture prior to the Civil War).

So, in response to the third form of your general question (any alternative to scientific method in resolving differences of opinion between groups of observers?), I say no—not that I can think of. In this I agree with the basic thrust of your APS award address, as well as your "Credentialed Persons, Credentialed Knowledge" paper.

I see no contradiction between the affirmation I have just stated and the conclusion drawn from Westen's very interesting Q study, i.e., that a surprising majority of psychodynamically oriented clinicians endorsed the same 5 propositions, now, per Westen, supported by a large body of empirical data. Why not? I consider some psychoanalysts whom I know [to be] muddle-headed, too strongly guided by unsubstantiated theory in their clinical practice, especially in their quasi-religious faiths about the role of transference in psychotherapy. To me, it is an empirical question whether it can be beneficial, as Arnold Lazarus, Al Ellis, & others say, or is uniformly harmful, as many psychoanalysts say, to extend relationships with clients beyond the therapeutic situation, as long as we agree on a clear set of ethical constraints, and the data, such as they are, favor Lazarus, et al. But most psychodynamically oriented clinicians are not stupid, and I find it more reassuring than contradictory that they agree on fundamentals, tho the degree of convergence Westen found is surprising. Indeed, if you had asked me, before I read Westen's paper, to list the Freudian concepts that I "believed in," my set, like yours, would have been very close to Westen's. I've never been analyzed. I do not identify my approach to clinical work as "psychodynamic." My knowledge of psychoanalytic literature, both theoretical & empirical, is spotty. But I too would have identified Freud's basic ideas of unconscious mental processes, conflict, ambivalence and parallel process, importance of childhood experience, mental representation of self, others, and relationships, and developmental dynamics as valid, important conceptions.

Actually, I did so in my teaching throughout a time when many experimentalists, with all their hard data, were claiming that most of the core ideas of Freudian theory were incorrect. Charlie Eriksen, who went through the Stanford clinical psy program about the same time I was studying at U of M but who devoted his long career at the U of Illinois to experimental research in visual perception, did some carefully controlled research that failed to show evidence of "learning without awareness" [as others had claimed], and went around the country giving colloquia under the title "Subliminal Perception, Unconscious Motivation, and Sounds That Go Bump in the Night." He considered the idea of unconscious mental processes a myth, and further, a damaging myth, because it led practitioners to fool their patients into paying high prices for allegedly therapeutic shenanigans that were based on error.

Why did I believe Freud and not Eriksen? Clinical experience, for the most part. I didn't see how anybody could spend much time doing psychotherapy and deny the importance of major defenses like repression. I didn't think Erik's lab provided a situation in which unconscious operations, as I saw them working in clinical practice, could be revealed. And I thought that Erik, for all his knowledge of scientific method & all his ingenuity as an experimentalist, had forgotten the first rule of statistical inference. One does not prove the null hypothesis.

I'm not surprised that 4 generations were required to separate, among all the theses Freud proposed, Westen's 5 propositions from those that are now largely ignored or discredited. <u>Eighty</u> generations passed between Hippocrates and Harvey, and 8 more between Harvey and Pasteur. I know—we psychologists had the advantage of reasonably well-developed scientific method from the start, and pre-Enlightenment bioscientists did not—but I consider Freud's subject matter, & even more the subject matter of soft psychology broadly conceived, far more recondite than theirs. Without making a direct comparison, you yourself have said so as persuasively as anyone I know. Of all your writings, the one I reread more often than any other is the "Theoretical Risks ..." article (Meehl, 1979). I do not do so primarily to dispute or deepen understanding of your central contentions about the futility of null hypothesis-testing research and the necessity of robust, multiply-determined observations. You assert those ideas with luminous clarity, and have of course advanced the arguments in subsequent statements. I reread Meehl, 1979 to ponder the 20 conditions, identified early in the article, that make the study of socially and personally vital phenomena in psychology so damnably difficult, & to muse upon your final "melancholy reflection": "It may be the nature of the subject matter in most of personology & social psychology is inherently incapable of permitting theories with sufficient conceptual power (especially mathematical development) to yield the kinds of strong refuters expected by Popperians, Bayesians, & unphilosophical scientists in developed fields like chemistry."

Here, perhaps, is where some differences between us lie. You clearly persist in the faith that mathematization of theoretical entities is possible, or at least sufficiently likely of attainment to devote a quantum of your talent to the effort. I admire work of the kind you do. In my heart, I hope you're right. But most of the work along these lines, by APS types who aren't as intelligent or sensible as you are, seems to me unproductive, pretentious, & sometimes downright silly. Let me try an example in a field of soft psychology that has occupied much of my attention for the past 20 years or so, i.e., the study of interpersonal relationships. I first took an active, focused interest in the area in the early 1970s, right after I had written my Clinical Study *book and saw the study of interpersonal relationships as (a) the most important, and (b) the most shabbily studied and poorly understood of all the phenomena that our science, and especially our profession, need to comprehend. Throughout the 1970s & into the 1980s there was a* huge *amount of research on game theory. Professors and PhD students across the land were sticking college sophomores into their labs to work out prisoners' dilemmas and other games. The work seemed pertinent to understanding not only decision making but interpersonal process more broadly. From the start, the theories were elegantly mathematized, and as the research went on the mathematical refinements became more & more complex. But like aspiration level, risky shift, and other "theories" you consider in your 1979 classic, work on game theory didn't die; it just faded away. I checked the last 5 issues of* Annual Review of Psy *& found* one *entry for the topic, as against dozens in the 1970s.*

To me, the problem of understanding interpersonal relationships seemed multifarious & exceedingly *complex. I did not and do not dispute your contention that a main flaw in the preponderance of psychological studies on problems of this kind lay in the readiness to accept Fisherian significance testing as the way to truth, and I agreed & still agree emphatically with your insistence on multiple measures, "triangulation" & more, in developing robust observational data. But it is on this last matter that I have chosen to focus my attention in research & practice. And it is here that I might differ with you on some of the arguments in your paper on the power of quantitative thinking (Meehl, 1998). I do not exactly wish to challenge, but I do propose to qualify some statements in the second paragraph of the article. You say, with Skinner, that the difficulties (in separating wheat from chaff) are not problems of observation, because the phenomena are relatively macroscopic & slow & can be recorded for leisurely analysis. Well, true enough for pigeons in a box, and even for interactional proceedings in the psychoanalyst's office. True as well, up to a point, in observing the interactions of, say, teachers & children in a classroom. But when we try to study the relationships that matter most to people,* close *relationships between husbands & wives, parents & children, brothers & sisters, etc., the problems of obtaining ecologically valid, dependable observations are* horrendous. *All 20 of the impediments to progress in soft psychology that you list in Meehl, 1979 come to the fore. How shall we define response classes? How shall we study situations (given, as I claim in Clinical Study, that we must study person–environment interactions if we are ever to develop a powerful science & a useful profession of psychology)? How do we overcome the other 18 difficulties that you claim to have tossed off "in 10 minutes of superficial thought"? (I never believed that.) How do we surmount an even more formidable obstacle that you only touch upon in your short paragraph on feedback loops, i.e., the reactivity of human beings to observation and the resulting indeterminacy that I consider qualitatively different from the Heisenbergian indeterminacy that pervades all science?*

So, I'm not quite as ready as you are to land on quantification as the key to scientific success, and even less as an essential ingredient of useful professional work in our field. I do believe, with you and Aristotle, that we should be as precise, in all our activity, scientific & professional, as our subject matter allows. But at this stage in evolution of the discipline I believe we are, if anything, overly eager to quantify in service of the illusion that quantification = science. To me it seems that we need a lot more time in the field, looking around, "noticing things," before we attempt anything more than crude inductive generalizations. In your terms, we need to extend our senses with improved observational techniques. Then it is helpful to numerify our observations, many of which will initially be registered in narrative form, and combine numbers in summary statistics. Ultimately, as you say & I agree, strong science requires mathematization of theoretical entities and rigorous linkage of the latter to quantified observations. But I believe we are far short of that stage now—more in company with Tycho Brahe than with Newton, and clearly short of advance from Newton to Einstein. Whether, in the soft areas of psychology, we shall ever have a strong science, in your terms and mine, I do not know. I personally do not foresee one. But short of that, we can do a great deal better than we have so far, and substantially better than competing disciplines, by improving observational procedures, examining phenomena by multiple means, and moving through the first 2 levels of quantification that you describe in your APS paper [numerified observations and summary statistics of numerified observations].

In my work against social prejudice at Rutgers University, work I conceive of as professional though not scientific, the importance of quantification recedes still further. Some forms of quantification are useful. By the time we got through organizing our efforts, some 150 people (administrators, faculty, & students) were involved. I was the only remaining psychologist on our executive committee, and the only one of the 150 members seriously committed to systematic study of our community. I was also chair of our task group on community assessment which, among other activities, ran a survey that elicited, among other data, narrative accounts of "interaction episodes" in which the respondent reported some kind of abuse apparently related to the race, religion, gender, or sexual ori-

entation of the victim. To readers of the report (for which we received more requests than anything else I've ever written, with one exception) the narrative accounts themselves were most persuasive in showing a sizable constituency in our community who didn't think we had much of a problem with prejudice and intergroup animosity at Rutgers that we did have problems. Many of the attacks were vicious and stories about them were poignant. But simple numerification and statistical summary of the accounts strengthened the case. It mattered to administrators, the RU Board of Trustees, & others that 22% of the respondents reported some kind of abuse; that 1/3 of the Black students, 1/4 of Latinos, 1/5 Asians, but only 1/20 of White students reported abuse; and that, proportionally (40%), the most frequently abused group of people were gay or lesbian. I didn't need any significance tests. Every differential finding I placed in the report far exceeded the usual limits of statistical significance. I certainly didn't mathematize any theoretical entities. Yet I was told the work was useful and believe that it was.

To me, the main issues I had to consider in doing the work were political (I could not repeat the survey because I was pretty sure our frightened, marginally competent president would not allow me to "stir up trouble") and philosophical matters—not of philosophy of science but of moral philosophy (the vision of community our efforts were designed to realize).

This letter is much too long already, but I cannot resist a final remark on Rorty. I disagree entirely with his main epistemological argument, but I'm still ready to read some of his remarks on the kinds of dialogue required to negotiate competing values in a pluralistic society, and I do not think he is especially dangerous. I trust the marketplace of ideas more than you do. Rorty's epistemic (and ontological) mistakes are there for all to see, however offensive his obscurantist sophistry may be, and he has plenty of critics. I'm counting on Haack, Bernstein, et al. to whittle Rorty down to size.

Nor do I think Rorty is stupid. Not in the same league as Peirce, nor James or Dewey, for that matter, but not downright stupid. In a related opinion, I do not necessarily regard anybody who is ready to find something in Rorty's loose writing that supports his or her own arguments a dummy. More generally, I am never surprised to find some otherwise smart people endorsing some blatantly wrong ideas. The g-factor intelligence of Nazi rocket scientists had to be high. How could they not see? Well, of course they'd get shot if they didn't go along, so we have to restrict consideration, as Rorty insists, to those who displayed unforced intellectual compliance and passionate affective commitment to arrantly & obviously wrong ideas. Still it is clear from the record (cf. Heidegger & the Nazi doctors) that many German intellectuals endorsed and implemented consequences of the idea that Jews were an inferior race. I've never known a stupid Jesuit, but there they go, reciting the Apostle's creed with straight faces. As you say, [D. G.] Paterson was right about the situational specificity of behavior. So were

Mischel and Peterson (1968), though situational variance is clearly smaller for the class of performances we call "intelligence" than for those we lump under the heading of "personality."

I've stopped beating up on myself for my part in the PsyD movement & thank you again for the RET you provided by mail & voice. I never did think I was a stupid fool for failing to predict how the movement would go. As you note, I had a lot of reputable company in that mistake. I don't know anybody who could have done a better job than I did in organizing the programs that I led. However, I am still disappointed and gravely concerned about those who have used a distorted, sometimes grotesquely perverted transformation of the PsyD concept (retaining little but the title) to justify perpetration of pre-Flexner-type diploma mills. I guess I shouldn't be surprised. If they wouldn't listen to Meehl, how could I dream that they would listen to Peterson? We're stuck with a social process and a history in which I had some influence but over which I had no control. Question for me now is "What can I do & say that will be (a) true, & (b) socially constructive?" Unlike the Solicitor General [in annual report to the Supreme Court], I can't just "confess error," because to do so would have (I'm confident) a demoralizing effect on people who are running PsyD programs in good faith, as well as they know how. For me, once past my depression, it's pretty simple. I shall continue to insist on the qualities a strong practitioner program must embody, help the best of the programs (they aren't all diploma mills) develop those qualities, work to stiffen accreditation standards (our main institutional means for weeding out bad programs; we cannot, in our contemporary litigious culture, do the kind of hatchet job Flexner & Co. did in medicine nearly a century ago), & count on economic forces (managed care will help here) to drive schools charging high prices for poor education and unpromising professional futures out of business.

Don

Ah—one more point. I do not "challenge" but wish to comment on the final paragraph of your APS address and Thorndike's famous epigram. ["Our ideals may be as lofty and subtle as you please, but if they are real ideals, they are ideals for achieving something; and if anything real is ever achieved, it can be measured. Not perhaps now, and not perhaps fifty years from now, but if a thing exists, it exists in some amount; and if it exists in some amount, it can be measured."] Yes, what "exists" exists in some amount and can be measured, but the phenomena with which we are concerned in psychology do not "exist" unless we reify them. They happen. And the processes with which we are primarily concerned in soft psychology are often so stripped of meaning by the unavoidable simplifications of quantification that they are better left in narrative form and interpreted linguistically. Disciplined inquiry, as I conceive it, admits both linguistic (I dislike the surplus meanings of "hermeneutic") and quanti-

tative interpretations, and integrates them, at least in the professional sector of our field, with primary focus on pragmatic consequences rather than scientifically established truth.

(Geez. I should have taped my response to your tape, or at least typed my letter. I hope you won't mind.)

I suppose it is conceivable that, some day, psychologists will solve all 20 of the problems you lay out so brilliantly in "Theoretical Risks," plus others none of us has even thought of yet but will surely encounter as we proceed, but my imagination is not so grand as to foresee it. We, you & I, may differ then in our visions of what psychology may become in distant millennia. To me, the aspiration of mathematizing not only all but even the most crucial features of subject matter in soft psychology is reminiscent of the quest for the Holy Grail: noble but childlike. I don't object to, indeed I strongly advocate, pushing quantification as far as it can sensibly go. I wish descendents of your fans in APS all the luck in the world. Meanwhile I am content to use the knowledge we can obtain, both quantitative and qualitative, in such efforts as reducing the evils of social prejudice, & to spend a considerable number of my remaining days trying to understand, with no mathematical concern whatsoever, how Rutherford B. Hayes could go along with the Bourbon aristocrats of the reconstructing American Southland in believing that they, the White plantation owners, knew how to handle "the Negro problem," and then watch the subjugative oppressions of Jim Crow take hold. Further, I consider it legitimate to develop this line of thought as a psychologist, though I shall acknowledge my debt to professional historians and biographers in early paragraphs of anything I may write on the topic.

The very next day, I reread my letter and got concerned about my remark that the effort to mathematize theoretical entities in psychology was reminiscent of the search for the Holy Grail: "noble but childlike." I feared that Paul, whose taxometric research was clearly directed toward the mathematical ideal, might believe I was referring to him. So I copied the page that contained the remark, underlined the relevant sentence, and mailed it to Paul with a note that read:

I don't know what I was thinking when I made this smart-ass remark. I was not thinking of you and your ingenious, meticulous, possibly epoch-making work, but of others in our field who seem to believe that if we can only transform all of our experiences into numbers, and do enough experiments, the mysteries of the human condition will be revealed. By the end of my letter I was tired, I got careless, & I guess I thought you might be amused by my clever comparison.

Paul replied immediately:

2/24/99

Dear Don: To your latest clarification, of course I would never interpret a harsh remark about fanatical quantifiers as directed at me. Have no fear. In social science, we see people failing to take the initial open-ended field observation stage (unlike, e.g., Jane Goodall!!) or being simplistic, non-empathic, clumsy about describing it. Then they build a weak, jerry-built "measuring device," after which they use feeble statistics (e.g., refuting the null hypothesis) to "test" their theory. I have no more esteem for those people than you do, and they preponderate.

I think I can formulate my view of quantification by a conjunction of methodological assertions that you will agree with:

1. *Quantification is never a sufficient condition for either strong theory-appraisal or technological power.*
2. *In social science, quantification is often abused—badly done and over-trusted. In some areas, more often than not.*
3. *It should be preceded by sensitive, open-minded, empathic field observation, to decide what is worth counting or measuring.*
4. *At some stage, it almost always becomes necessary. Hard to say when.*
5. *Observational quantification is probably more needed (at some stage) than mathematizing theoretical constructs. (Not sure I believe this, quite.)*
6. *In a powerful science, the 2 kinds of quantification become intimately connected. When we are doing both, but they are not so connected (e.g., much of economics), something is wrong.*
7. *Counting is often more valuable than measuring. A claim that qualitative properties correlate cannot be tested without counting (4-fold table!)*

Paul

P.S.: Remind me if I forgot to recount my experiences with "experts" that led me to invent taxometrics.

3/2/99

Dear Paul,

Exactly. A beautifully concise summary of your views and my rambling 30-page letter inspired by the questions & comments on your (also rambling but deliciously provocative) hour-long tape. I agree with all 7 assertions, both individually & conjunctively. On Item #5, my view is not so much that observational quantification is more needed than mathematizing theoretical constructs (for strong science, both are needed & I wouldn't know how to rank order their importance) but that in present, early stages of our science (soft psy anyway) observational quant. (following 3 & 4) is all we can sensibly do.

I don't remember hearing or seeing anything re your experience with "experts" that led to Meehl's taxometrics but would enjoy the story.

Don

**P.S. Is there anything left* that we disagree about? Not that I can think of, unless you count my readiness to credit some of Rorty's ideas & greater faith in dialectic to correct his epistemic nonsense.*

**I'd almost be relieved if there <u>were</u> some differences between us, as evidence of intellectual independence on my part. But much as I've been influenced by you (not to mention Feigl, Hathaway, Paterson, Elliott, Cronbach, Humphreys, Osgood, & the other fine minds I've been lucky enough to learn from) it seems to me we've reached many of the same conclusions on our own, guided only by a common way of thinking.*

3/5/99

DRP: No, nothing left we disagree on. We've settled the Rorty issue. He (and the others like him) make a qualitatively correct point, but overdo it. I hold the overdo has malignant consequences, and WORSE in the very fields where quantification is most badly needed, even if it is more difficult. Little or no danger that physicist Weinberg will screw up quantum mechanics because he's male, or Jewish, or whatever. But muddleheads in our field will <u>love</u> Rorty & Co., just as they abused Kuhn a few years back, for obscurantist reasons.

Separating math. of theoretical constructs from quantifying observations (and quasi-observations), the latter's necessity seems clear to me. I assert "observable O_1 correlates with observable O_2." ALL empirical science starts with such allegations; geology, physics, psychology, epidemiology, economics, whatever. Suppose I deny it, or at least doubt it. NO WAY EXISTS to check the allegation except to count and measure. Can't escape. Whereas the merit of a conjectural theoretical math model about unobserved entities or events may be very doubtful, do more harm than good.

On my taxometrics: In 1950s, partly due to my worries about psychotherapy, partly working on my Sc theory, the <u>Dx-category</u> problem was acute, no clear answer, numerous opinions, some dogmatic. I read, wrote letters, sought out people to talk with. Some psychometrists, some statisticians. They pontificated that Fisher (or Mahalanobis) had solved this. I *knew better, but when I explained why (no Gold Standard, or even Silver "criterion"), those who got the point explained that inverse factor analysis, or cluster analysis, had solved that situation. When I explained it hadn't and what it was needful to do by no-criterion, statistical boot strapping, what did they say? They solemnly and arrogantly informed me that, as I had formulated the problem, it was mathematically insoluble!*

But I finally thought, to hell with them. I may not be expert in the gamma function, and slow at matrix algebra, but I do know some math, and I know philosophy of science (which they disdained), and—big point—I'm smarter than they are, less rigid, and less slavishly conforming to "expertise." So I'll just invent my own home-baked method, and I did, and it works. Best there is.

Moral: Unclear. But I'm pretty sure brains + flexibility + cognitive chutzpah—a dash of Freud's "conquistador" in one's personality—is a needed composite. (Line between that & the schizy rebel, non-conforming reflexly, is hard to draw).

PEM

Before I received this letter, I found another letter from Paul in my mailbox. I was astonished to see that it was dated 2/23/99, that is, the day *before* the letter of 2/24/99 that contained Meehl's 7-point summary of the necessities and limitations of quantification in science. This, then, was the letter he had written immediately after receiving my 30-page monster, but it had been delayed in the mail by 2 full weeks while all the rest of our correspondence was flying back and forth:

2/23/99

Dear Don: WOW!! A great letter. I love it. But I can't respond as its depth deserves for awhile yet. On top of my congestive heart failure, I now am officially diabetic, Leslie tapping my blood every other day, etc. Dosage of pills (I'm not on insulin yet, thank goodness) is tricky—twice in last month I've had hypoglycemia on my walk. Rx is carry 3 glucose tablets. These somatic things have depressed us a bit, and my "mail-stack" is offensive. You, of course, have high priority. I assume I may dictate again. It's easier.

Short response: We hardly disagree. As to mathematics, I may have failed to parse (a) theoretical models [and] (b) empirical stats. I claim one cannot avoid (b), and I see you agree. As to (a), I have the same skepticism you have. Our intuitions are remarkably alike, e.g., I never took game theory seriously as a help to understanding psychopathology. I decided it could be OK for an MBA, and perhaps in government—but even there, to neglect primate ethology among rulers would be fatal. So I never bothered with it. Meehl and Peterson have sound instincts, whatever that is, hah?

On quantification, my papers may be misleading. I should parse necessary vs. sufficient. For math to help, one must notice the relevant things, measure them adequately, analyze them cleverly. Your complaints against dumb quantifiers I of course accept. And mathematizing the theoretical entities is useless if they are stupidly chosen. On all this we agree.

But here: Any alleged relation between observed properties, or between observed and theoretical properties, is inherently a mathematical claim, is it not? And do you know of any way to test such a claim that is not mathematical? This is not a question about theoretical models only, it's at the fact level, isn't it? In the 1920s, academic psychologists tried to test Freud "quantitatively" by dumb studies (e.g., "Do you like mother more than father?"). This shows quantification is not sufficient. But I contend it is necessary, and here is where we still disagree.

More later. My brilliant MS was rejected by Harvard U Press, so I must try elsewhere. I'm told MIT Press takes such things.

Paul

3/5/99

Dear Paul,

I just received your letter of 2/23 (reporting health problems) after responding to your letter of 2/24 (asserting 7-point conjunction on quant.) which arrived about a week ago. Snail mails get worse & worse, but I'm still resisting e-mail. My problem is not insufficiency & slow speed of info. but too much, too fast, and your load must be far greater than mine.

For God's sake protect yourself every way you can. I respond so quickly & at such length to your messages because I learn more & have more fun that way than by almost anything I do, but your list of correspondents is longer than mine & I don't expect any reciprocity beyond that which you enjoy. Any response from you—short or long, written or oral, sooner or later—will be welcomed with pleasure and appreciation.

Couple of comments on your letter of 2/23. Re your belief that we disagree about the necessity of quantification in testing claims of relations among observed properties etc. I don't think we disagree even there. Example: A recent book written by a historian who also happens to be a declared & published member of the political Christian Right claims to show that our best presidents were faithful to their wives. I can't think of any way to validate/invalidate that claim decisively except to correlate some measure of presidential quality with some measure of screwing around. In a crude way, the author does this. It ain't hard to show that the notoriously womanizing Warren Harding was a less effective president than A. Lincoln, who, despite fierce sex drive and plenty diddling in his youth, was, by every kind of evidence, faithful in his loveless marriage to Mary Todd. Even the slightly more subtle questions (any strong presidents who fooled around? Kennedy? FDR?) can be thought of in numerical terms. I agree that the core factual claims must be settled in some inherently quantitative fashion. It just seems to me that the more interesting questions (e.g., How can we understand the development, nature, & expression of Lincoln's "character"?) are trivialized by quantification and more fruitfully approached linguistically. And I'll add that some forms of linguistic analysis are more fruitful than others.

On rejection of your book. Fools! All publishers these days, including the U presses, are making their accept/reject decisions on financial grounds, and don't know what they are doing even in their financial projections. I can't imagine that your book wouldn't make the nut in the long run (cf. your 1954 classic) [his book on clinical and statistical prediction, for which he had trouble finding a publisher but sold more than 13,000 copies] let alone the (quantitatively non-measurable) contribution to clarity in scientific thought.

Please, dear friend, take all possible care of your health. I'll hold good thoughts for you.

Don

(Postdiction: When you first saw this envelope in your mail you said something like

"Jesus, another letter from Peterson.")

Meehl's instant reply to me was the page of my letter that included my comment about the trivialization of some interesting questions by quantification, and my belief that such questions were more fruitfully approached linguistically. Paul underlined the relevant sentences, and wrote in the margins:

Yes, because all we have [about Lincoln] is verbal text, by or about him. This is a tough one. If people disagree about his character (I do not admire him, as seems required), can the relevant verbal texts—tons of letters, anecdotes, speeches, news items) be assessed without counting something? I doubt it. Not where people disagree, that is. Some are quite clear, so no disagreement occurs.

And then, on the reverse, where I had written my "*another* letter from Peterson" comment, Paul wrote:

> *As when you appeared at my door, I think, 'Ah, good, it's Donald Robert Peterson.' Really, Leslie says, cheerfully (knowing my response, and that it's good for my health), "You guys are sure corresponding hot and heavy!"*

CHAPTER

12

Social Experience and Social Conscience

The correspondence continued, but much of the content over the following 2 months was confined to further obsessive rambling on my part about social constructionism in general and Rorty's arguments in particular. At first, Paul responded graciously, but then grew impatient, called a halt to further discussion of the topic, and wrote a version of constructionist thought that he considered appropriate to the subject matter of psychology. More on that later.

In one of my notes, I asked Paul to send me a copy of his contribution to *A History of Psychology in Autobiography,* a series that Gardner Lindzey had initiated partly to allow some of psychology's most influential figures to reflect on their careers, but also in recognition of the fact that scientific theories are human products, inevitably influenced to some degree by the personal histories and psychological dispositions of their authors. Understanding the author would help readers understand the author's contributions.

Like all the graduate students in my class at the University of Minnesota, I knew some vague truths about Meehl's personal history—that "Meehl" was not his original surname but rather the name of his adoptive stepfather; that some kind of cardiac condition had kept him out of military service in World War II; and of course I learned more in our subsequent correspondence, but I had never read the account that appeared in the Lindzey series. When I did, I had much the same reaction that Paul and Leslie had had to the autobiography I had sent to them previously. I found it fascinating to see, spelled out before my eyes, the antecedents of Meehl's valuation of intelligence, of his ethical principles, his contempt for bigotry, and a range of other attitudes, some of which we shared and others in which we differed. A few excerpts show what I mean and allow some understanding of the correspondence that followed:

> My father was a bank clerk who, despite extraordinary intelligence, quit high school to help support a widowed mother and unmarried sister. He was fond and proud of me in a cool way, and I knew it. Fortunately I got his "brain" genes, because he held Admiral Rickover's view that if a man is dumb he might just as well be dead. I identified strongly with him....
>
> Child rearing was permissive within firm limits. My parents laid down a few general rules, small in number, which to me seemed perfectly reasonable and which I therefore found easy to obey. The result has been an attitude toward the social group and toward authority figures which I consider healthy and rational, namely, it is foolish to break sensible rules imposed by persons in lawful authority over you; but given that, you are free to do your own thing and pay little attention to what other people expect, want, or approve. I believe that one reason I had such a good time both in high school and in college talking with my teachers is that I was totally devoid of rebelliousness or any chip-on-the-shoulder attitude.... I was a leader in my peer group in terms of what games to play and how. Puny and poor in sports, I suffered less from this than usual. As my father assured me, "That stuff doesn't matter, school work does. How many boys grow up to be baseball players?" I was aware of my intellectual superiority by age six or earlier. I liked school and was a "teacher's pet," but that rarely seemed to be resented by others, for I was regularly elected president of our grade school classes.

My parental home was wholly without racial or religious prejudice, although one grandmother admitted to a slight preference for Scandinavians. My mother's *n Nurturance* and liberal Methodism led her to view such prejudices as unloving, while my father considered them stupid, ignorant, and irrational. At age seven I had an experience that, with a succinct but powerful assist from my father, gave me insight into some unsavory features of the human condition, at least in its "herd" aspect.... The families in our neighborhood were mostly Scandinavian, with a few Irish, Polish, and German, but there was one Jewish family with whose son, a boy my age, I had fallen into conversation on the way to school and we became friends.... One day I saw a crowd of boys gathered on the playground, and when I got up close there was a boy confronting my Jewish friend who was simply standing, looking frightened, with a bloody nose and his glasses awry. The other boy kept poking him in the shoulder, daring him to fight, which the Jewish boy obviously did not want to do. I was frightened, puzzled, and angry, and I was ashamed of myself because I wanted to do something to protect him, but I feared the group who were standing around eagerly looking for more blood and calling out, "Hit him again," "Sock the dirty Jew," and the like. I must emphasize that this school had mostly children from the middle and lower-middle class; we were not in a slum nor a violent crime-ridden area, and yet here was my friend being subjected to this treatment, as far as I could discern solely because he was Jewish. Furthermore, it seemed that all of the group were eager for the fight, that I was a 1-in-20 deviate!

I was troubled by this episode and my own timidity (although in retrospect I realized that if I had got into the act all that would have happened was there would have been two bloody noses instead of one). I asked my father that evening why they did this, "What is the matter with them?" He put down his newspaper, looked at me somewhat skeptically, and said, "Paul, you mean you haven't figured out what's the matter with them yet?" I said no, I hadn't. He spoke three words, he tapped his head and said simply, "Dumb—no brains," and went back to his reading. This episode, and my father's three word diagnosis, "Dumb—no brains," carried more impact than my routine school experience that I could think, read, and speak better than my peers. I reflected on this for several days and my conclusion was yes, they were dumb. In fact, they were not just a little dumb—most of them barely had

> the wit to tie their own shoes or come in out of the rain. I have lived over half a century since then and have changed my views on a variety of subjects, but I must confess that I have never had occasion to revise that judgment.

Like Meehl, I had grown up in a home free of ethnic or religious prejudice of the common kinds, but unlike him I lived in a village so tiny, isolated, and homogenous—entirely White, mainly Scandinavian, and nearly 100% Protestant—that I had no exposure to prejudice. Still, I *was* exposed to cruelty and stupidity, and found a decency and wisdom in my parents' precepts and treatment of me that seemed comparable to some of Paul's experiences. In the autobiographical chapter I had written for Lisa Hoshmand's edited book, *Creativity and Moral Vision in Psychology,* I described an incident that had an indelible effect on me:

> From my mother, a rural schoolteacher, I got the idea that I might get a college education and "make something of myself," though it was not at all clear what I might take up for a career or how we could pay the bill. From my father, whom I helped build houses from foundation to chimney cap, I learned the importance of using the right tool for the job, of keeping my tools sharp, and of making sure that the foundation of any building we were putting up was perfectly squared and leveled before a single sill was put in place. Otherwise, we would have to make adjustments at every stage of the following construction.
>
> My father also taught me something about responsibility and redemption. As a 10-year-old boy with a new slingshot, out for adventure on a sunny Sunday afternoon, I broke all the windows in the west wall of a public building. To me, the windows were irresistible targets in a shooting gallery. With some excitement over awareness that my behavior was forbidden but mindless of effects, I fired carefully selected pebbles from the cover of a clump of bushes nearly 50 yards from the base of the building. With growing pride in my skill, I systematically plinked out 96 panes of glass. A few days before, after I had finished making the slingshot, I proudly showed it to my father. He examined my workmanship critically, nodded basic approval, and showed me how to improve the binding of rubber to the pouch. When word of

the window breakage got around, my father asked me if I was the one who did it. I would not have dreamed of lying to him. I confessed in tears and heard a brief, somber lecture on the consequences of behavior. Together, up and down ladders, over 3 sun-baked days, with contributions that depended on our skills, my father and I reglazed the window-panes I had broken. I was allowed to keep the slingshot but confined future fire to tin cans on fenceposts and an occasional unsuccessful shot at a rabbit.

In 1931, when Paul was 11 years old, his father committed suicide. He had embezzled some money to play the stock market, and the humiliation that followed exposure of his crime was more than he could bear. Five years later, Paul's mother died of ether pneumonia after surgery for a brain tumor. Her physician, a highly regarded internist, had diagnosed her as having Meniere's disease and failed to recheck her neurologically while her condition worsened over a year's time. A neurologist, called in against the patient's will, immediately observed the tell-tale choked disk in the eye-grounds and correctly localized the tumor. In his autobiography, Paul wrote, "This episode of gross medical bungling permanently immunized me from the childlike faith in physicians' omniscience that one finds among most persons, including educated ones. It has also helped me to avoid dogmatism about my own diagnostic inferences, to which I am tempted by my self-concept as a naturally gifted and well-trained clinician." For me, reading Paul's life story improved my understanding of many of his views. It also affected me in other ways:

4/21/99

Dear Paul,

I was delighted and moved by your autobiography. Many core similarities between your background and mine, tho plenty of differences too. Reading your story made me more grateful than ever for the lucky concatenation of circumstances that brought me into your world and put me in touch with you for lo these 52 years.

Don

4/25/99

Don—

You warm my heart, which it needs. Just went to Gordon Heistad's funeral (he ran a research unit, a PhD "over" MDs, a smart, under-productive, wise, good man, Dx lung cancer, dead in 2 weeks). The big difference between us is in your much stronger social conscience. I have n Nurturance to individuals, to patients & students (I know this partly because non-advisees sought me out for "help" of different kinds and said why they chose me as a helpful person), even strangers asking directions; but my urge to improve society is feeble, compared to yours. In youth, I was a socialist (for which I don't apologize; not to be a socialist in the Great Depression suggests dullness of mind or lack of compassion). I noted people were socialists because of (a) Hatred of the rich, (b) Love for the poor, (c) Snobbery of academics, [and] (d) Dislike for inefficiency. I had none of (a)–(c) but a lot of (d). So when the facts showed socialism wasn't efficient, I abandoned it—a purely rational change. No big "conversion," I did not join the right-wing Christers.

To what of the differences in our histories do you attribute this big difference? As we've said before, it's not groupiness, or an introversion/extraversion difference.

Paul

Psychoanalytic Addendum: I predict yr father was in some way group-active, d.k. how—a scout leader, community activist, church elder, in "lay politics," union—somehow involved in community's good? Mine was not, too narcissistic. Joined Masons but as a way to upward mobility. Ditto role in the big Norse-American "Viking Celebration." Had he had better group-feeling he might not have suicided (his friends would have lent him $$ to cover his embezzlement, I learned later from them). Somewhere, if not father, you must have had a role model that worked (or aspired, in thought) to make the damn world better. Who?

P.S.: I've written a fairly long letter saying how I would state a rational version of social constructionism (surprised?) It's now in Draft III, Leslie says it's an article, where publish? Hah!!

5/5/99

Dear Paul,

I don't know that my social conscience is that much stronger than yours, but I can definitely attest to your nurturant ways with individuals, not only with me but with the whole class of students who went through the MN program '48–'52 & many other MN grads I've talked to since. You weren't easy on us & you didn't appraise us all equally, but everybody I know trusted your judgment and appreciated the fair, non-punitive way you treated us. I felt the same way about Elliott, but not so much about Paterson or Hathaway. I admired them, and I learned that they thought well of me, but they were more forbidding and somehow less trustworthy than you were.

But I guess you're right about the urge to improve society. I've certainly written about it, every word I've written is heartfelt, & it shows in my work. I'm not sure where that came from. Not my father, who was very strong on personal responsibility (3 rules, implicit, never any preaching: no lies, keep your promises, & do the best job you can for your pay) but completely group-<u>in</u>active—apolitical and somewhat contemptuous of his brothers, who were big-time Shriners, church leaders, etc. He thought they were phonies.

My early playground & school experiences were very different from yours. [Paul enjoyed the company of a very bright group of friends, all of whom, influenced by the same teacher, shared something close to reverence for science and spent the time other youngsters might have spent in sports or mischief debating recondite questions, determining which participants would take which side of each argument by flipping coins.] In that tiny town, bounded by rivers & forests, physical prowess was highly valued—much more than brains—by my peers. Only 3–4 of my classmates went on to college & only one got an advanced (MA) degree. I had only one friend, a cousin, who was as interested as I was in the kinds of questions you and your high-bright buddies debated (and was smart enough to talk to). Boys in our primitive little town had to show how tough they were. Very early I won fights with a couple of bullies who were bigger than I was, never had to fight after that, & found myself coming in as protector when scared country kids in bib overalls & faded dresses came into high school from their 1-room schoolhouses, & were tormented by a few mean, dumb assholes from town. I was good-natured, never pushed anybody around, did well but not great in my studies, & like you kept getting elected president of my classes. Similar kind of fight-win-protect-the-new-kids business went on in my teens while I caddied with working-class kids from Brainerd at a golf course on Gull Lake. Got to be #1 caddy & was mighty proud of that at the time.

Maybe that mattered. I don't know. I'm pretty sure my military experience mattered a lot. I enlisted in the Army Specialized Training Program, not because I was eager to save our country or kill Germans but because I was bored with Pillager & Brainerd, wanted some adventure, & was promised a chance for some education, of which I got a little, in "pre-engineering," & a commission, which never materialized. I wound up as a company clerk in the medical battalion of an armored division, sort of like Radar O'Reilly in MASH, if you ever watched that, & had an entirely unheroic military career. Our division came in on the end of the Battle of the Bulge & then went south across the Rhine & into Bavaria. We were green & took a beating until we got some experience. I lost several friends, some of whom died horribly (burned to death in tanks & ambulances, which latter the Germans weren't supposed to shoot at but did). All through this, though, I was a few miles behind the lines keeping the company records, typing letters of condolence to parents when my combat medic friends were killed or typing citations for medals some of the guys received. I always felt embarrassed about the pussy job I had, & after the war ended in Europe I got our Co. Commander to promise me a different assignment—up front with the company—when we went to Japan, as we all thought we would at the time.

One of my jobs was to type the payroll, & when I brought that up to the line the first of every month I'd have to stick around a few days while the finance officer checked my figures & paid the troops. Those times I'd usually get sent on some special assignment, & on one of those I went into Dachau a few days after it was opened (had to be May 2–3, 1945). The corpses were still hanging out of the railroad cars where the Germans had stuffed them, trying to get rid of the evidence before we overran them. It was a dumb assignment. Someone must have made some kind of triage decision & called our ambulances in to move some injured prisoners from the camp to a nearby field hospital. Of course the hospital filled up after a few runs. Then the brass decided it was smarter to bring the docs to the camp than move patients to the docs & sent us back to our unit.

We'd heard something about these camps, but I'd never seen one. Some of the images are very vivid. The gate—ARBEIT MACHT FREI—the stench, long rows of barracks, looks on faces. Much is hazy. The war ended a few days later, and after that all I could think about was getting home.

I never talked much about my army days, not because they were so horrible but because I'd done so little. Our division was only in combat for 6 mo. or so, & knowing what the 1st Infantry, 101st Airborne, & some other groups had gone through, I knew I didn't have much to say. I kidded about the whole deal with my family. Never told my first wife about Dachau, for example, and in the "Daddy, what did you do in the war" talks with my children talked about the special assignment where we liberated a brewery or how my only injury came when I twisted my knee swinging a leg over the back of my typing chair. After the war I put all my army stuff—uniform, ribbons, battle stars, unit citation, etc.—in a duffle bag & left it there. When I opened it up a few years later & saw mold & moth holes, I threw it all away.

But I still have dreams about some of that, and just a couple of weeks ago when I saw a movie called "Life is Beautiful" about a man & his son in a concentration camp—the man convinces his son that the whole thing is a game & if the kid stays very quiet & keeps hiding from the "mean guys" they'll win a real tank as a prize—the tank that rumbles around the corner into the quad where the boy is hiding carried the insignia of my outfit—the 13th Armored Division—tho I'm pretty sure we were not the ones who came in first. When I saw the tank, I began sobbing uncontrollably, and I'm not exactly dry-eyed now. So maybe that had something to do with my urge to make things better.

Part of it, in psychology, is rational. Like George Albee, Seymour Sarason, & many others, I don't see how we can justify ourselves as a profession if our main stock-in-trade is individual psychotherapy. That's why I insist on disciplined inquiry as I've defined it—over individual, group, and organizational levels—as the distinctive core of practice in psychology.

Don

I'm not much impressed with my efforts to change society so far. I'm afraid the PsyD move has done at least as much harm as good & I can't show that my work against prejudice at Rutgers has helped in any fundamental, lasting way. Main thing I've learned is to be damned careful before meddling, tho I still think we have to try, as long as we keep checking and correcting as we go.

5/10/99

Dear Don: Your story is fascinating. I sure mis-predicted about your father. Score another against psy'dynamics, hah? Did I confess I was relieved to be 4-F? How's that for a big difference? And I never had a fist-fight as a kid.

My big letter is still being re-typed, sec'y back from Europe but swamped with stuff from others, higher priority. It's not a Big Deal but I want it correct. And some of it is useless, because you already know, or could infer, it. My main concession to social constructionists is perhaps stronger than you expect. I believe, regretfully, that in fields like ours, where (a) "Facts" are usually not "hard facts," [and] (b) Methodology is inadequately worked out and often bad, the appraisal of theories is so markedly "fact-underdetermined" (Quine et al.) that what the scientific community believes is more socially constructed than not. To be less so is a regulative ideal, which Rorty & Co. (by glorifying the subjective) tend to weaken. But the empirical part of social constructivism, aside from ideals of cognitive purity as motivators, is largely correct for "soft" fields. Anyone who argues from this sad fact that it's true of science in general should visit the chemistry building and contemplate that big table on every wall. Or does anyone who has been gravely ill, diagnosed and treated by medical science, seriously think the Hogo-Bogo's witch doctor could do as well? These people are in bad faith when they talk that way, they're phonies, crooks of the intellect.

CHAPTER

13

Meehl's Constructionism

Somewhere past the midpoint of our overlong exchange about radical constructionism, Meehl wrote, "I think we're both tired of Ol' Rorty, but here's a short easy task: Write me a sentence stating what Rorty says that's literally correct by your lights, that's helpful to you as a scientist, and that you didn't know before. Please, I don't ask you to defend it, merely write such a sentence. Then I'll ask (not you, but me) whether it applies to me as well." I knew immediately that I would not be able to find anything in the Rorty I had read that would satisfy all of the conditions Paul specified, but thought some of my colleagues might, so I sent the challenge to them, and several of them responded. I made the mistake of passing their efforts on to Meehl, whose patience with the whole issue finally gave way. He quoted a sentence from Rorty: "There is nothing to be said about either truth or rationality apart from description of the familiar procedures of justification which a given society—ours—uses in one or another area of inquiry." Then Paul wrote, "Take this *literally,* that there is 'nothing to be said.' I just read my philosophy center colleague Hellman's superb book on mathematical truth. Hellman has Feigl-level IQ. If Rorty's dumb remark—the CORE idea of his view mind you—is taken literally, that book is 'saying nothing.' My next letter is FINAL on the damn Rorty matter."

May 13, 1999

Dear Don,

I think your last letter pretty well clears up the Rorty business between us. It troubles me that I seem to have induced your superego (which I am beginning to think is a bit harsher than mine) to beat up on you for a kind of cognitive mistake in a complex matter, a failing to which we are all subject. The main thing is our treatability, right? Now I am going to surprise you by formulating a somewhat Rorty-ish position on scientists' beliefs, which I think some of our super-scientistic psychologist brethren do not sufficiently appreciate. And it's not merely that they don't fully appreciate it, it's that this lack of appreciation infects their thinking far more than most of them realize.

I have dictated because when I write by hand I sometimes find myself being condensed in a way that can be misleading, even by someone who reads carefully like yourself. I have read your long letter three times and do not comment on it because (except about Rorty and our mild (?) disagreement about quantifying) I readily accept all of it.

A minor cleanup on the passage in my "Quantitative Thinking" lecture that does not involve a disagreement but a malcommunication: (The trouble with giving convention talks is the time constraint, and this talk had to be mercilessly cut to get it down to fifty minutes, with the result that there are some obscurities.) You objected to my quoting Skinner as saying that behavior, unlike the phenomena of some other sciences, does not have primarily an observation problem, because its phenomena are "relatively macroscopic and slow." You objected to that on grounds of events in the patient's ecology that the therapist doesn't learn about, and I of course agree with this. I forget the names of the two psychotherapists who got into a terrible emotional fight, angry at one another, having lunch and realizing that they were treating spouses. After they cooled off, it struck them that their countertransference identifications were so intense, and their respective patients' accounts of husband/wife interactions so slanted, that they had been quite incapable of forming an accurate picture of certain emotional conversations between the spouses. They decided to see a series of such marriage pairs, and after doing a dozen or so wrote an article pointing out that the standard Freudian view that the analyst can always make appropriate corrections for his patients' biased reports is plainly false. (Do you know the study? It bugs me because I thought one of the authors was Waldo Bird and tried to track it down but it wasn't he, and have been unable to locate it. I'm pretty sure it was published in Harry Stack Sullivan's old yellow-page journal.)

Obviously, the fact that the actual raw phenomena of behavior are "macroscopic and slow" doesn't do us any good if we weren't observing at the time! Nor does it do us any good, even if we were observing, if we weren't observing what happened to the same people the day before. If a patient reports that his wife was needlessly sarcastic about his making a Dagwood sandwich at midnight, but doesn't realize—and hence can't report—that he unconsciously whispered another woman's name during intercourse, obviously the poor therapist doesn't have a clue about what is going on with the sandwich episode. In my talk, which dealt at the beginning with Hathaway's refusal to be impressed with a nice dream interpretation, what was the behavior I meant to refer to as macroscopic and slow? I was talking about the hermeneutics of the psychoanalytic session itself, not about other non-session behavior or situations. Even narrower, I was thinking of the theme-tracing problem proper (e.g., "patient's discourse is momentarily guided by negative transference impulses"), not even ecological inferences from the regnant theme (e.g., "probably caused by his father's recent visit"). Even the importance of gesture (as shown in Felix Deutsch's classic study of postures on the couch), or tone of voice, or speech rate—things that we customarily emphasize as important in psychoanalysis—I believe play a minor part except on rare occasions. I think 95% or better of all analytic interpretation hinges upon the verbal content (including, of course, things like parapraxes, or somewhat deviant but not Sc choice of language). Despite Freud's cute example of patient Dora inserting her finger in the reticule, Freud's own case material consists almost wholly of the content of the patient's discourse. So my Skinner quote was aimed at the ambiguities of interpretation of the psychoanalytic session, and I did not intend to make stuff that goes on outside easy of interpretation, let alone of access.

Now for my properly cleaned up Rorty-ish position. I don't believe there's anything here that would have been disputed by Herbert Feigl, even in his first year here, when he was still labeling himself a logical positivist. Nor would it be disputed by any of the philosophers that I have learned from, including nonpositivist analytic philosophers like Pap, Sellars, Popper, or Feyerabend. I have to start with some truisms.

The scientist is an organism with motives and emotions as well as perceptions and symbolic processes, pushed and pulled by a variety of forces. Whether we are strict determinists or only "statistical determinists," we can make a list of those kinds of forces, rational, nonrational, and irrational. Here I agree with the "strong program" people in the Edinburgh School (to the extent that I understand their thesis—they don't teach me much so I rarely read them, but I have read the standard quotes from them many times over). It's not as if there are two *kinds* of causes in the world, only one of which should be mentioned in interpreting scientific behavior. It's all part of the causal system & there's only one organism, the scientist. When we do philosophy of science we focus on the facts in their logical relation to the theories. The scientist learns some of these facts in the lab or the clinic, through his own receptors. But most of the facts he learns are about the verbal reports by other scientists. In disciplines where there are lots of "hard facts," and where the methodology has been very well worked out, this mass of facts tends to become quasi-determinative, at least in the long run. (Quine is wrong about underdetermination, as is becoming widely recognized.) If we ask why *all* chemists believe in Kekulé's theory that the benzene molecule is ring shaped, we are pretty sure that every organic chemist believes that because of hard facts plus rational argumentation from such facts. If he's not an organic chemist, he still believes it "rationally," on the authority of organic chemists. As Bertrand Russell (no lover of submission to authority) points out, most of us believe what we believe on the basis of authority. We learn the multiplication table as children solely on that basis. On the other hand, a chemist may have a few Jamesian overbeliefs in hypotheses that most competent chemists disagree with, because he was fond of his PhD advisor who held maverick opinions.

I don't need to go on with the list of the kinds of factors that are not rational. They do not arise from laboratory results, or from other competent observers' reports of laboratory results, but arise instead from any of a long list of nonrational influences including sex, age, nationality, race, class, geographics—all group membership stuff—and god knows what all idiographic neurotic complexes and sheer educational accidents and the opinions of one's college roommate. Now it happens in science, as it does in ordinary life, that some of these factors that are not rationally germane to a certain theory may work in opposition to what pure rationality would direct. What happens then? Well, I don't see anything deep or interesting about that. One simply accepts it and gets on with the scientific business, endeavoring to hold it to a minimum and to correct for it, in oneself and others. These corrective efforts will not always be successful. It is obvious that objective (truth-reaching) success will depend on the relative strength of the colliding influences. If the scientist is in a field replete with hard facts, and is not crazy, the facts will—in the long run—prevail over the irrational forces, internal or external. If there aren't very many facts, or most of the facts are "soft" facts, or if one is in a science in which even the methodology is not clear, then the relative potency of the nonrational and irrational factors will increase. As far as I'm concerned, it's like the beta weights in a multiple regression equation, and in this case we know that the beta weights are causal influences whereas in most statistical work we don't know that. One can view it as a field of forces on the scientist as a moving charged particle.

Now, if we are working in a field full of soft facts, and incompletely formulated methodology (like most areas of psychopathology), it follows from the above analysis that the relative influence of the nonrational factors in the equation will be increased. So what psychologists think about the inheritance of IQ, or the dynamics of schizophrenia, or the origin of sex differences in cognitive processes, or competition versus cooperation in group problem solving, will be heavily influenced by their political ideology, by their race, by their sex, by where they went to school, and so on. I recall statistical studies showing that psychologists who are political conservatives are more likely to be hereditarian about IQ. That's what any informed person would predict, but unlike the authors of the article, I do not conclude from that that IQ has nothing to do with genes. (I cannot be classified as either liberal or conservative; I just don't locate on that goddam newspeak dimension.)

Consider my brethren in Elliott Hall. The Minnesota psychology department is now ranked in the top half-dozen in the country overall, and in three fields (clinical, counseling, industrial) it is tied for first place. If there were national rankings on behavior genetics and differential psych we would also be in top positions there. With three or four exceptions, I have high esteem for both the intellect and the integrity of my colleagues. Yet, I am convinced there are two domains in which they are to some extent irrational.

The first is telepathy. The meta-analysis of the *Ganzfeld* experiments shows telepathy to be a robust finding, more robust than most of what my friends believe from the experimental journals. Radin's book compares the meta-analysis for the *Ganzfeld* studies with the meta-analysis for the efficacy of aspirin as prophylaxis against coronary disease, and the telepathy stuff is stronger. The reasons my brethren give are of three kinds, all disingenuous. (If I were being uncharitable, I would say dishonest.) They say, "Oh, I would accept telepathy if the findings replicated." They say that because they refuse to look at the meta-analysis even when I offer to lend them the book. Sometimes they say, "Well, I would accept these data if I had a theoretical explanation of them." Most of the data they accept about other topics—and I include the experimentalists—do not have a satisfactory theoretical explanation at the present time. I asked my colleague Bill Fox, who is a memory expert and therefore regularly reads the learning and memory section of the *Journal of Experimental Psychology*, what percent of all the articles whose empirical results he accepts as robust are explained (at least to his satisfaction) theoretically, and he said, "Oh, perhaps 5%." Think about the research on schizophrenia. I doubt that even the SPEM [smooth pursuit eye movement] anomaly is as robust as the *Ganzfeld* studies. Or finally, they say, "Well, there may be something to it, but I have far more important things to study and think about than telepathy." That's the most dishonest of all, because where else would a psychologist be able to say that he had discovered a new kind of causal influence not known to theoretical physics?

A second area is psychobiology and "evolutionary psychology." I think this work is very important and I don't think one can competently discuss the social group (even the dyad of one-on-one psychotherapy) in ignorance of the work of people like Goodall and Frans de Waal. When de Waal entitles his book *Chimpanzee Politics*, he is not making some sort of cutsie weak analogy; he means it quite literally. Politics is power relations in social groups, and his chimpanzees show all of the phenomena we get in studying Congress, such as coalitions to unseat the alpha chimp, sexual favors to the dominant males (in the military I believe it is called "status prick"), and so forth. A psychotherapist who has not read Jerome Frank's *Persuasion and Healing* is inadequately informed. I found Wilson's recent *Consilience* extremely interesting and certainly the man has a wider range of knowledge than most biologists do (although his earlier book's airy contemptuous dismissal of the great moral thinkers like Kant, Mill, and Aristotle was arrogant scientism of the worst sort). Having finally realized that deriving ethics from the termite colony (his technical field) is not as easy as he thought, he now tries to fix it up by saying that ethics should be seen as being analogous to art, a cop-out if there ever was one! Nevertheless, it's an important book. Nobody who knows me would suspect me of having a bias against the sociobiologists, despite their empire building and turf propensities. BUT: The theory of evolution is one of the most ad hoc and jerry-built of scientific theories. It is not "overwhelmingly confirmed," as all the books tell us it is. My colleagues in Elliott Hall take it as axiomatic that no one could conceivably have any doubts, even faint ones, about neo-Darwinism—the modern synthesis of the 1930s and '40s by Haldane, Huxley, Mayr, Dobzhansky, Fisher, Wright, & Co.—unless he was a barefoot Baptist from Tennessee with an IQ of 85. Well, I wear shoes and I don't have a southern accent and I never was a Baptist and my IQ is closer to 185, but I have read enough about neo-Darwinism to know that it is certainly not all it's cracked up to be as science. That doesn't mean I look upon "creation science" as science, which I do not. Nor does it mean that I have a good scientific alternative of my own. It just means that I have been able to recognize a shaky, ad hoc, speculative, jerry-built, and not very quantitative scientific theory for what it is. My colleagues are not capable of doubting neo-Darwinism, and what they see as its psychobiological consequences, any more than Thomas Aquinas was capable of doubting the Trinity. And I mean that literally. I mean that they are *literally not capable* of entertaining faint doubts about this.

Besides, assuming neo-Darwinism is correct, their use of it as window-dressing is irrational. They keep repeating (devoutly, a mantra) that human behavior "can only be understood in evolutionary terms." This is baloney. To understand (explain?) the behavior of *Homo sapiens*, one needs to know the environmental niche of Pleistocene man, what his hard-wired dispositions had to be to get food, a mate, rear young, avoid predators, etc., plus the fact that we have inherited 99.9% of his genome. Whether he evolved by natural selection from an ape-like species, or came on a spaceship, or was a Goldschmidt "hopeful monster," or was created by Zeus, or evolved not by natural selection but by Bergson's élan vital or Driesch's entelechy, is completely irrelevant to the explanation. Analogy: We understand a lot about diabetes from experiments on dogs, but that "works" because of the genetic similarity, not because we descended from dogs. It's an undergraduate error in causal reasoning.

Now why are these smart people, committed to being scientifically objective in the face of evidence, and usually striving hard to achieve that ideal—assuming I am right—so irrational on these two subjects? You need not be Robert Merton, let alone Rorty & Co., to see why. These two topics both *impinge on their secular faith*. Many of them would say that they are (reformed) logical empiricists, hence reject metaphysics, and therefore entertain no "metaphysical" doctrines. But this is false. They all entertain a metaphysic and its name is an old one, commonly employed in the Victorian age, to wit, *materialist monism*. They are absolutely certain that the universe is, as Lucretius said it was, "atoms and the void." If telepathy exists, something rather spooky is going on, and they are solidly against spooks. If evolution didn't occur (or at least didn't occur in the way Darwin said), something spooky must have been going on, and they are firmly against spooks, holy or unholy. I myself, as a scientist, dislike telepathy and wish it would go away. But I distinguish between science and "scientism," and I claim that my brethren are true believers in scientism. (If you don't know Eric Hoffer's *The True Believer*, you must read it.) Some of them would admit this; most of them would probably not. But I see this as a clear example of where what a scientist believes, even about a scientific topic, is powerfully influenced by exactly the sort of factors that Rorty & Co. are emphasizing. My recognition of this, which goes back to my high school days, if not earlier, does not lead me to make silly remarks that there is no such thing as objective truth, or that the benzene ring is nothing but a social construction, and so on.

Note well, I do not fault them for *holding* a metaphysic, but for being non-candid about it, and hence giving those three feeble and fake reasons instead of frankly admitting their metaphysical basis. Everyone has a metaphysic, whether he knows it or not. Although I practice TM regularly, and accept the meta-analysis showing its somatic and psychic benefits, I disbelieve the strong claims that the Maharishi levitated. This is definitely due to my metaphysical limits as to "mind over body," and I make no secret of it. How much alleged empirical evidence should (properly) lead to abandoning one's metaphysics is an unsolved problem in epistemology (cf. Hume on miracles; he can't be entirely right in his formulation, since if scientists followed it, we could not have replaced Newton by Einstein).

Finally, since there are at least 10 properties and relations of theories (you have the list in my class handout on scientific method) that correlate only imperfectly, that with respect to competing theories that point in opposite directions, it follows that theory appraisal is, except for huge collections of very hard facts, a judgment call, and scientists can differ about judgment calls when nonrational factors are held to a minimum. (See the three-fold classification of scientific errors at the beginning of my "Relevance of a Scientist's Ideology in Communal Recognition of Scientific Merit," *Psych Reports*, 1998). But going back to our multivariate causal equation, the more conflict there is among these 10 rationally relevant theory characteristics, the greater potential influence of nonrational and irrational factors. So, for example, whether psychologists in the broadly psychodynamic tradition are mainly Freudian or Sullivanian or Horneyan or Rogerian or Adlerian or Radovian is going to be determined more irrationally than not.

So what I am saying is that in ill-developed areas where most of the facts are soft (or for some of our super-quantifier friends, pseudo-hard), Rorty and other social constructionists are largely correct. All we have to delete is their own dogmatic denial that there exists an objective truth and that sometimes, in some domains, scientists can achieve a close approximation to it.

On nonrational factors, Marx and Freud had a bad effect on us. Educated persons tend to assume that all errors in reasoning must be due to the class interests of Marx & Co. or the personal neurotic complexes of Freud & Co. But as Nisbet and Ross's book (*Human Inference*, 1980) emphasizes, we often err from nonemotional causes. The brain, except for certain special things, is a poor computer. That's why I push cliometrics in meta-theory. We don't know how to weight the characteristics of scientific theories in appraising them. Nonoptimal weighting is not irrational, it's just "defective rationality," so to speak. But the looseness allowed in rough judgment calls—nobody's fault, the human epistemic condition—readily permits the irrational influences to prevail more than they can in "tighter" domains (e.g., rules of chess). I sometimes think that the biggest single impedance to scientific rationality is neither irrational (class and neurotic) forces, nor mal-computing, but sheer mental inertia. For example, you mention my weak grasp for the patient's ecology in my traditional one-to-one therapy. I explain that I don't disagree about it, have no prejudice against it, but that I don't discuss it because of my ignorance—that one should avoid talking about matters one knows nothing about. That's all true, as far as it goes. But why haven't I been motivated to read about it, and try it? Sheer mental inertia.

Why do [people who cite Rorty to support their arguments] think they *need* Rorty to do what they want to do? In the 1950s, Jim Jenkins kept harping on Kuhn's (vastly over-rated and careless) book, when Jenkins was abandoning connectionist psycholinguistics in favor of Chomsky. But he didn't need to do that; it was window dressing and self-reassurance. I told him he could defend Chomsky on the merits, that the *facts* (e.g., of children's grammar acquisition, and of Jenkins and Russell's own research) refuted the associationist theories then in vogue. Gassing about "paradigm shifts" was diversionary. One simply shifts paradigms, on *scientific* grounds, rather than *talking* about shiftings as a philosophical point. I believe Jenkins realizes now that my advice was sound. Despite my intrinsic philosophical interests, I have rarely invoked metatheory in examining theory, except when forced by uninformed or stupid philosophical objections to clear the air, e.g., my list of hyper-operational complaints about schizophrenia theory and research (*Psychodiagnosis: Selected Papers*, 1973, p. 196). I have to defend meta-notions like Pap's open concepts in discussing my schizophrenia theory or taxometrics, because several operationists (pre-1936!) have complained. But whenever I find a psychologist invoking a Rorty-type meta-theory, I become suspicious, because often—not always—the motivation is obscurantist; he wishes to ward off tough *scientific* (not philosophical) criticism by disarming the feared critic at the start. I'm sure some of your arrogant-stupid Illinois analysts played that game, whether or not they invoked any philosophers by name. It can be done in general terms, no names mentioned, by buzz words like "richness," "complex," "subtle," [and] "real life," all of which you and I recognize as pointing to important truths but commonly abused for obscurantist purposes.

I didn't mean to urge Horwich's *Truth* [mentioned in one of our less fruitful exchanges about Rorty] on you. I am merely skimming it; it's more technical logic and semantics than you or I can profit from. *True* is a funny sort of predicate (of meta-language). It does not designate a "property" in the usual sense. He says this is why efforts to *define* it explicitly (in the usual ways, as if it were like other, natural properties) are unsuccessful. My point in mentioning it was exemplary, that a whole book clarifying this indispensable meta-concept has to be dismissed as empty, devoid of content, if one accepts Rorty's view literally. Compared to an intellect like Horwich, Rorty is a philosophical clown.

Sincerely,

Paul E. Meehl, PhD, LP

Regents Professor of Psychology, Emeritus

File: Rorty, social constructionism

xc: Dawes, Faust, Grove

5/18/99

Dear Paul,

I have just finished my second reading of your great letter on Meehl's social constructionism. Both times, I felt much as I did in your lectures so long ago—learning something every step of the way, chuckling now and then, and sometimes feeling that I've been hit on the head with one of those truths that I should have known all along & vaguely sensed but had never seen that way before. That last response came to your exposé of neo-Darwinian faith. I was already with you on telepathy, already persuaded by data and then personally convinced (new faith) by the classroom demonstration I mentioned in a previous letter, but like your Elliott Hall colleagues considered the "theory of evolution" about as solidly grounded as any biological theory can be. You taught me better.

You arrived pretty close to the place I had reached on (a) the unavoidability of a metaphysic, & (b) the inevitability, tho not necessarily the merit, of social constructionist views in the soft areas of psychology, but you got there via a more coherent line of thought than I had ever managed, and completely free of the ridiculous and unnecessary claim that there is no such thing as objective truth. I might go further than you would in proposing that, in the professional assessment & evaluation of human conditions, a pragmatically constructive, functionally useful formulation, whether it is factually accurate or not, is our primary aim. I think the practitioner should attain as true & clear a view of the situation as possible, but the formulation he/she negotiates with the client is likely to contain many unknowns and unknowables, more narrative than historical "truth," as Don Spence would put it, and in the end it is more important to ask, "Did it work?" than "Is it true?" Not so, indeed the other way around, in science, though even in the latter, as you and I now agree, much of what we take as true is based on nonrational factors, faith & authority principally, rather than robust observation and rational inference. The balance is hugely on the nonrational side in the soft areas of psychology.

I do not know the study by the Sullivanian marriage counselors, tho I did quite a bit of reading in the yellow journal in my Close Relationships period. As soon as I began working clinically with couples & families, the utter impossibility of coming to a "true" view of what was going on hit me like a hammer. As the card-carrying family therapists say, I often wound up replacing destructive myths with constructive myths (or at least trying to), but myths in any case.

I bought Hoffer's True Believer soon after it came out, & then bought a couple more of his wise little books, including the Passionate State of Mind.

Helped me see dangers of zealotry, not only in others but in myself. Of course I agree with you about scientism in our field. That's why I'm ready to tilt with the hard-heads who claim practitioners should limit their interventions to those that have been tested and shown scientifically to be both harmless and effective.

Don

CHAPTER

14

Politics and Politicians, Psychotherapy and Psychotherapists, Paleontology and Paleontologists

Through the summer of 1999, the correspondence between Meehl and me slowed somewhat. Delays were incurred on my part because I spent the summer at our place in Vermont, to which my office mail is sent irregularly, and on Paul's part, I suspect, on account of health problems. In one of his notes, Paul wrote:

> *The soma looms large in my current life. My diabetes is a bit more erratic than it was when first diagnosed, blood sugar bounces around lately. Leslie has Achilles tendonitis that's refractory—but recently helped a lot by acupuncture (?!). My son Erik has been hospitalized with spontaneous pneumothorax, which in otherwise healthy persons is no big deal, but he has COPD [chronic obstructive pulmonary disease], which makes it pretty serious. He's just now out, and says it scares him enough to quit smoking. We're "hoping," but not betting on it.*

In addition to the delays, our exchanges lost some of the focus we had maintained while we were beating up on the radical constructionists. Three loosely strung threads run through the letters we wrote that summer. The themes are summarized in this chapter's title. To make sense of the first one, it is necessary to go back to previous correspondence we had exchanged about Meehl's strong position on quantification in science—that is, that *no* factual question can be decided firmly until observations are numerified in some way. In a letter dated March 8, I had written the following comment:

> *Re your notes on quant. & qual. supports for appraisal of "character" in the likes of A. Lincoln, we agree that all we have is verbal text, and I think we agree that that is why, despite mountains of linguistic "evidence," disagreements remain & are likely to continue. Still I think the question "How did Lincoln, with his history and temperament, in sway of the political/cultural conditions that evolved during his career, resolve the moral dilemmas that he encountered?" is of psychological as well as historical interest. And I consider some of the textual evidence on the question more credible, more plausible, than some other textual evidence, e.g., David Donald's historiography & critical biographical analysis are more even-handed, rigorous, & hence more persuasive than the historical/biographical material Carl Sandburg brought to bear on the subject. I share your limited admiration of Lincoln, though I doubt anyone could have handled the most difficult crisis in American history better than he did. In fact, as I move along in my course-of-American-bigotry project, I find little to admire or despise in any of the people whose lives & times I've chosen to examine. Jefferson, Jackson, Polk, Lincoln, Hayes, T. Roosevelt, Wilson, Truman, L. Johnson, Reagan—all emerge in my mind as complex, flawed, sometimes strong, sometimes weak, sometimes keenly insightful, sometimes blind—i.e., intensely human, characters. That's what makes them interesting to me, as a citizen-psychologist, trying to understand social prejudice. I don't mind that they are all controversial—that disagreeing opinions about them are passionately held & not likely to be resolved. All I'm trying to do is understand them as well as I can.*

3/19/99

> *Dear Don: Yes, of course, politicians—like all of us—differ a lot from one another, and on the whole range of traits. Yet I have concluded (without systematic survey such as you are doing, though I do read quite a bit of history & biography) that, as a group, I dislike and disesteem them. They are rarely first-rate brains (Jefferson was not a "career politician," and few of our Founding Fathers were), and usually are narcissistic, shifty, quick-change artists, thirsting for power & status. I voted for FDR, because he was what we*

needed for morale. But the more I read of him, the less I like him. Petty, vindictive, pathologically narcissisic, intellectually a lightweight (Keynes was amazed at his economic ignorance), and people who adored him (Tugwell, Ickes) complained about his downright lying. Johnson and JFK were awful people in ordinary relationships. Wilson is over-rated by academics because he's the only professor that ever got there. A rigid, self-righteous ideologue, and his speeches are blather, to someone like me.

I doubt anyone of 1st-class intellect and 1st-class ethics would go into politics. So my Utopia starts by not having "politics as a career." The whole idea of mass electoral democracy is of course absurd; it's just that Louis XIV or Nero or Hitler are worse!

Paul

3/29/99

Dear Paul,

The more I read the more I agree with your appraisal of politicians, including our Mt. Rushmore icons. Washington's mediocre intellect and his cruelty to others—a readiness to turn on anybody, loyal or disloyal, who threatened his position as top dog—tempers my admiration for him (he was what we needed at the time). Jefferson: 1st-class intellect and brilliant statesman, but ethically flawed, as p.c. critics are proudly showing. Lincoln we've discussed. TR: another 1st-class brain, in my opinion, but a class-conscious, Harvard Porcellian elitist, juvenile militarist, Aryan imperialist. Unfortunately, every society needs heroes, but the "characters" of the ones we've propped up on our pedestals do not impress me.

I think I'm more forgiving than you are, though, probably because my guiding conception of human behavior makes more of situational influences & less of trait dispositions than yours does. That's partly rational (Mischel, 1968; Peterson, 1968, 1991, 1997), but partly, I think, a consequence of my long experience (nearly 3/4 of my career, as it turned out) in university administration. Throughout that time, I held that any academic who actively sought administrative power should not be allowed to have it. Like you in the chair of the MN psy dept, I took on the jobs that came my way because "somebody had to do it," & in each case I thought I was the best equipped among available candidates to handle the task at hand. Once in position, I had to face the unavoidable political compromises and endure the silent hypocricies that effective administration requires. There are big differences between the presidency of a nation and the deanship of a tiny professional school, but there are some similarities too, and I have considerable sympathy for the poor boobs who wind up in presidential office, however they got there, dependent on the support of a grotesquely ignorant & irrational public, and of course, now, the big money of special interests, bearing enormous responsibilities, and at least in the cases I selected for my bigotry project, doing the best they can in the face of impossibly demanding and conflicting social/cultural/political conditions.

You've got it right, of course, in your view of mass electoral democracy as an absurdity. But I've never been able to move beyond Churchill's famous observation that our system of government is the worst in the world—except for all the others.

Don

P.S. I think my military experience might also have something to do with my tolerance for "character defects" among our leaders. Patton was an utterly contemptible human being, but boy were we glad to have that mean, tough son-of-a-bitch up front when the Tiger tanks came at us.

After this brief exchange in March, our sizable discussions of social conscience and constructionism intervened. Nothing else was said about political matters until late June, when Paul wrote, "Reading a recent biog. of Hamilton and his transitory disconnection from Washington, I am struck with the latter's narcissistic irascibility. Karl Menninger considered him a 'schizoid personality,' which would count in Rado as a compensated schizotype. Do you have an opinion about this from your study of Washington?" In my reply, I wrote:

I haven't studied Washington directly, but have gained impressions from the several bios. of Jefferson that I have read. In relationships with Jefferson too, as with Hamilton, and also Adams, I would say, Washington does come through as a narcissistic character. His aloofness, the distance he kept from everybody, his readiness to turn against loyal as well as disloyal inferiors, as long as he stayed on top, certainly fit a schizotypic pattern, about as effectively compensated as I can imagine. Built a political fortress around himself. No one could touch him.

And Meehl responded:

Your description of Washington is helpful. I incline to think Menninger was right, although the narcissistic component occurs in so many other "types" that without the other signs (e.g., over-reaction to touch, uncontrollable laughter even in dangerous situations, pathological rage) one could be led astray. And I never know what to make of academics who achieve, plan, etc.—can't be real psychopaths—but who have the egocentricity, shallow object relations, lack of ethics that the psychopath has. Do you have a label, and a psychodynamic, for such persons?

In August, I wrote:

I think you, Menninger, & I are right about GW, but the problems are just the ones you note. Without confirming signs of other components of the syndrome, we just don't know. The more I look into the lives and life situations of the 10 presidents I'm trying to understand for my bigotry project, the more cautious I get about simple DSM-type diagnoses. Lincoln is a clear-cut case [of major depressive disorder], I think, but the rest seem to me complex mixtures for whom even dimensional descriptions miss the point. Nixon (not one of my 10; I've eliminated scoundrels) is a case in point. Some kind of 46 [pronounced "four six"; MMPI code for combination of psychopathy and paranoia] I suppose, but the kinds of academics you describe—i.e., planful achievers, sometimes genuine contributors, hence not pure Pd [psychopathic deviate], but egocentric, treacherous in relationships with others, amoral—I cannot label nor do I have any good psychodynamic guesses about these characters. I used to toss them into the "secondary" class in the Cleckley/Lykken distinction between primary and secondary psychopathy, but don't think much of that idea any more either. Longer I live, the more I see need for taxometric research for better nomothetic understanding, and meanwhile close idiographic analysis to come at problem from the other side.

Paul's response to my comment about marginally psychopathic academics was brief: "I agree—DSM doesn't have good rubrics for what I call 'normal garden-variety ass-holes.' 'Narcissistic' is too laden with libido theory, etc., to be a useful term for them."

The same series of letters that touched upon our views of politicians also concerned other topics. The note that queried George Washington's possible schizotypy included an announcement of the Templeton Prize for contributions to positive psychology. This led to our discussion of the role of moral values in psychotherapy. The announcement read as follows:

The American Psychological Association (APA), with generous underwriting support from the John Templeton Foundation has created the Templeton Positive Psychology Prize to recognize outstanding mid-career research in positive psychology. The Templeton Prize, which will be the largest prize given in psychology today, is designed to recognize and encourage scientific excellence in the new science of positive psychology, including such topics as goal-focused living, self-control, character-building, future-mindedness, optimism, persistence, wisdom, work-ethic, thrift, courage, and moral identity. First Place Award totals $100,000. Nominators must hold the rank of professor or its equivalent.

Meehl had underlined the "topics," and wrote, in the margin of the announcement and in his letter:

These are all strongly ideological. What would hippies, Zen Buddhists, anarchists, some Blacks, etc., say about them? Even Ellis would dislike some of them! And what sort of "moral identity" is to be encouraged?

Seligman's "positive psychology" [Martin E. P. Seligman, president of the APA in 1998, advocated moving beyond clinical psychology's traditional emphasis on psychopathology to the study of "positive" aspects of human behavior] appeals to me, yet on reflection I see 2 big problems. First, how [to] train? If students really study the great life-style thinkers (e.g., Buddha, Aristotle, Epictetus, Russell) what do we drop from the curriculum? Second, the political/moral issues. Should a Baptist taxpayer pay Ellis to preach atheism, not to alleviate ulcers but to "raise quality of life?" When this surfaces, it will present a conflict as big as abortion, I would think. Do you have a view as yet?

7/12/99

Dear Paul,

... I've thought a lot about the political/moral problems in defining a "positive psychology" as required for award of the Templeton Prize. The boy-scout characteristics to be encouraged are all indeed ideological, and then we must ask, "Whose ideology?" Well, if Sir John Templeton is putting up the dough, I guess we have a simple answer: John Templeton's ideology. But the more general problem, as it arises, say in using tax money to educate professional psychologists, who are inevitably moral agents, defies any deep resolution that I've been able to manage. When (not if) we become secular priests as well as healers and truth-seekers, we are trapped in the prevailing ideology of the supporting society, and in a "free" society like ours, conflicts are bound to arise. In a small-time way—$1000 vs. $100K—we crash directly into the problem every year here at Rutgers in selecting the winner of the "Peterson Prize" for contributions to the "public good." We've agreed on some criteria: serious problem previously unattended; innovative, rigorously designed & evaluated "local" solution; etc., and our independent selections from short lists agree closely, i.e., "we know it when we see it," but if you asked me for a firmly grounded, ethically defensible justification for our procedure, I'd be unable to provide it.

The more general problem—what moral ideology underlies & pervades our educational program, in which we spend public money to educate practitioners of psychology—is one I think we solve mainly by evasion. We don't bring it up & hope nobody else does. I agree with you that if these issues were subjected to public debate, the conflicts would rival abortion. Our solution, such as it is, lies in defining the basic function of professional psychologists not as "raising the quality of life" but as disciplined inquiry or local science, in which the first step is to negotiate values and goals with each and every client, to be utterly honest and as open as we need to be about our own values, & see to it that we do our best to give all clients what they want by way of outcome. Here is where the neo-pragmatists, Bernstein, Toulmin, even Rorty, have offered some useful guidance that was not forthcoming from other sources. I'm not entirely unhappy that a considerable share of PsyD programs have developed in sectarian schools—Baylor, Fuller, Rosemead, Wheaton, Immaculata, etc. At least they are clear about the values they represent....

Don

7/18/99

DRP: ... Re pre-Seligman psychotherapy, I don't see it as value-soaked as you do. Set aside value-influence, not controllable, but a defect in technique, analogous to poor empathy, clumsy interpretation, etc., like stupid CPA's, unskilled surgeons, lazy lawyers. The client comes complaining, you, or Ellis, or I, don't drag him in. The client says, in effect, "I don't like the way I am," or "My wife doesn't, and I want to please her." One can view even Al Ellis's aggressive tactics (which I couldn't do, even if I wanted to) as instrumental, as applying means-end empirical relations. The moral rationale is Aristotle's pragmatic syllogism, "If you desire G, and A is (empirically, factually) a means to G, you should do A," The weak part of this argument is the doubtfulness about the causal A-to-G relation, of course. More research needed, as usual. But the dentist, engineer, economist, broker, CPA, etc. are in the same boat, as are all helping professions, right?

PEM

8/22/99

Dear Paul,

... On pre-Seligman/Templeton psychotherapy, I don't disagree with your argument that our main job is to help clients attain their goals by helping them consider ways to get there, and often helping them do what's needed (if desire G, & A = means to G, do A). But often the problem is not limited to

finding an effective A; it involves reconsideration of desirability of G. "Are you sure making all that money is really what you want?" "Is it that important to keep your mother-in-law from having a fit?" Here, I think T's values inevitably come into play, effects are subtle, & neither T nor C [therapist nor client] is fully aware of what's going on much of the time. Answer for T is to become aware, and be entirely up-front with C at least hint of conflict, and of course C can always walk out, but I think valuation of goals is a much bigger problem for us than it is for dentists, engineers, CPAs, or any other professional I can think of, including physicians.*

Don

**Do you think the "awareness" that results from successful psychoanalysis frees analyst and analysand from value issues? Doesn't seem so to me. More often, I see conversion to values of analyst.*

8/26/99

Dear Don: I agree with yr amendment to the A-to-G model, which is in line with John Dewey's axiology, if I grasp it. Somehow in my psyRx work, few clients came in to re-examine "basic" goals, they rather challenged their subsidiary ones, and the inadequate instrumental means to them. But the last 20+ years I saw mostly academics (had repute for being effective with them) and I think on average (numerous exceptions) academics' goals are not as crazy as other people's, plus being, on average, more realizable, and in the context of relative "safety." But I may have had some probe defects due to being an academic myself. Despite my n Achievement, I was, I believe, fairly good at explaining & challenging the excessive ambition, neurotic publishing pressure, concern with in-group status, intellectual insecurity....

Paul

9/2/99

Dear Paul,

I think you have hit on main reason you & I differ in emphasis on means vs. ends in psyRx. Sure enough, most of the academics I've seen in practice (not many, all told) were mainly concerned with minor goals & ways of reaching them. But much of my time in practice, esp. early days in Illinois, was spent with screwed-up adolescents, who didn't know where the hell they were going—occupationally, interpersonally, personally, spiritually, or otherwise. Later, both in IL and at Rutgers, I worked mainly with married couples, who often came in claiming, & maybe even thinking, they were there to "save the marriage," but who were sometimes—rather often, in my experience—in a counselor's office trying to find a guilt-reducing, socially acceptable way out of the marriage. Couldn't do much about means until we were all straight about what the goals were. Another set of couples during the "open marriage" fad were there because one of the partners wanted to screw around and the other one didn't. Despite my own not especially virtuous behavior while my first marriage was breaking up (I didn't see any clients during that period of my life), I couldn't keep my values out of the therapeutic process in those cases. Maybe some "open marriages" work, but I never saw one that did, & I let people (clients and students I was supervising) know how I felt about that once I went back into clinical work with the benefit of some painful personal experience behind me....

Don

9/8/99

Dear Don: ... On means-ends, your clientele surely presents harder task. Aristotle's pragmatic syllogism needs ceteris paribus clause, and cetera are not often paria. The difficult ethical issue for me, listening to Ellis tapes, is how explicit one may properly be in "forcing" value-exploration. Ellis does it up front, client may quit if he dislikes it. One can argue that explicit challenge is preferable to the unintended, subtle value-conveyance that others "commit" (I recall 1950–1960 studies showing that, altho the rs are not large). Also the means-end empirical relation is less solidly based than when an MD tells an obese patient to diet and exercise. However, I am as sure that holding tightly to Ellis' crazy life postulates is likely to hurt one's mental/physical health and relations to others and "life-success" (client's criteria!!) as I am that dreams have motivational meaning, or that Rogerian reflection tends to enlarge self-knowledge, etc., etc. I did a mini-study on Ellis's postulates and I'll send the research report. If your clinical experience strongly shows "open marriages" rarely work (I agree), that's an empirical fact, not a value-claim, so why isn't it OK to apply Aristotle's syllogism by so informing patient?

Paul

10/10/99

Dear Paul,

I just returned from Vermont to find your letter of 9/8 (re ... Aristotle's prag. syllogism, open marriage, etc.). Slow communication my doing. We had so much to do during last weeks in VT—yard care, social obligations, mainly—that I asked sec'y to hold my office mail until I got back....

On Aristotle's syllogism re clinical advice about open marriage, you're right. If data, even my clinical experience, show that open marriages rarely "work," i.e., fail to enhance satisfactions of both partners, often lead to di-

vorce, etc., all I'm doing in cautionary counsel is offering clients benefit of knowledge about means to end of "good" marriage. In my work with couples, though, the issue came up, following publication of the O'Neills' book [title, Open Marriage; message, advocacy] before I had any experience with clients who had tried it, and the O'Neills claimed that their "data" (clinical & personal experience) showed positive outcomes (enrichment of the marriage). During this time, I didn't claim any special professional expertise on the question "Should we or shouldn't we?" so when the question came up I would pose a prior question: "What do you, Mr. H, and what do you, Mrs. W, consider to be a 'good' marriage?" Big differences between H and W often emerged, and in working those out I'm pretty sure my own values came into play. I'm far from Puritanical in matters of this kind, but less liberal than Ellis, for example, & much less liberal than another colleague of mine who actively encouraged open marriage for some of his clients (said so), talked his second wife into living that way and 20+ years after the O'Neill book came out, died of AIDS, and left his widow furious with him for infecting her with HIV. I suppose that outcome can be seen as a simple predictive error in a means-end relationship, but it seems to me a more complex risk/benefit calculus of values is also required....

Don

In a brief following note, Paul asked:

When one has neither research data or wide clinical experience as to the empirical premise in a pragmatic syllogism (as with your first experience with questions about open marriage) then what? Can one claim some "expertise" via theory, or via extrapolation from related clinical experience? Dangerous. I d.k. what I think there, and I daresay I have varied rather haphazardly as to when I did, when not. Lawyers & brokers & CPAs don't tend to ask these questions as we do, hence they are more comfortable, even bright learned ones.

Meehl's questions seemed to me more rhetorical than substantive. We were both ready to let the matter of values in psychotherapy stand where we left it.

The same series of letters that concerned political issues and the questions just discussed also brought up the third matter suggested by the title of this chapter, on paleontology and paleontologists. In my letter of July 12, I led our correspondence into some exchanges about neo-Darwinian theory:

Jane and I were browsing in a used bookstore recently, and I picked up a copy of The Science of Life. It was written by H. G. Wells, Julian Huxley (grandson of "Darwin's bulldog," T. S. Huxley), & Henry George's son, like J. Huxley a paleontologist. The book was originally published in 1929, when the stew over the Scopes trial was boiling, & a long section, nearly a third of the book in itself, is entitled, "The Incontestible Fact of Evolution." Of course the authors wrote the book to quash the prevailing Creationist nonsense of the time, but I must say I was impressed with the way the authors marshaled evidence from the rocks, embryology, chemistry, geographical distribution, etc. to support the basic propositions of the "theory of evolution." I could see considerable ad hockery going on, & I suppose there are other flaws I don't recognize (your long dictated letter shocked me into the realization that I had accepted the "theory of evolution" nearly as reverentially as pre-Darwinians accepted creationist myths, tho I never did take the "human-behavior-can-only-be-understood-in-evolutionary-terms" line seriously), BUT, all in all, the core propositions seem impressive to me as scientific theory based almost entirely on observational data, conceptually integrated by rough comparison rather than inherently impossible precise quantification. Eminently falsifiable. One human tooth in a coal deposit would knock it all apart. High marks on parsimony, seems to me, & also number, diversity, & novelty of facts derived. Short on quantification, of course, but we're not talking quantum mechanics or modern cosmology here. Different questions, different data. I would be hugely pleased if any theory in psychology, hard or soft, did half as well as Darwin, Wallace, et al. did in making sense of biological history. I'm curious to know in more detail what your objections are, tho I don't expect a letter to tell me.

Meehl's comment on this was that:

Evolution is too much to discuss by mail for sure. My skepticism is, briefly, from (a) Lack of phylogenetic trees, even incomplete ones—which gave rise to Eldredge–Gould paper—and (b) Highly implausible mechanisms (random mutations) for variation. But as I have no decent (= scientific) alternative theory, I avoid disputing it. I sent Gould a reprint of my fossil paper, and a letter, which (as I predicted) he lacked the courtesy to answer. He's a conceited over-rated fake polymath.

The "Gould" to whom Paul referred was the popular paleontologist, Stephen Jay Gould, who died in 2002. The paper Gould had written with Eldredge was concerned primarily with the scarcity, often absolute absence, of transitional forms in the fossil records that are often adduced as the primary evidence for Darwinian gradualism—the progression, say, from eohippus to the modern horse or the descent of man from the apes through the earliest hominids to present-day *homo sapiens*. Darwin himself did not regard the paleontological data as the strongest evidence for his theory. Rather, because of its incompleteness, the lack of transitional forms, the fossil record offered "the gravest objection that could be urged" against his theory. He hoped that further paleontological research would provide the "missing links," but paleontologists have been digging ever since and findings have been scant indeed. For example, no proto-rhinoceroids have been found. All of a sudden, there is a fully formed rhinocerous! Furthermore, most species, once formed, do not change much morphologically even though they survive extreme environmental changes over millions of years. Gould and Eldredge recognized the problem, argued that many breaks in the fossil record were "real," proposed a theory of "punctuated equilibrium" as an alternative to Darwinian gradualism, and acknowledged that the rarity of transitional series remained as a "persistent *bugbear.*"

The "fossil paper" to which Meehl referred defined four nonredundant methods for quantifying the completeness of the fossil record. Meehl considered it a potentially important contribution to methodology for testing Darwin's theory, but had published the paper as a chapter in the highly regarded but somewhat obscure Minnesota series on the philosophy of science, the paper was never cited by scientists who might have followed up on Meehl's lead, and of course Meehl himself was not in a position to do the necessary research. He had sent his paper to Gould in the thought that one of Gould's students, if not Gould himself, might be interested in following the lead to theoretical inquiry that Meehl's methodology could provide. He had no way of guessing what Gould might do with his research proposal, but thought it reasonable to expect at least an acknowledgment of his letter. In my letter of September 2, I offered some observations about Professor Gould.

I have much to learn about evolution, but I've seen enough to be suspicious about Gould on other grounds, & I agree with your personal size-up of him as an over-rated phony. A few years ago, when Fran Lawrence, RU president, excited near riots by mentioning the dread words "genetic hereditary background" in some discussions of drop-out rates & other affirmative action problems with African-American students, a group of students sought to calm the waters by inviting Gould to speak here. He came, said essentially that there was nothing to the "bell curve" argument, & as scientific basis claimed that factor analysis had shown there was no such thing as "general intelligence." He charged $16,000 for the talk, exhausting the students' paltry speakers' fund, and left as soon as he finished his lecture.

9/8/99

Dear Don: Wow!! Yr Gould story sure confirms my view of the man. Amazing how these slick characters fool "intellectuals." Sometimes seems intellectuals fool easier than non-intellectuals of = IQ. I almost believe that—match academics, writers, the "chattering class," for IQ with business executives, engineers, lawyers, army generals—I wouldn't be surprised if the latter were less gullible about efflorescent pseudo-scholarly bullshit. Would be fun to research that....

Paul

10/10/99

Dear Paul

... In fairness to Gould, I should tell you that I did not attend his talk, so am not directly qualified to comment. My info. about his message came from an article in the campus newspaper & reports from 2 of our students who did attend & basically confirmed accuracy of the press account. Facts: SJG <u>did</u> charge $16K for the talk, which pissed off students who would have liked to bring in some other experts & couldn't because G took all that was left of their speakers' fund; he <u>did</u> claim that factor analysis questioned value, if not existence, of <u>g</u>; he <u>did</u> leave in a hurry after his talk, tho according to the newspaper he stuck around long enough to answer questions about Fran Lawrence's "genetic hereditary background" remark re African-American students and was quoted as saying FL's comment "didn't amount to a hill of beans." His presence & opposition to the "bell curve" argument, however ill-founded, probably helped calm the political waters,

which were boiling at the time. None of this changes my opinion of Gould as over-rated and marginally fraudulent.

Don

Six months later, the following April, I reread Paul's article on the statistical estimation of completeness of the fossil record more closely than I had at the time of our autumn correspondence, and wrote a brief note to Paul to express my reaction:

It's a wonder to me how serious paleontologists can ignore a path to better knowledge as clearly marked as this (tho given our shared view of S. J. Gould's shallowness, no mystery about his failure to respond to your proposal). For my part, thanks again. Two main effects on me: better understanding of limits of evidence supporting Darwin's theory; improved acceptance of discrepancy between my view of value of some things I've written & social response they received. I suspect r between "true" value of works in science & their public acknowledgment (=) .50; in art, .30, in professional work, ??

Please, no reply. I hope your taxometric studies are going well & that there have been no bad turns in your state of health.

Don

CHAPTER

15

Factor Analysis

Shortly after I arrived on the faculty of the University of Illinois in 1952, I joined Raymond B. Cattell in research on personality structure in children. Cattell was a pioneer in the use of factor analysis as a method for defining the "elements" of which the conglomerate human "personality" was composed. He was an internationally recognized expert in the conceptual and mathematical foundations of the method and taught me everything I knew about the techniques. We published a series of research reports with which I was, at the time, entirely content. Later, however, as I followed another line of research on children's behavior disorders, I found Cattell's methodology to be less dependable than it had seemed during our collaboration. I discovered that I could obtain more decisively replicable results by a simple but radical modification of Cattell's procedure. I reanalyzed the data Cattell and I had collected jointly, using my revised technique, and found the same improvement in structural definition for those data that I had found in analyzing my own. I published the findings in the *Psychological Review* in an article entitled "Scope and Generality of Verbally Defined Personality Factors." The abstract read as follows:

Factor analyses of verbal personality measures have typically generated highly complex multidimensional structural systems. Available evidence now suggests that the most dependable dimensions drawn from conventional factor analyses of ratings and questionnaires are simple, familiar dimensions of broad semantic scope. It also appears that most of the initially obscure, apparently more precise, more narrowly defined factors many investigators claim to have revealed are either trivial, artifactual, capricious, or all 3. Verbal descriptions of personality were reduced to 2 factors, and the 2 factors were reduced to 2 ratings, 1 concerning perceived adjustment and the other related to introversion-extraversion. Convergent and discriminant validities for the 2 simple ratings are evidently equal or superior to those for any of the more cumbersome and expensive questionnaires examined in the review. Implications for theory and method were discussed.

I liked the article, and such knowing colleagues as Lloyd Humphreys and Ledyard Tucker shared my opinion of it, but it appeared to have no effect on the field. It seemed to me that the way my work was ignored was not unlike the failure of paleontologists to follow Meehl's methodological proposal for studying the fossil record, so I sent him a reprint with an accompanying comment: "The enclosed article in the *Psy Review* I considered the best work I had done up to that time. Several of my previous articles had been anthologized—most of them actually—but nobody picked up on this one, tho it was fairly widely cited."

10/28/99

Dear Don: Hoo!! The Psy Rev (1965) is terrific. My explanation of its being neglected is simple. It's threatening....

How do you react to worry #3 of the enclosed? This has bothered me for many years, and no one gives me a good answer. (As Sewell Avery said to Congress in 1933, about the Depression, "Unfortunately I have no friends who are able to explain this to me"—a beautiful quote from an honest baffled businessman, who later got carried out of his office by troops, the famous photo).

I can see that if a physically real non-arbitrary inner variable (e.g., count of anxiety-producing polygenes) saturates many dispositions, "intrinsically" so ubiquitous, then the hyperspace dots will tend to densify in a region—if many traits are anxiety-loaded, we will find a factor, as we should. But couldn't introversion-extraversion show up mostly because humans have named many dispositions involving how people relate to others, that being important to us? (In Cattell's 1946 book, he says dogs would have many differentiated trait-names for how humans use their feet. Like the Eskimo with many terms for kinds of snow.) I know this worry is an oldie, but why hasn't anyone been able to help me with it?

Paul

Meehl enclosed an article entitled "Four Queries About Factor Reality" that began with the following remarks:

> When I first learned about factor analysis (as an undergraduate over a half-century ago) there were four methodological questions that troubled me. They still do. Although I have used factor analysis in research, with excellent results, it is disconcerting to realize that these basic issues remain unsettled, and are rarely examined with the incisiveness and depth they deserve. I have neither the expertise nor temerity to "answer" them, so I shall only try to put them clearly and forcibly.

The queries were: (1) What sort of existential status do we—and ought we—impute to factors? (2) What is the purpose of factor analysis if one is a fictionist rather than a realist? (3) How dependent are results on the choice of tests? (4) What is the role of parsimony? Each query was elaborated briefly but succinctly. For "worry" #3, about which Meehl had specifically inquired in his letter to me, he began by saying, "Everyone agrees with the clichés, 'You cannot get more than what you put in,' 'Garbage in, garbage out,' [and] 'Test building is more important than the formalism.' I am not challenging these accepted principles. But I do not find them helpful in answering the question, *'How dependent?'*"

Jane and I went to Ireland that fall, so I could not answer his question until we returned:

11/16/99

Dear Paul,

Just back from Ireland. Went to Ulster for the first time. Spectacular beauty and fascinating history. Prehistory too. Carbon-dated relics in recently excavated passage tombs place them around 7000 B.C., and on the west side of the island, suggesting that the first inhabitants might have sailed in from the Mediterranean and then, following the Gulf Stream, up the west coast of the island rather than crossing over from the larger island, and before that the continent to the east, as previously supposed. Fine time on our trip all in all, tho cold & rainy much of the time, & economic boom has, among other consequences, put far more traffic on Ireland's narrow, winding roads than they can safely bear. Doesn't help that most natives drive cars the way they race their horses. Competitive sport.

I don't know that I can help you much with your query about dependence of factor analytic results on choice of tests, but I have thought a lot about it & my "answers," such as they are, are reflected in my work. When I first began my studies of children's behavior disorders I examined previous descriptive research and could not make any sense of it. Results went all over the place. Authors of most factor studies seemed to have selected variables & their measures (ratings & questionnaire items more often than "tests") arbitrarily. As I remember my review of the lit. I concentrated on 3 studies of the "same" domain that produced 3 utterly divergent outcomes for the simple reason that the authors had entirely different conceptions of the area they were trying to map. I didn't exactly attempt a "solution" to the problem, but I did say that authors owed readers a rational description of the process by which they had arrived at the initial variable set, & that either theory-based definitions or ecologically reasonable, empirically defined descriptor sets be employed in forming any matrix worth the trouble of factor analysis.

In my own work, I took the second route. My Behavior Problem Checklist was developed by writing down the presenting problem of every child who had come to our U of I clinic over its 15-year history, counting the frequencies & factoring the 55 most common problems. Results: big "conduct problem" and "personality problem" factors, much (maybe just) like Tom Achenbach's "externalizing" & "internalizing" factors.

I wasn't satisfied with the measure, tho it was widely cited (my only "citation classic") & apparently useful as a rough clinical screening device & as a research tool. I was concerned with the existential status (yr Query 1) of the factors, which were based on teacher & parent ratings. As I've mentioned to you in some letters about Hans Eysenck, I set out to replicate a study by Himmelweit, using Cattelian/Eysenckian "objective tests" that both H and E claimed to show clear, strong neuroticism and introversion-extraversion factors. No clusters. No nothing. Led me to distrust Eysenck, or at least question Himmelweit's data, & also led me to the same questions you raise in "Four Queries." I couldn't justify FA as a fictionist, saw no sign of "reality" in the factors I was finding, & set off on the course that led to my clinical-study-of-social-behavior argument (multiply-determined study of situated behavior in process a better way of finding out what people were thinking-feeling-doing).

Herb Quay retained interest in the checklist, however, extended it into the adolescent age range, did a lot of research on & with it himself, & became a collector/coordinator of research of others. Many studies. Hundreds, I think. By and by, Herb saw signs of other factors besides the "conduct" and "person-

ality" problem pair. Something like attention deficit popped up in some of the studies. Occasionally an autism/psychoticism cluster. Maybe. The original data set didn't include enough descriptors to allow those factors to show, even if they were "really" there. So Herb wrote 100+ new items, not entirely off the top of his head, at least partially based on hints in the many studies he had done or seen, did 4 separate factor studies of the new data set, and lo! the Revised Behavior Problem Checklist "measures" 6 factors.

So an (not the) answer to your Query 3 is: Results of factor analysis are hugely dependent on choice of measures. Which is one reason why I no longer do any, tho I still believe the procedure can be useful in the quantitative simplifications needed for nomothetic research on intelligence, temperament, "personality," etc. The Quay–Peterson checklist seems to be useful as a screening device for school psychologists, tho I sometimes wonder whether they couldn't get the same info more simply just by asking teachers which kids are doing what.

On long flight back from Ireland, I finished reading John Horgan's latest: The Undiscovered Mind. Smart science writer, Mr. Horgan, claiming now that (a) mind-science hasn't taught us much about the most interesting questions, (b) isn't likely to (for many reasons like those laid out in Meehl, 1979), & (c) should & certainly shall go on ad infinitum anyhow. I found myself agreeing with 85% of what Horgan said & found the book oddly reassuring.

Don

12/2/99

Dear Paul,

Got stuck on something I was trying to write, eyes fell on our latest correspondence re dependence of factor analytic results on choice of tests, reread exchange, & felt mildly embarrassed at realization that I didn't tell you anything you didn't already know (tho some of anecdotal stuff might have interested you). To me, the most important of yr 4 queries is #1 re existential status. Cattell, as you know, was a thorough-going metaphysical realist & firmly believed that his procedures would uncover fundamental elements of personality. At first, I hoped so too, but later saw dependence of factor outcomes on the way we (happened to) name phenomena in the fields that interested me (personality and social behavior).

I still factor correlation matrices, but only as a way of deriving summary statistics (yr 2nd level of quantification), useful because of cognitive limitations of human beings in thinking about themselves & others (7 ± 2) [well documented claim that human beings are limited to dealing cognitively with somewhere between 5 and 9 ideas simultaneously], not as a way of discovering real elements of any kind. Like Sewell Avery, you & I would both like to have some of our friends help us understand these matters.

I enclose 2 articles results of which do not at all surprise but sorely sadden me. No question any more about effects proliferation of professional schools & availability of weak PsyD programs have had on dumbing down our profession nationally. Locally, I still think we do a good job & am organizing a comparative study of performance records of grads. of Rutgers PsyD & clinical PhD programs over past 25 years. We're the only ones who can do the comparison in any very interesting way (selection ratios about same in PsyD & PhD programs; same core faculty). We'll let the chips fall where they fall. When that is done, I think I'll have the info needed for an AP piece titled "Thirty Years of Practitioner Training in Psychology" (cf. Peterson, 1985, "20 years of ..."). I hope by then I can find something constructive to say about our situation. Can you?

Don

12/11/99

Dear Don: Oh, no, u helped me. Having used FA only 3–4x in resch, I have no self-confidence about methodological belly-aches, and am readily squelched by "experts" who swear by it. Your comments, and the reprints you sent earlier, made me feel more comfortable. Also, in my rare research reliance, the task for FA was to assist key-construction by finding relatively "purer" items to make subkeys, so the big issue of inferring existence of a real latent entity was not present. But I note your view on g is more realism-compatible, so is mine. That's due to converging evidence, isn't it? Not just the FA, but foster-child data, twin data, even the recent brain-size & other physical correlates. Also, the Jensen–Cheng comparison of half-dozen seemingly "different" hierarchical methods, showing they give identical results for inferred factor scores on g, is reasoning from a purely statistical viewpoint, and answers Gould's complaint. Even the plausibility of fairly simple polygenic substrates (e.g., # of dendritic twigs on CNS neurons) is involved in one's readiness to reify g.

As to the Templer studies, I d.k. what to say, or at least what would cheer us up on that discouraging subject. The non-test outcomes don't bother me much, do they you? Why should we expect or desire, that PsyDs publish as much as PhDs? Or get kudos that are correlated with that? My old speech (in Holt's book) didn't say that. It praised my physician who didn't publish. My harping on seminars to teach "research-consumers" who aren't expected to create new scientific knowledge would be inconsistent with my deploring lesser article-production, wouldn't it? Especially as my Sacred Cows MS takes a dim view of most research articles, hah?

The only non-test predictand that bothers me is the lower ABPP rate. But since I have no confidence in how ABPP examines today, even that isn't a big depressor. For you?

Paul

12/29/99

Dear Paul,

Quick note to thank you for your letter of 12/11. I'm glad my experience with FA was of some help to you. As usual, it seems your views & mine on such matters as theoretical status of g *are in accord, & the questions that you raised in "4 queries" still linger in my mind as well. I conflate all 4 in a pragmatic form: "What would it take (by way of improved instrumentation, conceptual clarity, etc.) for FA to be decisively useful as a tool for educing strong, existentially real, elemental theoretical entities in personality, interpersonal process, and the other domains of soft psychology that are most important for scientific understanding of the human condition?" When I ponder that question, I conclude that current and immediately foreseeable measures and theoretical formulations are so weak that factor analysis is nearly useless, except in a few cases as a bootstrapping operation, & I foresee merit in it through a long time into the future restricted almost entirely to the uses you & I have made of it, i.e., "purifying" item sets for sake of psychometric efficiency. Enough of that.*

On poor performance of PsyDs in every comparison so far, I agree that all non-test indices, including ABPP rate, are poor indicators of performance we need to measure, viz. "How well do grads do in their day-by-day professional work?" We'll do our best to move ahead on that one in the comparison of Rutgers PhDs & PsyDs I mentioned in my last letter, but the core assessment problems have stumped us all so far.

Off to the Wright Institute Jan. 9. Only 2 months this time, rather than 4.

Happy New Year,

Don

During my time in Berkeley, I spent such leisure time as I had reading and enjoying the pleasures of the Bay Area. I didn't write to Paul nor he to me until the following spring, when he was evidently vexed by some results in his taxometric research and thought my experience in factor analysis might provide a useful perspective:

5/31/00

Dear Don: Puzzle why tests separate groups as well as they do (MMPI keys, interest tests, Gough's scales, etc., many examples), often show mean differences 2–3 SDs [standard deviations] apart, but tapping, say, latent Sc, taxometrics do worse. Leslie says, "Careless job leads to feeble indicators." Query to you, as to a Big Example: We thought Cattell was sloppy & lazy in building his damn tests, after all those years of getting at the (alleged) latent factors. People research Sc using goddam 7-item questionnaires, "testing" my theory that way. Irks me.

Your opinion? Other scientists hone their instruments carefully, I suspect we don't.

Paul

6/15/00

Dear Paul,

Your letter of 5/31 asking why yr efforts to tap latent taxa are less successful than the tests you mention in discriminating groups only reached me today. I've moved around so much and [the] Rutgers delivery system is so bad that some of my mail is long delayed.

Anyway, I believe strongly that Leslie ("Careless job leads to feeble indicators") has hit the key. My experience with Cattell, Himmelweit/ Eysenck too, points in that direction. I helped Cattell build all the tests—some 30–40 "objective" tests, an oral questionnaire, teacher & parent ratings (Cattell's "life record" data)—for our studies of personality factors in preschool children. We both felt rather pleased with the battery we had assembled. Cattell actually seemed delighted with some of my inventions. We went ahead with the study, came out with all our numbers, shoved them through ILLIAC, refined the analytic rotations "visually," & published 4 reports. We both wrote as if the factors we educed were reasonably clear expressions of those Cattell had previously "discovered" in adults.

Only later did I begin to question our conclusions, especially when I tried to replicate Himmelweit's study allegedly showing clear conduct disorder & dysthymic factors in troublesome and troubled children, and found nothing but random swarms of data points for all my efforts. I realized then that the problem lay in the unexamined reliability & validity of the elemental measures themselves. I now think the "oral questionnaire" Ray & I inflicted on those kids was a joke. I do not know what, if anything, all those "objective tests" measured. In our "time-sampled" observations, the times were so brief, & the sample situation (nursery school) so restricted, that the logs our assistants recorded told very little about what the children were like "inside," where their latent traits presumably resided.

So Leslie is right. Poor measures reveal nothing. The tests you mention were empirically derived.

Don

P.S. You bet other scientists "hone their instruments" very carefully. One of my sons is head of the astrophysics program at Carnegie-Mellon. Every year, he goes to the South Pole to point a radio telescope, which he designed, at the Big Bang. And every year he makes tiny adjustments to improve the sensitivity and precision of the instrument he's using. His data, along with all the rest from Hubble and the other devices cosmologists are using these days, are clearly closing in on some real truth.

CHAPTER

16

History and Historians

Then came summer, with another lull in correspondence, except for some brief exchanges about Robert Holt's severely critical review contrasted with Brewster Smith's enthusiastic praise for Dan Fishman's book, *Pragmatic Psychology*. In our short notes, Meehl and I did little more than note the ironies of critical appraisal. Then, in October, Paul sent me another audiotape (which I can't find; it must surely be resting alongside the tape that inspired a previous letter). Paul said he had had a "medical summer," as Leslie described it. Probably return of endocarditis, he thought, with severe septicemia, high fever, loss of blood platelets, plus failing vision and a "big backache" that forced him for a time to hobble around with a walker. "Not good for the spirits," he said. Now, as I look at my notes on Paul's tape and at my lengthy written reply, I see little content that we hadn't discussed previously. I think we both just wanted a friendly visit. But I told him I would hold good thoughts for him in his struggle with an ailing body, and I had brought up one topic that led us into new territory:

These days I'm headed off on the study of the course of American bigotry from Jefferson to Reagan. That's history & biography, not science, but I see no reason for a psychologist to avoid the topic. I'm not a trained historian, & will say so, but neither were Gibbon (who went to Oxford for one year and said he got nothing out of it) or Churchill. In fact I think my training as a psychologist (on reliability of eyewitness testimony, distortions of memory, etc.) will help me avoid some of the errors I see professional historians & biographers making, so I'm not bashful about taking on the subject, though only the product (if there ever is one; I'm still "collecting") will tell whether or not I can write an interesting, informative account.

10/26/00

Dear Don: On historians, I incline to think they are often poor thinkers. (W. S. Miller had data that PhD candidates in History have Miller scores at bottom among "social sciences," about same level as Education PhDs. Psy and Econ are at top, predictably. The more quantitative, the brighter—can't get around it.) So it wouldn't bother me either to write on something "historical" without their union card. I think only a few technical things may sometimes matter. Not many!

You may enjoy recent book Isaac's Storm, on the Galveston hurricane-flood of 1902. Fascinating examples of denial as a mechanism, plus the inefficient power-driven federal bureaucracy. The idiographic component limits "scientific" possibilities in all sciences where it occurs, whether geology, meteorology, or personology. I have never disagreed with ole Allport on that, although he thought I did. Nor with Paterson, who waffled a bit.

I've been ruminating about history lately, like you. About to re-read Marx's 18th Brumaire, have re-read Gardiner's book on historical explanation. Georgii Plekhanov (despite his dogmatic Marxism, a VERY smart, learned man) did a good job in his little book (1898!!). One of [the] best is Sidney Hook, The Hero in History. Hook almost never wrote anything silly, in my opinion, although I disagree with many of his views. But Croce—widely esteemed—strikes me as a complete muddle-head. I puzzle why some muddleheads gain repute as deep thinkers.

I see idiographic element in historiography as closely analogous, almost identical, with that of personology. It will never be like visual perception theory, for example. No sense in pretending it will, or trying to make it so.

Paul

ADDENDUM

If you find Croce useful, don't suffer cognitive dissonance. I haven't, but have read little of him. He may be one of those clever muddle-heads that at times perceive a "deep truth," like Jung. (Even Hitler in Mein Kampf saw some social truths that many sane people missed). It's the Frank Barron creativity thing—high Sc correlated with creativity but needs high ES [ego strength] (re-

versing the usual correlation) to sift wheat from chaff. Hathaway's schizotypy showed this tendency if one knew him well. It was frustrating to me.

But 2 Croce arguments to make my point:

1. *He says term "cause" doesn't apply in history, because if y is caused by x, then we may ask what caused x? So infinite regress, therefore....*
2. *He says history is "not in time," because an event occurs, later a historian writes about it, so the same event exists at different times, therefore....*

I could think better than that in 9th grade science, probably even in 6th grade. You know, there's a difference between the scientific and pre-scientific intellect that has nothing to do with test tubes, instruments, or even use of mathematics. The pre-scientific mind often thinks crappily even when only words are involved. That's why Glymour (no positivist!) wrote, "If I have to choose between the logical positivists and the goddam English professors, I'll take the positivists." Of course one knows English profs who can think clearly—I know a world authority on Coleridge who is a clear thinker—but there is a marked statistical trend. Partly education, partly self-selection. I note few people with clear heads become anthropologists, but a few do. I've known three.

11/13/00

Dear Paul,

Miller's data on MAT [Miller Analogies Test] scores of PhD candidates in history and other fields do not surprise me. I'm inclined to the view Lloyd Humphreys held re PhDs in education, i.e., the very best are the equal of scholars in any field, but the bar for entry is lower so the variance is greater & mean is less. History is easier than math or chemistry as a subject for grad study. Isaiah Berlin mentions in passing another historian (Buckle, I think) who attributes the poor thinking evident in many historical accounts to the low IQs of their authors. Says history as a discipline does not attract the finest intellects. No Leibnizs or Newtons in their ancestry. So there's a huge mass of junk out there & the main challenge for anyone in my position—trying to write a coherent, "accurate" account of the course of American bigotry—is to separate the credible & significant from the implausible & trivial.

In this, I find my career-long preoccupation with the vexations of personology relevant & my early studies in the "philosophy of science" as solid a grounding as I could possibly have wished. As you, Feigl, & your philosopher colleagues defined the territory in those days, coverage was very broad. Feigl wrote & talked about the "scientific outlook" & included history among the social sciences in readings. (I just checked, & sure enuf found essays on history by Sidney Hook & Ernest Nagel in Feigl & Brodbeck's Readings in the Philosophy of Science (1953).

Speaking of Hook & recalling your letter of 10/26, I just took The Hero in History & Patrick Gardiner's book on historical explanation out of the library & have read enough to know they'll be useful to me. I think I'll skip Croce (135 refs. in RU library alone). Writing history, I find, is tougher than writing about it. More or less as an archival duty, I decided to write a history of our school at Rutgers. I'm about half-way through now & am finding out the hard way how tough it is to reconstruct even relatively recent, not particularly controversial events, e.g., a hearing that determined the location, hence the decisively important surrounding culture, of the school. I called four people who were present at the meeting and got 4 different accounts. This allowed me to piece together a reasonably coherent, nowhere downright inaccurate rendering of the event, but if any of my informants had written the history it would not have come out the same as mine. I also called Norm Garmezy [who had been hired as a consultant by the New Jersey Board of Higher Education to help decide whether the school should be located in Rutgers University or in the independently administered medical school] to verify a statement attributed to him. Norm frankly admitted that his memory of the hearing was so cloudy that he was not a very reliable witness but figured the remark was the "kind of smart-ass thing" he might have said. Through a series of discursions I do not recall, we wound up talking about our experiences in the Battle of the Bulge.

Don

11/15/00

DRP: Yes, for Pete's sake, skip Croce. One should always remember the point Humphreys makes (I tend to forget it, d.k. why, strange) that the BEST persons in even half-way scholarly fields are as smart as the BEST in any field. Miller told us that in his aptitude testing class. I'm sure top sociologists are as smart as top physicists, but "top" here is a smaller area of their curve. The smartest psychologists I know are smarter than the average chemists I've known, for example.

I'm reading Jacques Barzun's latest (he's 92) and he's damn bright despite his "humanistic" bias against quantification. Clio and the Doctors is a fun read, if you haven't.

PEM

12/5/00

Dear Paul,

I found Sidney Hook's Hero in History so clear, sound, & timely (still right to the point re current political situation nearly 60 years after original publication) that I intend to buy a copy of the 1990 Transaction [Publishers] issue.

It'll go on the growing stack of my books that I want to reread from time to time. Gardiner's Nature of Historical Explanation is sound & useful too, or so it seems to me. Thanks for mentioning them. I wish I could join you in reading some of the other items noted in yr. recent letters & may do so, but most evenings I'm tired, have a drink, & after dinner (horrors!) watch TV, or less often, listen to music or play the piano.

On more general questions of scholarly inquiry, the resemblance between the issues faced by historians and those encountered by clinical psychologists & personologists in their idiographic, biographical, & historical investigations continue to impress me, as do the differences between the issues faced by historians and those encountered by clinical psychologists and personologists in their nomothetic, observational, contemporary studies. In the field of psy. at large the main confusions seem to arise from those, like Gergen, who write as if psy were entirely a history-like enterprise, or on the other side from those, like McFall, who either see psy now, or would like to make it, just about like physics, or at least microbiology. I see no reason we can't keep both kinds of inquiry within our purview, as long as the necessary distinctions are maintained, or, as in Lamiell's idiothetic analysis & my disciplined inquiry, judiciously combined.

Don

P.S. Note on quantification & conviction: Seems to me Hook's argument that the Russian Revolution of 1917 would be "unthinkable" without the work of Lenin—the objectives, policy, controlling strategy, day-by-day tactics, were all his—and that without the October revolution we would be living in a vastly different world today, is as convincing an argument as any scientific proof I've ever seen, in psychology at least. But there's not a number in sight. Purely verbal, logical argument. I remember your quoting C. S. Lewis once as saying, "If nothing is nearly certain, then nothing is probable." How does this square with your insistence on quantification as a necessary condition for settling factual questions?

12/11/00

Dear Don: Glad u find Hook useful. An amazing man! I disagree with him about many important matters (Freud, socialism, IQ tests, philosophy—he's basically a Dewey disciple). But of his books & articles I've read, even his personal correspondence, where one feels free to be loose & even dogmatic at times, he NEVER says anything I consider downright silly or stupid. Given the range of his interests, and the big role of ethico-political issues, that's an amazing track record. Query, what is the mental trait apart from sheer g (and wide learning) that does that? Whatever it is, it makes all the difference. I don't claim Hook's record, but I'm pretty close to it. Mistakes, yes. Plainly stupid or silly, no. I know a number of people who approach "foolish-free" dis-

course—you, Feigl, Grove, Faust, Jenkins, MacCorquodale—but I can name many more who are high Miller + learned who have said, and written, quite a few pretty dumb things. I d.k. what that is. It's not just a matter of being "skeptical"; one form of being foolish is being (safely) hyper-skeptical. SRH [Starke Hathaway] did that at times, to the point of folly.

Your example of a non-quantitative but solid Hook argument, crucial role of Lenin, is well taken. Same could be argued for Hitler, and FDR. So the tough question is "Under what knowledge conditions can a completely unquantified inference be so clear & potent that only a hyper-skeptic would withhold belief?" I have never managed to formulate that even halfway decently. See my psychoanalytic examples of dream interpretation, in Minn. Studies Philos. Science. But SRH was unpersuaded. Why is it so hard to explicate this simple, obvious point? I give up.

Paul

12/19/00

Dear Paul,

I wish I could offer a confident answer to your query "What is the mental trait apart from sheer g (& wide learning) [that permits demonstrably intelligent, learned people to say, and write, downright stupid, silly things]?" At the first level, the muddle-headed/simple-minded dichotomy comes to mind, of course, and your comment about the occasional foolishness of hyper-skeptics suggests that dumb arguments can be seen among the simple as well as the muddled, tho I presume we'd also agree that frequency is higher among the latter. I think your term "safely" hyper-skeptical moves us toward a plausible guess. Seems to me most of the really silly ideas I've read or heard come from people who have an axe to grind—who are passionately insistent that their views be accepted by others (cf. Hoffer)—and that they are so nervous about social approval of their views because they haven't been able to separate their arguments, which will stand or fall on their own merit, from their feelings of personal worth. They have to prove themselves. Among commonly well-known, reasonably well-defined traits in the psy lit, I'd say ego strength comes closest.

Of all the people I know personally, you have the best record of avoiding foolish statements over a wide range of recondite issues, tho, like you, I've known quite a few others who approach "foolish-free" discourse, including the Minnesotans you name and several I met at Illinois, especially Cronbach & Humphreys. In the scholarly world at large (or at least the part with which I have some familiarity) Hook & Popper top my list.

The second question in yr. letter of 12/11 (generalized form of my Hook/Lenin example)—"Under what knowledge conditions can a completely unquantified inference be so clear and potent that only a hyper-skeptic would withhold belief?"—is equally tough, and I'll bet my response will be equally uncertain. Isn't this the basic question the hermeneuts have been trying to answer? I think so. That's why I've tried to find some wisdom in their writings and may see more there than you do. But the knowledge conditions favored by the hermeneutical crowd, near as I can tell, seem to boil down to three: freedom from logical error, coherence, and rhetorical persuasiveness, with social consensus, the political consequence principally of Condition #3, as the main criterion for acceptance/rejection of a knowledge claim. And then, when I read these birds closely, I find their own writings anything but free of logical error (you are much sharper at spotting those than I am; you know more logic), not particularly coherent, especially when arguments of several authors are considered as a group, and even if rhetorically persuasive & widely endorsed (e.g., Hitler, historicist arguments of Marx), just plain wrong. We've traded many letters on this topic and I give up, as you do, on hope of going much further.

Don

P.S. I picked up a copy of Isaac's Storm yesterday and am enjoying it greatly. A dreadful story of human denial & bureaucratic stupidity, beautifully told, and carrying along the way lessons in the history of meteorology. I have about 4´´ of file space devoted to episodes of this kind, starting with the story of the WASA, a 17th century Swedish man o' war that capsized and sank, drowning all aboard, on her maiden voyage. Maybe you know the story. The WASA was to be the grandest vessel on the sea. The shipwright loaded her with more cannons than any other ship afloat. Questions arose about stability, so an admiral had the vessel towed out into the harbor and ordered 30 swabbies to run back & forth on the deck. After 3 runs, WASA rolled so far that she came close to capsizing. The admiral responded by halting the test. After all, the King had approved the plan. So, on the maiden voyage, the WASA set sail, pennants flying, crowds cheering, then caught a gust, shipped water through her multitudinous gunports, and sank. I've collected numerous comparable stories, including the Galveston flood (Isaac's Storm is much better than any account I'd seen before) and chunked them into a file labeled "Disaster Principle" (for "The Disaster Principle of Social Reform") whose major tenets you can easily guess.

Have you read Earnest May's "Lessons" of the Past? Shows we've learned damn little from history, so far.

12/21/00

Paul,

Afterthought on yr. query re silly arguments by smart, learned people. Isn't intellectual arrogance often a factor? I think of Pauling, Leakey, & some others who started believing their press notices and ignored Popper's insistence that we all need the editorial help of others in appraising our statements, tho each of us has to be his own best critic. I'll bet some such arrogance was at work in Croce's case. In the Italian culture (still highly authoritarian when I spent a Fulbright year there in 1959–1960, with the status of "expert" going unquestioned and the "experts," in response, saying whatever came to mind dogmatically) arrogance is encouraged. I haven't read Croce and don't intend to, but I suspect he, saying silly things with nobody around to raise a question about the Emperor's clothes, just kept getting by with anything that came squirting out of his head. Mebbe the other end of the trait is something like confident humility—i.e., sufficient intelligence & scholarly depth to be pretty sure of the validity of anything you do say, but at the same time a readiness to admit there are some questions that are just beyond your ken. As you say in your letters & fairly often in your writings, "I haven't been able to figure that one out."

With best wishes for the new year and beyond, Don

CHAPTER

17

The Scientific Mentality

The next set of letters Paul and I wrote to each other meandered considerably. Comments on health, scientistic hyper-skepticism, and a paradoxical finding in taxometric research popped in and out. At one point, Paul sent me, without comment, a single page from Joseph Ellis's book, *Founding Brothers*. This page quoted some of the famous correspondence between Adams and Jefferson that resembled ours, both in content and spirit. The most persistent theme, however, was a continued effort to make sense of the occasional outbreak of foolishness on the part of otherwise bright and rational people, and the corruption of an authentically scientific mentality implied by the lapses:

12/27/00

Dear Don: Vision after 2nd cataract operation still impaired (not always "miraculous") but improving; hence big script and short note.

Yes, the too intimate fusion of doctrine with self-concept is a big one, probably biggest after g and mis-education, followed by narrow exposure to selected sub-groups and biased reading. My self-concept is "I try to be a rational person," from 9th-grade science + peer group + Feigl, etc. If one's self-concept is not about method but doctrine, "I am a Catholic" ("Freudian," "Behaviorist," "Rorschacher," "Multiphasiker," in psy), this corrupts the mind.

Challenger disaster due partly to poor graphics—literally—along with dumb NASA bureaucratic PR "urgency." I've seen one simple scatter-plot of ring rigidity against temperature that clearly advised delay.

Paul

12/29/00

Dear Don: I sealed last letter before your 12/21 afterthought. I agree with your postscript on sheer arrogance; believing in group adulation encourages dogmatism. I believe we can now list (without weights) factors leading high-g people to say silly things at times, fusing our thoughts.

1. *Poor education; a dept. that's too ideological, few scientific (or clinical) alphas, no bright, critical peer group to challenge & hone the mind. Political-religious atmosphere.*
2. *Self-concept tied to doctrine more than method: "I am a Freudian, proud of it."*
3. *Neurotic insecurity aiding and abetting (2).*
4. *Being adulated and swallowing it. [David] Lubinski would add a purely cognitive (non-emotional/motivational) dimension of clear thinking. Some brights "just don't think clearly," a factor like poor spatial reasoning, poor mechanical ability, poor musical talent, whatever. No good tests available. I d.k. what I think about that.*

I saw [Richard] McFall [with whom I, DRP, had argued in print about the limits of a "science-based" profession] at an APA meeting. He assumes I agree with his extreme view. I just gently warded him off. Should our list include "drive to be special," when a sub-culture reinforces a radical hobby-horse? I disagree with him, of course, but if he said, "Someone should help troubled people, but WE—scientific psychologists—shouldn't be the ones, absent proof," could we answer that? He could point to history of useless medicine.

Paul

1/4/01

Dear Don: Vision still marginal, saw retina experts yesterday—not a fun way to spend my birthday. Life is spelled HASSLE, as Ellis says (ditto the Enlightened One 500+ B.C.E.).

Ruscio & Ruscio (J. Abn. Psy. recent) use TX [taxometrics] on huge N, conclude major depression not taxonic. I can't believe it. So Meehl in strange position of believing "clinical experience" against my own statistical method! This suggests a paper on why (not attack on Ruscios, instead some reflections on this eternal bugaboo question). If I want to cite McFall and Peterson on hyper-scientism vs. disciplined clinical inquiry, what are best single references for each of you?

Hunch! The Ruscio finding comes from using indicators not sensitive enough in the right region to capture taxon. E.g., "I feel discouraged" is too weak to detect gross irrational hope loss, found in severe Depr. but not in reactive, OCD [obsessive-compulsive disorder], anhedonic, etc. depressions. But I can't prove this, alas.

Paul

1/8/01

Dear Paul,

I'm sorry to learn about your visual problems, tho glad to see improvement (smaller script, longer note) between letters of 12/27 and 1/4. Yes, life is HASSLE. Jane is still struggling with the pain and uncertainty of 2 herniated discs; I spent 2 days in local ER couple months ago following brief, mild, but unmistakable TIA→ many tests→mainly favorable results but fairly high residual risk of stroke→closer focus in work + resumption of regular exercise (which I had stopped with first visit to Berkeley) + resumption of regular meditation (which I had stopped out of sheer laziness 5–6 years ago). Sure enough, the Enlightened One had it right, but I seem to need a kick in the butt every so often to boot me back on my path.

In your inimitable way, you have listed probable determinants of the high g/silly statement syndrome about as concisely as our common observations & rationality allow, tho I'd prefer to distinguish ideological culture from absence of bright, critical peer group as separate items rather than conflating them under "poor education," e.g., our clinical faculty at Illinois consistently included several very bright, critical peers, but became increasingly ideological (not merely behavioral but "operant") to point of foolishness (e.g., Ullmann & Krasner's 1969 book which disputed the occurrence of schizophrenia as a disease. Lenny Ullmann used to go around giving talks entitled, "Schizophrenia: It Ain't"). So I come up with:

1. *Ideological educational culture.*
2. *Absence of bright, critical peers.*
3. *Valuation of self tied to doctrine more than method (at least partly in defense against neurotic insecurity).*
4. *Intellectual arrogance (resulting at least partly from incorporation of public adulation into self-concept).*

I don't know either what to think about existence of "clear-thinking" factor distinct from g. Could be. I think the question is worth asking & might ultimately be answerable, but am inclined to view the "clear-thinking" factor as a mixed disposition closest to the characteristic we're trying to parse, i.e., the freedom from silly statements by highly intelligent and learned people that emerges as resultant of 1–4 above. Enuf on that.

On McFall & his various arguments: I think he does say "[Perhaps] someone should [try to] help troubled people [even if they don't know just what they are doing scientifically] but WE—scientific psychologists—shouldn't be the ones to do so, absent proof." I consider that an arguable point of view which McFall not only preaches but embodies in the IU [Indiana University] clinical program. As I understand the IU program, students there learn only empirically supported treatments, which they then hand off to others, and devote themselves to the scientific development and evaluation of additional methods. Go Indiana! say I.

I do not think, however, that the history of useless medicine would provide a strong basis for his argument as a moral imperative, which is the way McFall states it. My reading of the history of medicine does not tell me that the development of safe, useful procedures typically started in the laboratory and then made its way into the hands of practitioners. It usually went the other way around, starting with Hippocrates, the scientific practitioner, doing his best to heal the sick, first doing no harm, and then doing whatever available knowledge (not doctrine), his own observations, and rationally determined action in the interest of the patient might suggest. The decisive experiments came later. I don't object if McFall decides to restrict his own practice & the tutelage of his students to the tried and true, & in fact applaud his emphasis on training students to try other procedures under clearly defined experimental conditions to find out what else is true. But in our infant science and our even more infantile profession, I see room for my "disciplined inquiry" as well. If McFall's restriction had been generally accepted all along, we'd have had no Freud, no Rogers, no Ellis, no Wolpe, no Lazarus.

Best single reference to McFall's position is his "Manifesto For a Science of Clinical Psychology," The Clinical Psychologist, 1991, 44, 75–88. Best single ref. for my position is my piece on "Connection & Disconnection of Research and Practice in the Education of Professional Psychologists," which I enclose. Best reference on the McFall–Peterson dialogue is the enclosed series in Applied and Preventive Psychology.

In your response to Dick's assumption of your agreement with him at APA, I think you responded the way I do to deans of free-standing schools who assume I approve their opening of new, under-funded, ill-conceived operations. (I have visited several of these. A few good ones. Many awful.) They sometimes tell me how deeply informed & inspired they have been by my writings, but it's clear they haven't understood the fundamentals. Like you, I find the situation awkward but can't think of anything better to do than gently ward them off and trust that our (grossly inadequate) accreditation system & economic forces (provided we see a reversal of Gresham's Law) eliminate the worst of their creatures.

I read the Ruscio & Ruscio (2000) with interest, surprise, &, like you, serious doubt (if you ask me to vote, disbelief) about the validity of their conclusion. My hunch about the failure to detect taxonicity is the same as yours: weak indicators. The authors are correct in noting that the instruments they used are the most widely used in the profession, probably the "best" available for use in their study, & the indicators they subjected to taxometric analysis appear to be as well defined as the raw data allow, but dammit they are still depending entirely on responses to individual questionnaire items of unknown empirical status. However sophisticated & powerful the statistical analysis, there is only so far one can go with flabby observations. I still hold to the opinion I came to in Clinical Study (1968), i.e., the tests on which so much of our science and practice depend are never going to provide the robust information needed for strong science and a solidly grounded profession. This doesn't mean, of course, that we shouldn't do the best we can with what we have, or that my suggestions (extend senses by direct observation, functional analysis, & other means) will free us from ignorance & uncertainty. I just doubt that we have a sufficiently advanced technology of assessment to provide the data required for a decisive test of the taxonicity hypothesis. In the case of severe D, I have an additional hunch we'll need some hard signs (e.g., improved neural imagery, better measures of vegetative functions) to give the latent taxa a chance to show their peaks. If you go ahead with a paper, I would be very interested in your reflections on "this eternal bugaboo question," as you describe it.

Don

P.S. Interesting coincidence: When your single page from Ellis's Founding Brothers arrived I already had his book at the top of my evening reading list & had been reading around in an old selection of the Jefferson/Adams letters. Editor of the latter wrote, "Ambition had no further bait for them, they had no further favors to ask. They waited in the twilight, and gossiped, and speculated, and gave their ideas and convictions free rein...."

1/13/01

Dear Don: Lubinski intends his "clear-thinking" factor to be like other sheer ability group factors, such as emerge in factor analysis, minimally influenced by emotion, motivation, or even experience. So it will be hard to get at even if it exists. He doesn't press it, just an option.

I agree better to parse the education thing, separate bright critical peers.

Those damn disks—did I tell you about mine? Hospitalized for septicemia (and maybe S.B.E., they never found the focus, that's a bet from history and known valve lesion), on 3rd day I get acute back pain & hardly get out of bed or walk. Feared spinal abscess ruled out by 2 MRIs. After discharge I needed a walker & pain pills for a cpl weeks, than a tetrapod cane (and some pills), then plain cane. But now all OK, take my walks. Cause of (verified inflamed) protruding disk? Unknown. Relation to the septicemia? Unknown. Perhaps sheer coincidence. I presume your wife knows the stats, they recover without surgery in very high %.

Too easy to get careless about meditation. I did after hospital, but now regular again. My wife has been slipping so I remind her. Did you know Tim Beck is a meditator? But Ellis pokes fun at it. And this is one where we have fairly good data, even a meta-analysis. Alas, "People believe what they want to believe," as Mencken said. Try to keep well!

Paul

CHAPTER

18

Meehl's Scientism

My Meehl correspondence file for the following 7 months is more than a half-inch thick and contains 11 items, but the coverage is so scattered that it exceeds my talent as a synthesizer. In the stack I find exchanges about actuarial prediction in selecting graduate students, behavioral episodes as evidence in trait attribution, and several other matters, plus several one-page clips on journalistic idiocies that Paul sent to his "gene gang," but much of the weight in the pile is contributed by two long "memoranda" that Meehl addressed to other correspondents. To Will Grove he wrote a 24-page typed statement on "interest in evolution." To David Faust he wrote a 12-page typed statement on "rationality on social issues." In both cases, I was included in the "minuscule reference group" that received copies, but saw no call for response beyond thanks and occasional brief comments.

In July 2001, I had a rare chance to visit Paul and Leslie in person. An "all-school reunion" was scheduled in my hometown of Pillager, Minnesota, a village so tiny that everybody who ever went to the local school is routinely invited to every reunion. At approximately 5-year intervals, swarms of graduates, young and old, descend on the little river town in the sweetness of a Minnesota summer. I never fail to attend, although only a few of my 20 high school classmates are still alive and sufficiently free of disabilities to join the crowd.

I had never been inside Paul's home before, but Leslie gave me clear directions so I had no trouble finding it, and not long after my flight from Newark landed I rang the doorbell of their house on East River Terrace in Minneapolis. Leslie greeted me warmly. Then into the living room, where Paul was seated in a lounge chair, reading a large-print book through a magnifying lens in the bright shine of a powerful light. Long handshake. I remembered the time a grad school classmate, Joel Cantor, had remarked on the small size of Meehl's hands. Somehow we expected the hands of an intellectual giant to be larger. "Let's go to the sunroom," said Paul. "We'll be more comfortable there." Tea by Leslie, and then the beginning of a talk that went on for 2 hours. I felt much as I had in Meehl's office 50 years before. The same cheerful animation. The same comfort in exploring any topic whatsoever. We covered a lot of ground, from Lord Kelvin's Baltimore lectures, which he delivered in 1889, and the Pillager band of Chippewa Indians, who in 1898 fought federal troops in the final battle of the American Indian Wars, to Paul's latest work in taxometrics (he had written a reply to the Ruscios) and my current writing project, which I had entitled "Science, Scientism, and Professional Responsibility," but had only begun to frame. Paul and I had both read William James on the topic of overbelief, and thought the concept might be useful as a way of thinking about scientism.

I spent the summer writing the piece, saying what I thought needed to be said regardless of length (the first draft came to 95 pages) and only the vaguest of plans for publication—perhaps a chapter in a book Roger Peterson, Jules Abrams, and I were planning to compose. I was still working on it in September, when I found a memo from Meehl in my mailbox:

To: Donald R. Peterson

From: P. E. Meehl

Date: 9/25/01

Re: Scientism

These thoughts on scientism are probably not directly relevant to your current writing project, but I send them along, thinking that some of them might be useful indirectly by stimulating your cerebrations. In any case, your project provides me with an excuse for formulating my own ideas on paper. There will be a certain element of academic free association; no harm done.

As I wrote a while back, and also in a couple of memos to others on evolution and on rationality, I try to use the term "scientism" in a purely descriptive value-neutral sense, realizing that it is not usual. What makes a belief system an *-ism* is a cluster of features, some of which are perhaps intrinsically a bit pejorative; but that can't be helped. For example, a hyper-rationalist like W. K. Clifford, who in his famous essay on belief made the astonishing remark, "It is wrong always, everywhere, and for anyone, to believe anything whatsoever on insufficient evidence." On this view, the element of overbelief, a belief possibly supported by evidence and argument but held with higher conviction than rationality allows, would be intrinsically a bad thing. As you know, William James, in his writings on pragmatism, poked fun at Clifford, saying that the latter apparently thought the worst possible thing that could ever happen to a man would be making a mistake by believing a false proposition! There is no way I can avoid the negative connotations of some of the features that enter into the notion of an *-ism*, but to denigrate such *-isms* is not my intention in using the suffix.

I think it is possible to divide scientism in the broadest sense into five levels which, as usual in these matters are not sharp but nevertheless distinguishable. Each level is expressed by a belief statement in italics.

1. *In the well developed sciences, and in some portions of the less-developed sciences, there are clearly established facts (I would call them "hard facts") and well confirmed theories that statistically speaking are quasi-certain to survive.* I am willing to say that we know that the liver stores glycogen; that genes are sections of a double helix with backbone ribose and phosphate radical, with codons that are triplets of bases adenine, guanine, cytosine, and thymine corresponding to the twenty amino acids; that the sun is not Apollo's chariot or a hot ball

but a globe of gas, mostly hydrogen. (Philosophers of science have overdone the overthrow of theories by emphasizing Einstein's surprising refutation of Newton.) No one is ever going to discover that the liver doesn't store glycogen after all, or that the backbone of the double helix is sucrose linked to the carbonate radical. Suppose, on contemplating the periodic table found in every lecture room and laboratory in the chemistry building, a social constructionist were to say that chemistry was invented by White males, and that if it had been invented by Black lesbian Marxists the atomic weight of carbon might have been 13 instead of 12. We know that person is either insincere (the usual case) or a candidate for a mental hospital.

2. *Science is not only pretty much correct, but is far and away the most trustworthy kind of knowledge that we have*. There are of course pre-scientific facts and generalizations that can be arrived at from ordinary life and common sense that humans discovered long before Galileo & Co. You don't need to do experiments or collect statistics to know that the thunder follows the lightning, that if you eat unrestrainedly without exercising you will become obese, that if you make a practice of saying cruel things to people, they won't like you. But we as psychologists, of all people, know that even some very "obvious" and "universally held" generalizations about ordinary life can be false and many such have been scientifically disproved. This level of scientism holds that the knowledge claimed by physicists, chemists, physiologists, and some kinds of psychologists is almost certainly more accurate than the cognitive claims of metaphysics, theology, ethics, aesthetics, history, biography, jurisprudence, or literary criticism. This strong claim offends most—not all—humanist scholars, but if they don't admit it, they are just plain mistaken. I co-taught jurisprudence in the Law School for several years, and believe that I knew some things that a layman does not know; but to claim that what I know about the facts and "theory" of appellate court decisions is as clear and solidly established as the chemist's periodic table would be absurd. I earned part of my living for a half a century practicing psychotherapy (psychoanalytic and rational emotive) and I believe that I was sometimes successful because I relied on factual generalizations and a bit of theory; but to say that that knowledge was of the same quality as what I did as an experimenter on latent learning would be crazy.

3. There are a few hard-nosed scientists who affirm (2) so strongly that they seem to be saying, in effect, that *these other pre-scientific or nonscientific disciplines have almost no claim to credence*. I have not met any scientists who state this explicitly as a generalization. But I have known a few who, whenever a controversy arises concerning an al-

leged truth from one of these less-developed disciplines, feel free to dismiss statements they dislike, apparently on the ground that these disciplines have no valid claim to intellectual respect. You and I are familiar with this in our field where one knows experimentalists or psychometricians that dismiss *anything* based on clinical experience with patients as not deserving of respect.

4. At this level, the view is not only that the only kinds of explanations are scientific explanations, but that science *will ultimately explain almost everything*. One allows for some very small number of questions that science may never succeed in answering such as questions about the fundamental nomologicals (e.g., Maxwell's equations) or questions about historical origins (e.g., origin of life).

5. *Science will ultimately explain everything.*

I have no trouble locating myself in these strata. I am firmly convinced of (1) and (2), and I equally firmly reject (3), (4), [and] (5). I predict that you will locate yourself at the same point with equal ease and firmness.

For a clinician, the problem is that clinical experience is similar to common sense and folklore in that one can learn things that way, without doing experiments or statistics, and—something you and I agree on and some of our nonclinical brethren deny—that one would probably not learn without clinical experience, relying solely on experiments and statistics. But as I emphasized in my paper "Credentialed Persons, Credentialed Knowledge" (Meehl, 1997, *Clin Psy: Sci & Practice, 4,* 91–98), the trouble is, as with common sense and folklore, one also "learns" many things that are not true. This unpleasant fact about the human mind is what gives critics like Dawes and McFall some powerful ammunition.

I don't recall whether I have mentioned Emil DuBois-Reymond's famous lecture on the seven mysteries of the universe [DuBois-Reymond, E., (1882). The seven world-problems. *Popular Science Monthly, 20,* 433–447]. I believe he was of the super-scientism school of scientists like Helmholtz and Freud's mentor Bruëcke, and certainly no obscurantist or defender of mysticism. But he thought that among the seven unsolved problems of his day there were three that might conceivably be solved by science, and four that could not possibly be solved by science. He apparently held that you could rule out any solution of these four from the armchair just by contemplating their content in relation to how science "explains" things. Here is the list.

1. The origin of matter and force;
2. The origin of motion;
3. The origin of life;

4. The teleological features of living organisms;
5. The origin of language and rational thought;
6. The origin of simple sensations;
7. The contradiction of free will and determinism.

This is a fascinating list from a man who was a first-class scientist and probably would have got the Nobel prize if he had lived longer, and who I assume (given his Helmholtz mid-Victorian ideology) would have much preferred to think all seven of these mysteries were scientifically solvable. As you might expect, my own views on that list are somewhat deviant. I would be curious as to yours, but I won't worry about poisoning your mind with mine. I don't understand why he distinguishes (1) from (2), since the fundamental nomologicals of the physics he believed in defines force in terms of its capacity to accelerate motion, so that if you have force and matter, you have motion. I would tend to collapse them and one way to state it would be to ask, "Why is there anything rather than nothing?" This question, put in that broad, abstract way, almost suffices to show me from the armchair (by the very meaning of the words) that the fifth level of scientism [science can explain everything] can't be right. When we use the word "explain," in either scientific or common language, we mean to deduce (derive, infer) the explanandum from *premises*. In talking about the empirical world, whatever we take as the premises in an explanation are not derived, *any* more than they are in formal logic and mathematics. So those premises themselves are not "explained," and hence the existence and properties of the entities they speak of are not explained. One may of course aspire to deriving some of his premises from more basic premises, as the progress of physics to nuclear physics shows. But one knows that at any stage of knowledge, including some "ultimate" stage of science, one will always require premises, primitive propositions from which the others are deduced and which themselves are not deduced. It seems to me that's an obvious matter of formal logic, so that the notion that everything will be explained in the sense of no underived propositions is incoherent.

As to (3) [origin of life], there is no currently accepted view among evolutionists; and the discovery of DNA, with the richness of the code, has made that more mystifying than it was before. I don't think an explanation is possible. (4) [teleological features of living organisms]: Here it hinges upon the theory of evolution. By 1882 that theory had been fairly widely but not universally accepted in biology, and I don't recall whether DuBois-Reymond expresses an opinion about it, but at least there was a theory that, if it survived and developed, would explain it. So, he counted (3) and (4) [as] possibly soluble, although they hadn't been solved in 1882. Neither had

(5) [origin of language and rational thought], but he didn't preclude it from solution. He thought that (6) [origin of simple sensations] was insoluble, and I agree with him. I don't recall whether he explained why he used the adjective "simple," but my formulation would be that the properties of complex sensations might be derivable from appropriate psychophysical laws relating brain states to sensations. The puzzle is why there should be any raw feels at all. If I knew the psychophysical relations of the experienced spectrum to brain sites in the calcarine cortex, then I might be able to derive the quality of orange as a mixture of red and yellow produced by the color wheel or by a pure spectral orange frequency, so in that sense, the location of orange would be in a sense derivable. But given a complete description of my cortical activity in the language of chemistry and physics, a language which does not include raw feel terms, how could a sentence containing the raw feel predicate "red" or "yellow" be derived? I may be wrong, but it strikes me as almost as a point in formal logic; that is, one cannot in general derive a sentence containing a term from premises that do not contain it. That I take to be his point about the origin of simple sensations. You may recall that Feigl, also a kind of materialist monist with a dislike for anything spooky, experienced somewhat the same feeling of puzzlement about raw feels, despite his having done the best job anybody did in formulating the mind–body identity theory.

As to (7) [contradiction of free will and determinism], which DuBois-Reymond considered one of the insolubles, I am inclined to disagree with him on several counts. First, he assumed that psychophysical determinism must be true, because he believed that about physical events generally, and the brain is a physical entity. Whether the indeterminacy of quantum mechanics applies to the micro-events at the synapse is, I believe, unknown, although some physicists (Jordan, Eddington) and neurophysiologists (Eccles) have speculated to that effect. Whether indeterminacy at the level of the neuron gets rid of his puzzle, I don't know, but I have written a paper showing how it might (Meehl, 1989, "Psychological determinism or chance: Configural cerebral autoselection as a tertium quid," in M. L. Maxwell & C. W. Savage (Eds.), *Science, mind and psychology: Essays in honor of Grover Maxwell* (pp. 211–255). Lanham, MD: University Press of America). I will send you a reprint if you are interested. Although that volume has some degree of visibility among philosophers and I sent reprints to some three dozen philosophers who have published on the determinism question, nobody has paid any attention to it pro or con, so I don't know whether there is something defective in the argument. Feigl used to say that quantum indeterminacy in the brain wouldn't help, because the alternative to determinism is chance and nobody wants to think that his free choices are made by chance. That's the position of the logical empiricist and other philosophers that I have talked with but my article attempts to show that plausible as that dichotomy sounds, it is not correct because strict determinism and chance are contraries but not contradictories. I believe I am the only person who takes that position and so I am frustrated by the fact that the paper fell into limbo. It was reprinted in my *Selected Philosophical and Methodological Papers* (1991), which probably had more readers than the Maxwell memorial volume, but still, nobody has written a reply or commented about it to me except Wesley Salmon, who in reviewing that volume for the University Press stated that he disagreed with it. But even if we assume strict psychological determinism, there need not be a contradiction. The subjective experience of "willing freely" involves mainly the belief that, however one decided, one could have chosen otherwise, because there is absent a feeling of constraint as when one is forced to do something because one lacks the requisite skill, strength, or knowledge. To have such a subjective feeling that I could have chosen otherwise because nobody or nothing compelled me to do what I did is not equivalent to the statement that the events in my brain involved in that choice did not instantiate physico-chemical laws. On that analysis, the mystery disappears. Instead of relying on the subjective feeling of free choice, one may invoke the *moral* necessity of metaphysical freedom—as in Kant's "Ought implies can." That argument I have never understood, since it seems to impose a requirement upon the world of facts arising from our impulse to praise or blame. In that connection there is, as you probably know, a sizable group of moral philosophers who are compatibilists, who believe that imputation of free responsible accountable choice to moral agents is not inconsistent with their choices being determined when described at the brain state level. So there are several alternative ways out of the alleged mystery (7) which were not available to DuBois-Reymond in 1882.

cc: Bryden, Faust, Ruscio

circ: Gene Gang

CHAPTER

19

Farewell

I spent the following autumn and winter writing my paper on "Science, Scientism, and Professional Responsibility." I intended it as my swansong on the topic that above all others had preoccupied me for the preceding 35 years: relations between science and practice in psychology. As it came out, the paper started with a strong definition of science, continued with a nonpejorative definition of scientism, proceeded at length through implications of those concepts for responsible practice and rigorous education in psychology, and ended with a proposal for embracing William James' philosophy of pluralism (which he propounded so brilliantly in 1908 that no one has ever improved it) as a conceptual and attitudinal framework for respectful political cooperation and effective working relationships between researchers and practitioners in our field. During the many months I was working on the project, I mentioned it to a considerable number of colleagues in the "what are you doing these days?" conversations that professors have, and several of them asked to see the paper when I completed it. So I sent copies to them, as well as a few other people whose opinions I valued. Of course I sent a copy to Meehl.

Somewhere along the line of the several brief exchanges we had in the interim, I told him my essay was 30% Meehl, 30% William James, 30% Peterson, and 10% everybody else.

I warned Leslie by e-mail that a long manuscript was on the way, and included an apologetic letter that I hoped would relieve Paul of any pressure to read beyond the material that required his permission before I could attempt publication. Leslie replied in her usual cheerful way:

Thu, Apr 4, 2002

Hello Don,

It's good to hear from you. We're doing better, started walks again last week but were snowed in by the Great Minnesota April Fool Joke—8 inches of white stuff. It seems to be melting fast, and I'm hoping the walks will be clear enough for us to get back on a walking routine, maybe by tomorrow. We will have to see how Paul handles unexpected obstacles and unevenness in the sidewalks, but I'm optimistic that he will be able to walk solo again after a while. We'll look for the MS and give you feedback when we can. Stay well!

Leslie

Three days later, Paul's e-mail response, typed by Leslie, arrived:

DRP: As promised, we will scan your selected passages for accuracy. "We" because I am reading blind so have to have Leslie or my secretary read aloud. At last I have a doctor's excuse not to read journals. Blindness aside, I find I have almost totally de-cathected psychology, as an intellectual interest and as a profession. American Psychologist devoted 14 columns to letters advocating post-modernism. Would a journal of genetics, geology, or even economics do this? And Fowler officially apologizing to those clowns in Congress for publishing a scientific paper? I'm ashamed to be a psychologist. Have to practice RET on myself to rise above it. Now I think of myself as a "psychologist, retired" whose current professions are philosophy of science and statistics. Niels Waller and I have a paper to appear in Psychological Methods that is path-breaking and may become a minor classic. I doubt I shall live to see my cliometrics book published, but I am completing 2 articles that contain its main points. I am reconciled to philosophers reacting as clinicians did to my 1954 book, but that's OK.

PEM

At the time, I was so concerned about imposing my 95-page paper on Paul, blind and obviously depressed as he was, that I limited my response to repetition of my request for permission to publish quotations from his personal correspondence, which Paul, through Leslie, immediately granted. I did not comment then about his alienation from psychology, but his remarks require comment now. The preceding October, Kenneth Gergen—often considered psychology's strongest advocate of postmodern views—had published an article on "Psychological Science in a Postmodern Context" in the *American Psychologist*. Gergen proposed that psychology move beyond its outdated, modernist position to adopt a constructivist, postmodern approach to its subject matter. In Gergen's view, traditional research was still worthwhile, but only as one language among many in useful discourse on the human condition. The article elicited nine letters of commentary that occupied 30 columns of journal space. Most of the letters were critical of Gergen's argument, but to Paul that didn't matter. To him, the whole discussion of "postmodernism" was diversionary blather. He had lost patience with colleagues who took it seriously.

The background of Meehl's remark about Fowler and "those clowns in Congress" is more complex. In July 1998, Bruce Rind, Philip Tromovitch, and Robert Bauserman published a meta-analysis of 59 studies on the psychopathological correlates of child sexual abuse in the *Psychological Bulletin*, one of the oldest and most respected of the journals sponsored by the American Psychological Association. Using quantitative procedures, the authors found that correlations between self-reported histories of abuse and symptoms of psychopathology were weak, with mean *r*s ranging from .04 to .13. Contrary to common belief that sexual contact between adults and children was uniformly and permanently damaging to the children, many appeared to have survived the experience with no lasting deleterious effects! Several other findings, particularly that sexual encounters were reported to be consensual in some cases and that short-term reactions were sometimes positive, were equally provocative. The authors ended with their most controversial conclusion, that at least some cases of child sexual abuse, particularly those with positive reactions, be described with the value-neutral term "adult–child sex." They were careful to add the caveat that "lack of harmfulness does not imply lack of wrongfulness," and that their findings did not imply abandonment or change in moral or legal views of behavior commonly defined as abusive.

Not surprisingly, the findings were frightening to some and infuriating to others. Through a cascade of events, an avalanche of media and political abuse poured down on the authors of the study, the editors who had approved publication of the article, and most heavily on the American Psychological Association for allowing the article, derided as "junk science" by talk-show personality "Dr. Laura" Schlessinger, to appear in print. Letters and postcards condemning the article, and psychology and psychologists indiscriminately, for trying to "normalize pederasty" flooded the offices of members of Congress. Representatives and senators responded with their own forms of indignation, making sure that their constituents did not perceive them as condoning sexual abuse of children. On July 12, 1999, a bill demanding that the APA reject the conclusions of the article by Rind et al. passed 355 to 0 in the U.S. House of Representatives, with 13 members voting "present." Two weeks later, the bill passed by voice vote in the Senate.

For several months prior to these actions, APA staff were in turmoil, laboring mightily to avert the impending political disaster. As Chief Executive Officer, Raymond Fowler took the lead in defending the credibility of the article and the peer review process that led to its publication. A few days before the House bill came to a vote, Fowler signed a carefully written, much reviewed letter to Republican Majority Whip Tom DeLay. The letter set forth an array of actions the APA had taken and intended to take to put to rest charges that the association supported "normalizing" pedophilia. In all, the letter Fowler wrote to DeLay was a reasoned statement, but it included a contention that the assertions by Rind and his colleagues "should have caused us [the APA] to evaluate the article based on its potential for misinforming the public process." To Meehl, this was a gutless concession. How could a man of his convictions not be galled by the apparent surrender of psychology's scientific authority to political pressure? The angry despair in his message to me was sad to see but not surprising.

However he felt about psychology in general, Paul had "read" my remarks about scientism in the draft articles I had sent to him. As usual, Paul's thoughts and mine ran along nearly parallel lines, but I saw the main issue that divided psychology into separate and opposing cultures not only as a matter of varying degrees of confidence in science as a way of examining human behavior but somewhat more complexly as a matter of relative faith in scientific versus humanistic approaches to the understanding of human behavior and experience. I thought the division might be bridged by placing different balances between the two approaches on a continuum. My formulation drew heavily on Meehl's idea of levels of confidence but reduced the markers on the continuum to three:

> ***Level 1.*** *Science can answer some important psychological questions, primarily in psychophysiology and a few other fields of inquiry that can be examined experimentally. In "soft" areas, such as clinical and counseling psychology, scientific methods are largely useless. Deep understanding can only be gained by way of humanistic inquiry.*
>
> ***Level 2.*** *Science can not only answer questions in hard psychology but is also the most trustworthy means of answering questions in soft areas, including personality, social, clinical, and counseling psychology. It is therefore desirable to "scientize" as much of psychology as the subject matter allows. For questions that do not yield to quantification, controlled investigation, and other conditions inherent in the most rigorous forms of scientific research, other methods, such as narrative accounts and qualitative analyses, can be employed.*
>
> ***Level 3.*** *The superiority of scientific approaches to psychological knowledge over all other modes is so marked that other pre-scientific or nonscientific approaches, such as clinical experience and hermeneutic analysis, have little or no claim to credence and should be excluded from serious scientific consideration.*

By e-mail from Leslie, I learned that Paul was puzzled about my reduction of his five-level scheme to three and wondered whether my decision had something to do with the scalability of the items. No, I replied.

> I don't know about Guttman scalability of scientism levels, either your 5 or my 3, but concern about scalability was not the reason I chose the 3-level formulation. I went for the briefer scale partly because it's easier to grasp—somewhat like the alpha-beta-gamma order among intellectuals—but mainly for reasons of presumed ecological validity. Your top level, for example, is an interesting abstraction, but I can't

> think of any psychologists who actually believe that science can explain everything, and I can think, easily and immediately, of psychologists who belong at each of my three levels, as well as others whom I locate beyond the pale on grounds of anti-scientific, "post-modern" constructionism (Gergen) or hyperskeptical exclusivity (McFall). I could make long lists of social scientists at all three levels I consider conducive to reasonable discourse and scientific advance, e.g., Level 1, Carl Rogers (especially in late years, he was closer to Level 2 in the 1950s); Level 2, you and me (and, I suspect, majority of other clinical psychologists); Level 3, Dawes (bordering on hyper-skeptical fringe) and any number of strict experimentalists I have known.

By this time, I had divided my long paper in two for journal publication. From the total philosophical and empirical discussion of relations between science and profession in the discipline, I extracted an internally coherent critical analysis of education for practice in psychology, and after 2 months' work sent the manuscript to the *American Psychologist* under the title "Unintended Consequences: Ventures and Misadventures in the Education of Professional Psychologists," saving the title "Science, Scientism, and Professional Responsibility" for an essay I expected to publish later on.

Late in July 2002, I received a phone call from Melissa Warren, managing editor of the *American Psychologist*, telling me that she and an associate editor had decided that I "had a right to say all those things I said at the end of the article," which consisted primarily of proposals for improving education for practice in psychology, but needed to "get rid of all that stuff at the beginning," which contained the historical background and data supporting my contention that quality of education in professional psychology had declined with the rise of professional schools and PsyD programs in departments of dubious reputation. Warren noted correctly that there was "nothing new" in the history or factual information I offered in my introduction. In an e-mail to Leslie and Paul a week later, I mentioned where my article stood in the editorial process:

> Melissa Warren called last week to tell me my "Unintended Consequences" article will be published in the AP, but one of the editors—she didn't say who—wanted me to "get rid of all that stuff" at

> the beginning.... I'm reluctant to do that for several reasons, but suppose some abbreviation is possible and will try to negotiate an acceptable compromise.

Paul replied the following day: "Don't let referee make you get rid of 'all that stuff'.... Those right nostril specialists are pathetic. One must resist them." It was the last personal message I was to receive from him. True to his injunction, I objected to removal of material I considered essential to my argument. Melissa Warren, with whom I had a long, cordial relationship that grew out of previous work I had done for the journal, responded by sending my manuscript to 13 reviewers representing a broad spectrum of interests and ideological positions in psychology. Except for two critics who considered my critique of professional psychology unduly harsh, all the reviewers recommended publication, and several offered excellent suggestions for amendments. I accepted those cheerfully and revised the manuscript. At this writing, it is in press awaiting a "companion piece" to be written by an author whose views differ from mine. The essay on "Science, Scientism, and Professional Psychology" took longer to revise, but it too is now in press in *Clinical Psychology: Science and Practice*.

For his part, Meehl continued to teach and publish into his final months. During the spring quarter of 2002, he gave his customary guest lecture in Will Grove's philosophy of psychology seminar. Leslie wrote, "He can't see much any more but he sure can talk." I have no doubt he was as engaging as ever. In July, she wrote again:

> We're settling down more into our new circumstances. Paul has almost finished tapes of Autopsy of an Empire by Matlock (former ambassador to USSR). He has a bunch of choices now (MN Reading for Blind has been terrific about getting books on tape for him) and we have several machines so he can have more than one book going at a time. We're listening to Russell's History of Western Philosophy in bed each night. (Yep, I tend to fall asleep.) Hope you're having a good summer.

I was. Except for a return to New Jersey to revise the *American Psychologist* article, I spent the summer and fall in Vermont. When I returned to my Rutgers office, I found two reprints in my mailbox. One was a monograph on "Cliometric Metatheory," Meehl's radical proposal for employing statistical methods in the study of scientific theory by sampling episodes from the history of science and subjecting them to formal psychometric treatment. The other was an article jointly written by David Faust and Paul Meehl that concerned the same fundamental prospect. Long before, Faust had hit on the idea of using statistical methods to resolve questions in the history and philosophy of science. Faust and Meehl had developed the proposal collaboratively. The article I found in my mailbox was an advanced statement of the "Faust–Meehl Thesis," as Paul had come to call it. I wrote to thank him for the reprints:

Fri, Nov 22, 2002

Greetings, Leslie and Paul,

Jane and I are just back from Vermont enjoying a second autumn. NJ is about a month behind VT in the foliage cycle. Had a fine time up north, pleasured by the beauty of the area, leisurely visits with good friends, and lots of reading. Among books that might interest you, Stephen Toulmin's Return to Reason (which succeeds in vindicating practical thinking about particular events without trashing scientific method) and Louis Menard's Metaphysical Club (which taught me a lot more than I knew before about Holmes, Peirce, James, Dewey, and pragmatic ways of thinking) stood out as special joys. I'm winding up, at long last, to begin writing about the course of American bigotry. I finally feel sure enough of myself to give it a whirl.

It was a special treat to find Faust & Meehl (2002) and Meehl's Cliometric Metatheory II in my mailbox. I don't think I have ever read anything you wrote, Paul, without at least one gasp (when a truth hits home) and some chuckles. It takes a special kind of mind to write about the Big Crazy Committee in the Sky.

I often wonder how you are doing. I miss the CALIGULA FOR PROCONSUL envelopes, always the bright spot in my day when one arrived. But at least the reprints continue, and I'm counting on staying in touch as the years move on.

Don

That last sentence was more hopeful than realistic, and beneath my cheerful prose I knew it. I received no reply. Often I thought, "He must be seriously ill." When I learned of Paul's death, I e-mailed a note of sympathy to Leslie and followed it with a letter:

> Dear Leslie,
>
> I have thought about you and Paul many, many times over the past few months, ever since our correspondence stopped. A question would come up and I'd wish for an opinion from the wisest person I have ever known personally. Less often, given the narrowing of Paul's interests following his blindness and his disgust with the idiocies in our once so brightly promising discipline, I would have a thought, or come across the ideas of another that I might have relayed to Paul in earlier times, but would suppress the impulse to contact you. I figured you were probably going through some tough times, & didn't need any extra burdens from me.
>
> I learned about Paul's death from the obit in the NY Times. As free of sentimentality as Paul was....

I continued with the comments that appear at the beginning of this elegy.

Notes

I have not attempted to provide references for all the works that are mentioned in this book. I have not read all the materials that Meehl noted, and do not want to suggest that I have. Many books are mentioned only in passing and are of little relevance to the main themes of the text. References are therefore limited to those I considered most likely to be helpful to readers in understanding the correspondence between Meehl and me.

Page	INTRODUCTION
vi	The Buddhist quotation was brought to my attention by Scott Lilienfeld.
ix	Meehl's obituary: Goode, E. (2003). Paul Meehl, 83, an example for leaders of psychotherapy. *New York Times*, Wednesday, February 19, p. A23.
ix	1962 presidential address: Meehl, P. E. (1962). Schizotaxia, schizotypy, schizophrenia. *American Psychologist, 17*, 827–838.

x 1954 book: Meehl, P. E. (1954). *Clinical versus statistical prediction: A theoretical analysis and review of the evidence.* Minneapolis: University of Minnesota Press. Reissued in 1996 with a new preface by the author; the reissue was published by Jason Aronson, Northvale, NJ.

x The now-classic paper: Meehl, P. E. (1973). Why I do not attend case conferences. In *Psychodiagnosis: Selected papers* (pp. 225–302). Minneapolis: University of Minnesota Press.

x One of the scales of the Minnesota Multiphasic Personality Inventory: McKinley, J. C., Hathaway, S. R., & Meehl, P. E. (1948). The Minnesota multiphasic personality inventory: VI. The K scale. *Journal of Consulting Psychology, 12,* 20–31. With his characteristic generosity, Meehl listed himself as last author of the report, although he was clearly the inventor of the scale.

x Central role in developing taxometrics: Brief introductions to taxometrics are offered in Meehl, P. E. (1992). Factors and taxa, traits and types, differences of degree and differences in kind. *Journal of Personality, 60,* 117–174; and Bootstraps taxometrics: Solving the classification problem in psychology. *American Psychologist, 50,* 266–275. More comprehensive treatment is provided in Waller, N. G., & Meehl, P. E. (1998). *Multivariate taxometric procedures: Distinguishing types from continuua.* Newbury Park, CA: Sage.

xii I have described elsewhere: Peterson, D. R. (1997). The education of a professional psychologist: A personal introduction. In D. R. Peterson, *Educating professional psychologists: History and guiding conception* (pp. 5–27). Washington, DC: APA Books.

xiii The Great Struggle of the Psychoclinician: See Meehl, *Psychodiagnosis: Selected papers,* pp. vii–viii. Ibid.

xiii Niels Waller on taxometrics: See Waller & Meehl, *Multivariate taxometric procedures: Distinguishing types from continuua.* Ibid.

xiii The Faust–Meehl Hypothesis: Faust, D., & Meehl, P. E. (2002). Using scientific methods to resolve questions in the history and philosophy of science: Some illustrations. *Philosophy of Science, 69,* S185–S196.

xiv David Lubinski's research: See Lubinski, D. (2004). Introduction to the special section on cognitive abilities. *Journal of Personality and Social Psychology, 88,* 96–111.

xiv Susan Haack's views: Haack, S. (1998). *Manifesto of a passionate moderate: Unfashionable essays*. Chicago: University of Chicago Press.

xiv The Meehl Reader: Waller, N. G., Yonce, L. J., Grove, W. M., Faust, D., & Lenzenweger, M. F. (Eds). (2005). A *Paul Meehl reader: Essays on the practice of scientific psychology*. Mahwah, NJ: Lawrence Erlbaum Associates.

1. MEEKL

2 My latest try at the science x practice issue: Peterson, D. R. (1991). Connection and disconnection of research and practice in the education of professional psychologists. *American Psychologist*, *46*, 422–429.

3 Meehl–Dahlstrom rules: Meehl, P. E., & Dahlstrom, W. G. (1960). Objective configural rules for discriminating psychotic from neurotic profiles. *Journal of Consulting Psychology*, *24*, 375–387.

2. HERMENEUTICS

6 Article in *Psychological Inquiry*: Meehl, P. E. (1990). Appraising and amending theories: The strategy of Lakatosian defense and two principles that warrant it. *Psychological Inquiry*, *1*, 108–141.

6 Essay published in 1978: Meehl, P. E. (1978). Theoretical risks and tabular asterisks: Sir Karl, Sir Ronald, and the slow progress of soft psychology. *Journal of Consulting and Clinical Psychology*, *46*, 806–834.

8 Effort to reduce racial tension: Peterson, D. R. (1990). Working against prejudice in a large state university. In G. Stricker, E. Davis-Russell, E. Bourg, E. Duran, R. Hammond, J. McHolland, K. Polite, & B. Vaughn (Eds.), *Toward ethnic diversification in psychology education and training*. Washington, DC: APA Books.

9 Lee Cronbach's good works: Cronbach, L. J., et al. (Eds). (1980). *Toward reform in program evaluation*. San Francisco: Jossey-Bass.

9 Adverse effects of reverse discrimination: Meehl's position on this issue, like mine, was more complex than might be suggested by the remarks that appear in our letters. In a 26-page memorandum, "On Reverse Discrimination," addressed to David Faust and dated January 15, 1999, Meehl described in detail the kinds of affirmative action he considered ethically just and socially effective, as contrasted with forms of reverse discrimination he viewed as ethically unjust and socially ineffective. He would have approved—and I do approve—the position toward which the U.S. Supreme

Court appears to be groping in its 2003 decision to allow consideration of race as a factor in admissions to undergraduate study and the law school at the University of Michigan.

9 Black intellectuals: At the time (1991), I was thinking of two works: Steele, S. (1990). *The content of our character: A New vision of race in America*. New York: St. Martin's Press; and Sowell, T. (1981). *Ethnic America: A history*. New York: Basic Books. Both authors have published more since then, but have not changed their views on the infelicities of reverse discrimination.

10 Interest in philos. of science: Bridgman, P. W. (1927). *The logic of modern physics*. New York: Macmillan; and Pratt, C. C. (1939). *The logic of modern psychology*. New York: Macmillan.

10 Symposium on hermeneutics: Messer, S. B., Sass, L. A., & Woolfolk, R. L (Eds). (1988). *Hermeneutics and psychological theory: Interpretive perspectives on personality, psychotherapy, and psychopathology*. New Brunswick, NJ: Rutgers University Press.

10 Study of close relationships: Kelley, H. H., Berscheid, E., Christensen, A., Harvey, J. H., Huston, T. L., Levinger, G., McClintock, E., Peplau, L. A., & Peterson, D. R. (1983). *Close relationships*. San Francisco: Freeman. Reissued in 2002 with a new introduction by Kelley & Berscheid, by Percheron Press, Clinton Corners, NY.

10 Research methodology chapter in *Close Relationships* book: My statement that "the people who wrote the research methodology chapter … wound up *defending* most conventional null hypothesie-refuting research" is flatly untrue. No defense of such research appears in the chapter, which in fact proposes an array of more powerful approaches to inquiry and is one of the strongest chapters in the volume. What I was trying to say to Meehl was that, in my opinion, several of the substantive chapters gave undue attention to studies reporting statistically significant but conceptually and technologically worthless findings, and that I did not object although I had ample opportunity to do so during the many meetings we authors had in critique of one another's efforts.

11 Feigl as an "empirical realist": Feigl, H. (1950). Existential hypotheses: Realistic versus phenomenalistic interpretations. *Philosophy of Science*, *17*, 33–39.

12 Kuhn on history of science: Kuhn, T. S. (1970). *The Structure of scientific revolutions* (2nd ed.). Chicago: University of Chicago Press.

12 Gergen on social process as history: Gergen, K. J. (1973). Social psychology as history. *Journal of Personality and Social Psychology*, *26*, 309–320.

12 Gergen on generativity of theory: Gergen, K. J. (1978). Toward generative theory. *Journal of Personality and Social Psychology, 36*, 1344–1360.

12 Spence on narrative vs. historical truth: Spence, D. P. (1982). *Narrative truth and historical truth.* New York: Norton.

12 Idea of hermeneutic circle: Packer, M. J., & Addison, R. B. (Eds.). (1989). *Entering the circle: Hermeneutic investigation in psychology.* Albany: State University of New York Press.

12 My 1968 book: Peterson, D. R. (1968). *The clinical study of social behavior.* New York: Appleton-Century-Crofts. Reissued in 2004 with a new introduction by the author, by Percheron Press, Clinton Corners, NY.

12 Mischel on contextualism: Mischel, W. (1968). *Personality and assessment.* New York: Wiley.

12 Constructs, construct validity, nomological nets: MacCorquodale, K., & Meehl, P. E. (1948). On a distinction between hypothetical constructs and intervening variables. *Psychological Review, 55*, 95–107; Cronbach, L. J., & Meehl, P. E. (1955). Construct validity in psychological tests. *Psychological Bulletin, 52*, 281–302.

3. KUDOS AND CONFUSIONS

14 Meehl's philosophical and methodological papers: Anderson, C. A., & Gunderson, K. (Eds.) (1991). *Paul E. Meehl: Selected philosophical and methodological papers.* Minneapolis: University of Minnesota Press.

15 Book on the history of psychotherapy: Freedheim, D. K. (Ed.). (1992). *History of psychotherapy: A century of change.* Washington, DC: APA Books.

16 ABPP Prize lecture: As Meehl predicted, his submission to the *American Psychologist* was rejected. The paper, titled "If Freud Could Define Psychoanalysis, Why Can't ABPP Do It?" was published in 1993 in *Psychoanalysis and Contemporary Thought: A Quarterly of Integrative and Interdisciplinary Studies, 16*, 299–326.

17 "Ways of Knowing" paper: Peterson, D. R., & Peterson, R. L. (1997). Ways of knowing in a profession: Toward an epistemology for the education of professional psychologists. In D. R. Peterson, *Educating professional psychologists: History and guiding conception* (pp. 191–228). Washington, DC: APA Books.

18 Carnap's paper on testability and meaning: Carnap, R. (1953). Testability and meaning. In H. Feigl & M. Brodbeck (Eds.), *Readings in the philosophy of science* (pp. 47–92). New York: Appleton-Century-Crofts. (Original article published 1936).

18 Bridgman's relaxed operationism: Bridgman, P. W. (1959). *The way things are*. Cambridge, MA: Harvard University Press.

4. PRIZEWINNERS, PERILS, AND PARAPRAXES

21 Eysenck published an article purporting to show: Eysenck, H. J. (1952). The effects of psychotherapy: An evaluation. *Journal of Consulting Psychology, 16*, 319–324.

23 Study Hilde Himmelweit had done in Eysenck's lab: A factorial study of "children's behavior disorders." (1953). Cited in H. J. Eysenck, *The structure of human personality* (pp. 88–89, 334). London: Metheun.

25 Early work at the University of Illinois psychological clinic: Peterson, D. R. (1997). *Educating professional psychologists: History and guiding conception*, p. 14. Ibid.

26 The book was published in 1997: Peterson, D. R., *Educating professional psychologists: History and guiding conception*. Ibid.

5. MORALITY

27 Invited addresses: Meehl, P. E. (1996, August). Credentialed persons, credentialed knowledge; and Eysenck, H. J. (1996, August). Progress and revolution in clinical psychology. Presented at 104th annual convention of the APA, Toronto, Canada.

27 Autobiographical narrative: Peterson, D. R. (1998). The professional psychologist as a moral agent. In L. T. Hoshmand (Ed.), *Creativity and moral vision in psychology: Narratives on identity and commitment in a postmodern age* (pp. 29–49). Thousand Oaks, CA: Sage.

28 The best scholarship: In his autobiography, Meehl mentioned that he read more than 300 treatises on theology during his dozen years as a communicant Lutheran.

30 Obituary of Hobart Mowrer: Peterson, D. R. (1982). In memoriam—O. Hobart Mowrer, 1907–1982. *Child and Family Behavior Therapy, 4*, 99–101.

31 Trotter's "Herd Instinct": Trotter, T. F. (1921). *Instincts of the herd in peace and war.* London: Unwin.

32 Citation of Mowrer on Q technique: Mowrer, O. H. (1953). *Psychotherapy: theory and research*. New York: Ronald.

32 Research on Mowrer's theory: Peterson, D. R. (1963). The Insecure child: Over-socialized or under-socialized? In O. H. Mowrer (Ed.), *Morality and mental health* (pp. 459–471). New York: Rand-McNally.

33 Mowrer's moral imperatives: Mowrer, O. H. (1967). *The new group therapy*. Princeton, NJ: Nostrand.

7. MEEHL'S RESPONSE TO CAMPBELL

45 Campbell's APA presidential Address: Campbell, D. T. (1975). On the conflicts between biological and social evolution and between psychology and moral tradition. *American Psychologist, 30*, 1103–1126.

46 "Law and the Fireside Inductions": Meehl, P. E. (1971). Law and the fireside inductions: Some reflections of a clinical psychologist., *Journal of Social Issues, 27*, 65–100. Reprinted in C. A. Anderson & K. Gunderson (Eds.), *Paul E. Meehl: Selected philosophical and methodological papers* (pp. 440–480). Ibid.

8. SELLING AN UNPOPULAR BOOK

58 Otherwise excellent contribution to Holt's book: Meehl, P. E. (1971). A scientific, scholarly, nonresearch doctorate for clinical practitioners. In R. R. Holt (Ed.), *New horizons for psychotherapy: Autonomy as a profession* (pp. 37–81). New York: International Universities Press.

64 If sales continue: Sixty-nine copies were sold in 2003. My royalties on 11 copies at 10% and 58 copies at 12.5% totaled $135.04. The 69 copies sold out the first and only printing. The book is no longer available except online through PsycBOOKS.

9. DISCOVERY AND JUSTIFICATION

66 Differentiation of context of discovery from context of justification: Reichenbach, H. (1938). *Experience and prediction*. Chicago: University of Chicago Press. (See pp. 6–7 of Reichenbach's book.)

66 Conversation with Thomas Reid and George Allen: Peterson, D. R., Reid, T. A., & Allen, G. (1999). Reflections on training: Donald Peterson talks with the first PsyD and a PhD Classmate. *Professional Psychology: Research and Practice, 30*, 74–82.

68 Distinction between contexts of discovery and justification: Reichenbach, H. (1938). *Experience and prediction*. Ibid., pp. 6–7.

10. CONSTRUCTIONISM, REALISM, AND INTELLECTUAL HONESTY

72 Foreword to Dan Fishman's book: Peterson, D. R. (1999). Foreword. In D. B. Fishman, *Pragmatic psychology* (pp. xv–xviii). New York: New York University Press.

74 Rorty's radical, "postmodern," constructionist argument: Rorty, R. (1991). *Objectivity, relativism, and truth*. New York: Cambridge University Press; and Rorty, R. (1998). *Truth and progress*. New York: Cambridge University Press.

78 Westen's "Freud legacy" paper: Westen, D. (1998). The scientific legacy of Sigmund Freud. *Psychological Bulletin, 124*, 333–371.

78 Rattle yr cage: Radin, D. (1997). *The conscious universe: The scientific truth of psychic phenomena.* New York: Harper Collins.

80 "Conversation" between Richard Rorty and Charles Sanders Peirce: Haack, S. (1998). "We pragmatists ...": Peirce and Rorty in conversation. In S. Haack, *Manifesto of a passionate moderate: Unfashionable essays* (pp. 31–47). Chicago: University of Chicago Press.

11. RECONCILING DIFFERENCES

81 Meehl's APS Award address: Meehl, P. E. (1998, May). The power of quantitative thinking. Address delivered on receipt of the James McKeen Cattell Fellow award at meeting of the American Psychological Society, Washington, DC.

84 "Credentialed Persons, Credentialed Knowledge" paper: Meehl, P. E. (1997). Credentialed persons, credentialed knowledge. *Clinical Psychology: Science and Practice, 4*, 91–98.

87 Survey on prejudice at Rutgers University: Peterson, D. R. (1990). *Students speak on prejudice: A survey of intergroup attitudes and ethnoviolent behavior among undergraduate students at Rutgers University*. New Brunswick, NJ: Rutgers University.

94 My brilliant MS was rejected: Meehl's book was not rejected outright. Editors told him he might submit a revised version. But Paul knew he did not have the energy or time to undertake a task of the required scope or duration, so he decided to complement a previously published monograph on cliometric metatheory with two further articles that contained the core content of the material he had elaborated in the book. References for the three articles, all by Paul E. Meehl, are as follows: Cliometric metatheory: The actuarial approach to empirical, history-based philosophy of science. (1992). *Psychological Reports, 71*, 339–467; Cliometric metatheory II: Criteria scientists use in theory appraisal and why it is rational to do so. (2002). *Psychological Reports, 91*, 339–404; Cliometric metatheory III: Peircean consensus, verisimilitude, and the asymptotic method. (2004). *British Journal for the Philosophy of Science, 55*, 615–643.

94 Lincoln's "loveless marriage": Of course, Abraham Lincoln's marriage to Mary Todd was not entirely loveless at the beginning. He declared that he "would love her forever" and his devotion to Mary and their children is legendary. Even so, Mary's extravagant, demanding ways taxed Abe's tolerance sorely. The best single descriptor for their marriage in the later years might be "vexatious."

12. SOCIAL EXPERIENCE AND SOCIAL CONSCIENCE

97 Meehl's autobiography: Paul E. Meehl. In G. Lindzey (Ed.), *A history of psychology in autobiography* (vol. *3*; pp. 337–389). Stanford, CA: Stanford University Press.

100 Incident from autobiography: Peterson, D. R. (1998). The professional psychologist as a moral agent. In L. T. Hoshmand (Ed.), *Creativity and moral vision in psychology: Narratives on identity and commitment in a postmodern age.* (pp. 31–32). Ibid.

13. MEEHL'S CONSTRUCTIONISM

107 Hellman's superb book: Hellman, G. (1980). *Mathematics without numbers: Toward a modal-structural interpretation.* New York: Oxford University Press.

114 "Relevance of a Scientist's Ideology": Meehl, P. E. (1998). Psychology of the scientist: LXXVIII. Relevance of a scientist's ideology in communal recognition of scientific merit. *Psychological Reports, 83,* 1123–1144.

14. POLITICS AND POLITICIANS, PSYCHOTHERAPY AND PSYCHOTHERAPISTS, PALEONTOLOGY AND PALEONTOLOGISTS

120 Historiography of David Donald and Carl Sandburg: Donald, D. H. (1995). *Lincoln.* New York: Touchstone; Sandburg, C. (1929). *Abraham Lincoln: The prairie years.* New York: Harcourt Brace; Sandburg, C. (1939). *Abraham Lincoln, the war years.* New York: Harcourt Brace.

121 So my Utopia starts: In a brief note that I have omitted from this selection, Paul said, "I have started to write my Utopia—a well-known sign of senility." According to Leslie, he cogitated for many years on the possibility of devising a political system that would carry the benefits but avoid the problems inherent in modern democracy, and had dictated a good deal of material for a book on the subject.

121 Cites of Mischel, 1968; Peterson, 1968, 1991, 1997: See previous notes for full publication information.

124 Seligman's "positive psychology": Seligman, M. E. P. (1998). *Learned optimism* (2nd ed.). New York: Simon & Schuster. Research on positive psychology has advanced rapidly since 1998. Especially as presented by Seligman in his 2002 book *Authentic Happiness* (New York: Free Press), positive psychology moves beyond the ideological presumptions implicit in topics chosen for award of the Templeton Prize to an empirical foundation. Seligman's formulation is clearly consistent with Aristotle's pragmatic syllogism: "If you desire G [happiness] and A [e.g., maintaining positive illusions, perceiving one's work as a calling] is empirically, factually a means to G, you should do A." See also Seligman, M. E. P., & Csikszentmihaly, M. (Eds.). (2000). Happiness, excellence, and optimal human functioning [Special issue]. *American Psychologist, 55,* 5–183.

129 Wells, H. G., Huxley, J. S., & Wells, G. P. (1934). *The science of life*. New York: Literary Guild. (Original work published 1929).

130 Darwin, "the gravest objection that could be urged": Darwin, C. (1964). *On the origin of species* (p. 280). Cambridge, MA: Harvard University Press (Original work published 1859).

130 Eldredge–Gould paper: Eldredge, N., & Gould, S. J. (1972). Punctuated equilibrium: An alternative to phyletic gradualism. In J. M. Schopf (Ed.), *Models of paleobiology* (pp. 82–115). San Francisco: Freeman, Cooper.

130 Meehl's "fossil paper": Meehl, P. E. (1983). Consistency tests in estimating the completeness of the fossil record: A neo-Popperian approach to statistical paleontology. In *Minnesota Studies in the Philosophy of Science*, vol. *X*, Testing Scientific Theories (pp. 413–473). Minneapolis: University of Minnesota Press.

131 The "bell curve" argument: Herrnstein, R. J., & Murray, C. (1994). *The bell curve: Intelligence and class structure in American life*. New York: Free Press.

15. FACTOR ANALYSIS

133 We published a series of research reports: Cattell, R. B., & Peterson, D. R. (1958). Personality factors in nursery school children as derived from parent ratings. *Journal of Clinical Psychology, 14*, 346–355; Cattell, R. B., & Peterson, D. R. (1958). Personality structure in 4–5 year olds by factoring observed, time-sampled behavior. *Rassegna di Psicologia Generale & Clinical, 3*, 1–21; Peterson, D. R., & Cattell, R. B. (1959). Personality factors in nursery school children as derived from teacher ratings. *Journal of Consulting Psychology, 23*, 562; Peterson, D. R., & Cattell, R. B. (1959). Personality structure in 4–5 year olds in terms of objective tests. *Journal of Clinical Psychology, 15*, 355–369.

133 Article in *Psychological Review*: Peterson, D. R. (1965). Scope and generality of verbally defined personality factors. *Psychological Review, 72*, 48–58. (Abstract p. 48).

135 "Four Queries About Factor Reality": Meehl, P. E. (1991). Four queries about factor reality. *History and Philosophy of Psychology Bulletin, 3*, 16–18.

136 My Behavior Problem Checklist: Peterson, D. R. (1961). Behavior problems of middle childhood. *Journal of Consulting Psychology, 25*, 205–209.

136 Tom Achenbach's factors: Achenbach, T. M. (1966). *The classification of children's psychiatric symptoms: A factor analytic study*. Washington, DC: American Psychological Association.

137 Revised Behavior Problem Checklist: Quay, H. C., & Peterson, D. R. (1983). *The revised behavior problem checklist*. Miami: Franklin Press. (The instrument is now available from Psychological Assessment Resources, Inc., Odessa, FL.)

137 John Horgan's latest: Horgan, J. (1999). *The undiscovered mind: How the brain defies replication, medication, and explanation*. New York: Free Press.

138 2 articles which do not at all surprise: Templer, D. I., Tomeo, M. E., Pointkowski, S. R., Mitroff, D., Niederhauser, R. N., & Siscoe, K. (2000). Professional school and traditional program graduates: comparison on measures of success in clinical psychology. *Psychological Reports, 86*, 951–956; Yu, L. M., Rinaldi, S. A., Templer, D. I., Colbert, L. A., Siscoe, K., & Van Patten, K. (1997). Score on the examination for professional practice in psychology as a function of attributes of clinical psychology graduate programs. *Psychological Science 8*, 347–350.

138 Peterson, 1985: Peterson, D. R. (1985). Twenty years of practitioner training in psychology. *American Psychologist, 40,* 441–451.

138 My old speech (in Holt's book): Meehl, "A scientific, scholarly, nonresearch doctorate for clinical practitioners." Ibid.

138 Meehl's Sacred Cows MS: Meehl, P. E. (1979). *The seven sacred cows of academia: Can we afford them?* Unpublished manuscript, University of Minnesota, Minneapolis. Improving the cost efficiency of higher education was yet another subject of Paul's ruminations over many years.

16. HISTORY AND HISTORIANS

141 Robert Holt's severely critical review: Holt, R. R. (2000). Case dismissed. *Contemporary Psychology, 45,* 108–111.

141 Brewster Smith's enthusiastic praise: Smith, B. (2001). Pragmatic psychology, point-counterpoint. *Contemporary Psychology, 46,* 216–217.

142 Sidney Hook's *Hero in History:* Hook, S. (1992). *The hero in history: A study in limitation and possibility,* New Brunswick, NJ: Transaction. (Original published 1945, by Secker & Warburg).

144 Jacques Barzun's latest: Barzun, J. (2000). *From dawn to decadence: 500 years of Western cultural life: 1500 to the present.* New York: Harper Collins.

146 Psychoanalytic examples of dream interpretation: Meehl, P. E. (1991). Subjectivity in psychoanalytic inference: The nagging persistence of Wilhelm Fliess's Achensee question. Most easily available in *Paul E. Meehl: Selected philosophical and methodological papers* (pp. 284–337).

147 A copy of *Isaac's Storm:* Larson, E. (1999). *Isaac's storm: A man, a time, and the deadliest hurricane in history.* New York: Crown Publishers.

17. THE SCIENTIFIC MENTALITY

150 The Enlightened One: Meehl was referring to the Gautama Buddha. Buddha is not a name but rather a descriptive adjective that literally means "The Enlightened One." Paul was profoundly interested in religion, both intellectually and in a personal, spiritual way. After leaving the Lutheran church and as he entered his later years, he was drawn more closely to Buddhistic beliefs and practices than to those of any other organized religion.

150 Ruscio & Ruscio: Ruscio, J., & Ruscio, A. M. (2000). Informing the continuity controversy: A taxometric analysis of depression. *Journal of Abnormal Psychology, 109*, 473–487.

151 Ullmann & Krasner's 1969 book: Ullmann, L. P., & Krasner, L. (1969). *A psychological approach to abnormal behavior.* Englewood Cliffs, NJ: Prentice-Hall. The authors' position on biological influences in schizophrenia was not altered in the second edition of their book, published in 1975.

152 "Connection & Disconnection": Peterson, D. R. Connection and disconnection of research and practice in the education of professional psychologists. Ibid.

152 McFall–Peterson dialogue: This dialogue took the form of three consecutive papers in a single issue of *Applied and Preventive Psychology*: Peterson, D. R. Making psychology indispensable; McFall, R. M. Making psychology incorruptible; Peterson, D. R. Making conversation possible. *Applied and Preventive Psychology, 5*, 1–18. (Issue published in 1996).

18. MEEHL'S SCIENTISM

162 Paul's "gene gang": This was an informal list of Paul's Minnesota colleagues who were interested in behavior genetics and to whom he routinely sent relevant memos and notes.

19. FAREWELL

164 Niels Waller and I have a paper: Meehl, P. E., & Waller, N. G. (2002). The path analysis controversy: A new statistical approach to strong appraisal of verisimilitude. *Psychological Methods*, 7, 263–300. Their reply to commentators on the article is an article in itself: Waller, N. G., & Meehl, P. E. (2002). Risky tests, verisimilitude, and path analysis. *Psychological Methods*, 7, 323–337.

165 Kenneth Gergen's paper on postmodernism: Gergen, K. J. (2001). Psychological science in a postmodern context. *American Psychologist, 56*, 803–813.

165 Nine letters of commentary: *American Psychologist, 57*, 455–464. (Issue published in 2002.)

165 Meta-analysis of 59 studies: Rind, B., Tromovitch, P., & Bauserman, R. (1998). A meta-analytic examination of assumed properties of child sexual abuse using college samples. *Psychological Bulletin, 124*, 22–53.

166 A cascade of events: Commentary on the article by Rind and his colleagues, the story of its interpretations in the popular media, and uses by various political constituencies to further their divergent political agendas, along with lessons learned by APA leaders in the process, occupy an entire 2002 special issue of the *American Psychologist, 57*, 161–227.

167 Levels of scientism: Now published as Peterson, D. R. (2004). Science, scientism, and professional responsibility. *Clinical Psychology: Science and Practice, 11*, 196–210.

168 Critical analysis of education for practice: Now published as Peterson, D. R. (2003). Unintended consequences: Ventures and misadventures in the education of professional psychologists. *American Psychologist, 58*, 791–800.

169 I found two reprints: One was Meehl, Cliometric Metatheory II. The other article was Faust, D., & Meehl, P. E. (2002). Using scientific methods to resolve questions in the history and philosophy of science: Some illustrations. *Philosophy of Science, 69*, S185–S196.

Additional references are provided in the text.

Author Index

* Page numbers in italics indicate reference information in the "Notes" section.

T

U

V

W

Y

Subject Index

D

E

F

G

H

I

J

K

L

M

N

O

P

For Product Safety Concerns and Information please contact our EU
representative GPSR@taylorandfrancis.com
Taylor & Francis Verlag GmbH, Kaufingerstraße 24, 80331 München, Germany

www.ingramcontent.com/pod-product-compliance
Ingram Content Group UK Ltd.
Pitfield, Milton Keynes, MK11 3LW, UK
UKHW022119190926
475702UK00013B/1535
9780415654647